Beyond Orange and Green

Belinda Probert

Beyond Orange and Green

The Political Economy of the Northern Ireland Crisis

Belinda Probert

Zed

Zed Press Ltd., 57 Caledonian Road, London N1 9DN.

Beyond Orange and Green was first published by Zed Press,
57 Caledonian Road, London N1 9DN in June 1978.

Copyright © Belinda Probert, 1978

ISBN Hb 0 905762 16 9
     Pb 0 905762 17 7

Printed by Billing & Sons, London
Typeset by Lyn Caldwell
Designed by An Dekker

A Special Edition of Beyond Orange and Green has been
produced in conjunction with The Academy Press,
124 Ranelagh, Dublin 6, for distribution by them exclusively throughout the whole of Ireland.

This work was undertaken with the aim of redressing what seems to me to be a central weakness in most marxist interpretations of the current political crisis in Northern Ireland: the treatment of Protestant politics and ideology. Not surprisingly marxist studies of Irish affairs have, in the past, been primarily concerned with the national struggle for independence, and the nature of Britain's continued intervention in Ireland. From such a perspective the present conflict in Northern Ireland is dominated by the political and military confrontation between the forces of republicanism and the British State. The role of Unionism and loyalism is thus reduced to that of a 'dependent variable' in this broader struggle. The object of this book, however, is to develop a class analysis of Protestant politics in Northern Ireland which clearly reveals the relative autonomy of these dimensions to the conflict, and which can account adequately for such central events as the Ulster Workers Council strike in 1974. Such a study must necessarily be situated within a broader politico-economic analysis of Anglo-Irish relations which recognises the decline of local capital in Ireland, both North and South, and the increasing dominance of international monopoly capital.

My aim in this book is primarily interpretative, and I have relied heavily on the already available historical and empirical material. I am grateful to both Lancaster and Murdoch Universities for their financial assistance, and would like to express my sincere thanks to John Bayley, John Frow and Meredith Beevers.

Belinda Probert

Murdoch University
Western Australia

December 1977

INTRODUCTION

For almost fifty years after the Government of Ireland Act of 1920, under which the six North-Eastern counties retained their status as an integral part of the United Kingdom, Northern Ireland attracted little interest from the outside world. Then, in 1968, a series of civil rights marches were staged in the province to protest about the existence of widespread, institutionalised discrimination against Catholics, gerrymandered electoral boundaries, denial of one-man-one-vote in local elections, and the repressive powers of the Unionist Government. In October of that year the civil rights cause was brought dramatically to the attention of television viewers all over Ireland and Britain with coverage of a large demonstration in Derry. They were astonished to see over 2,000 peaceful marchers, including two prominent opposition MPs, being batoned and hosed with water cannon by the Royal Ulster Constabulary. In the following ten months the civil rights campaign provoked increasingly violent opposition from sections of the Protestant community, leading to attacks against Catholics which the police failed to prevent. Indeed, on several occasions members of the RUC, and in particular the part-time B Special Constabulary, actively participated in such attacks.[1] In August 1969 sectarian rioting exploded in Derrry and Belfast, resulting in several fatalities, mostly Catholic, and the destruction of 150 Catholic homes in Belfast. The Unionist Government had no choice but to support Westminster's decision to send in British troops to prevent further bloodshed.

Between August 1969 and March 1972 when Westminster suspended the Stormont Parliament and imposed direct rule, conflicts proliferated and the violence continued to escalate. The Irish Republican Army re-emerged as the defenders of the Catholic ghettos and renewed their struggle against the British presence in Ireland with a military campaign against the British Army. The exclusively Protestant Unionist Party, which had ruled continuously since the partitioning of Ireland, lost its hegemonic position because of determined loyalist opposition to the reform programme which Westminster and a liberal section of the party sought to introduce. Westminster's decision to suspend Stormont early in 1972 was made in the face of an apparently insoluble political crisis in the province. The Catholic community had withdrawn from parliamentary politics, having despaired of winning economic and social equality from any

Unionist Government, while at the same time the Unionist Party was splintering under pressure from those sections of the Protestant community who were totally opposed to any further reforms. Since 1972 all attempts to resolve this political crisis, and restore self-government to the province on the basis of equal rights for Protestants and Catholics, have foundered on the implacable opposition of the Protestant working class and petty-bourgeoisie. These loyalists succeeded in sabotaging the power-sharing Northern Ireland Assembly which was introduced in 1973 with support not only from the Westminster and Dublin Governments, but also from much of the Catholic community in the North and from the reformist section of the Unionist Party.

Many commentators on Northern Ireland politics have characterised loyalist intransigeance as a purely ideological phenomenon. The persistence of uncompromising Orange beliefs amongst Protestants, who are engaged in the great battle of Biblical Protestantism against popery, is explained either in terms of a 'cultural lag' or by asserting the independence of ideological relations from economic or political influence.[2] Alternatively, it is seen as the product of ruling class ideological manipulation designed to perpetuate divisions within the working class; a problem of false-consciousness. Still others have asserted that 'the Protestants of Northern Ireland appear impervious to theories and explanations'.[3] In a review of Peter Gibbon's marxist study, *The Origins of Ulster Unionism*, John Harbinson claims that 'by concentrating on the purely economic argument he totally ignores the real soul of Unionism, the gut reaction of the average Ulster Protestant which is emotional, racial and frequently irrational. In other words Ulster Unionism cannot be "scientifically" dissected and analysed.'[4] The complexity and intractability of the present crisis in Northern Ireland have driven many observers to similar agnostic conclusions.

This book, however, takes as its starting point the assumption that the elaboration of general theoretical concepts is an essential component of the 'concrete analysis of a concrete situation'.[5] It is an attempt to analyse the political crisis that has prevailed in Northern Ireland since 1972, using the method of historical materialism. Within this perspective political and ideological relations can only be analysed as a part of a total social formation which is historically determined by a given mode of production, and specified by a particular articulation of its different economic, political and ideological levels. The salience of religious and nationalist forms of conflict in Northern Ireland makes this enterprise particularly complex. However, as Gustav Therborn has argued:

> A Marxist analysis would involve the assumption that the emergence and character of religions and nationalism are related, but not reducible to men's different experiences in different modes of production and particular classes in ways that the analysis must disclose. It would imply that religions and nationalism where they exist . . . have a different character and function in different modes

of production and that they play different roles for different classes
... Further, Marxists would argue that religions and nationalisms,
religious and national conflicts, develop in and through the class
struggle.[6]

Apart from Gibbon's important historical study on the origins of
Unionism there have been very few marxist analyses of Protestant politics
in Ireland. Traditionally, socialists have been far more interested in Irish
Nationalism than Ulster Unionism, and in the years between the partitioning of Ireland in 1920 and the start of the 'troubles' in 1968-9, Northern
Ireland attracted little outside interest. After partition British governments
systematically avoided the question of the province's problems on the
grounds that, by convention, the internal affairs of Northern Ireland should
not be discussed at Westminster. The convention did not only apply at
Westminster. The Sunday Times Insight Team reported that shortly after
the British Army was sent in to keep the peace in 1969, 'the Labour
cabinet solemnly asked themselves if there might not be some Oxford
academics who could perhaps advise them on Northern Ireland matters.'
However, 'Westminster's self-imposed ignorance of Ulster's affairs was
such that nobody else knew anything about the place.'[7]

Similarly, anyone interested in a marxist analysis of Northern Ireland
politics found little that could not have been written fifty years previously.
The failure of socialists to provide a consistent and coherent analysis is
symptomatic of their virtual exclusion from practical politics in Ireland.
In Ireland, both north and south of the border, politically organised labour
movements capable of developing new and critical perspectives on Ireland's
problems are conspicuous by their absence. In the years since 1968
marxists and socialists have begun to re-analyse the Irish question, but as
yet little has been added to the work done by James Connolly at the
beginning of this century in fusing socialist objectives with the national
struggle.

It is beyond the scope of this work to trace out in detail the historical
development of Irish socialist thought, and its fusion with a traditional
republican ideology which is centred on the concepts of national
oppression and national liberation. However, it is important to outline its
major assumptions since they have influenced most marxist interpretations
of the present struggles in Northern Ireland, as well as the political
strategies of the IRA, People's Democracy and the Communist Party of
Northern Ireland. Within this perspective the struggle towards socialism in
Ireland is inseparable from the struggle for national reunification and
independence from the domination of Great Britain. Writing in 1914,
Connolly warned of the disastrous consequences that the exclusion of
Ulster from Home Rule would have for the Labour movement in Ireland.
'All hopes of uniting the workers, irrespective of religion or old political
battle cries will be shattered, and through North and South the issue of
Home Rule will be still used to cover the iniquities of the capitalist and

landlord class.'[8] And in 1916, committing himself to a rising planned by 'bourgeois nationalists', Connolly declared that, 'the cause of labour is the cause of Ireland, the cause of Ireland is the cause of labour. They cannot be dissevered. Ireland seeks freedom. Labour seeks that an Ireland free should be the sole mistress of her own destiny, supreme owner of all material things within and upon her soil. . .'[9]

More recently it has been argued from this traditional position that, in granting independence to the twenty-six counties whilst depriving them of sovereignty over the six North-Eastern counties in which the island's industry was concentrated, Britain effectively sabotaged the Irish nationalists' hope of real independence, and with it the possibility of socialism in Ireland. 'If the state of the six counties remains fundamentally colonial that of the twenty-six is classically "neo-colonial". That is to say that while the old colonial Government has been replaced by a Government based on native interests, those upholding these interests are content to work the old colonial system subject to certain reforms necessary for its preservation.'[10]

A succinct characterisation of this perspective is provided by Anders Boserup:

> British domination is thus seen as the root of all the problems of Ireland. In the socialist ideology British domination becomes British imperialism. In this way everything fits nicely into place in what appears to be a consistent socialist theory. The severing of the links with the British oppressor becomes the precondition for socialism in Ireland . . . Most important: the existence of the common enemy, British imperialism, fuses Catholics and Protestants into one "people" in so far as their *objective* interests are concerned. National differences conveniently recede into the background. Divisions among the people are the result of "false-consciousness", itself the consequence of the divide-and-rule policies of imperialism and its local executioners. [11]

Thus, C. Desmond Greaves, in criticising various suggestions for a federal solution to Ireland's problems, argues that 'the significance of having a united Ireland has been missed. It is not only a means of liberating six county Catholics from Unionism, it is a means of liberating also the men of the Shankill Road, and the surest road to socialism, which is what their best representatives desire.'[12] In this way the Northern Ireland problem is subsumed under the broader 'Irish question'; the age-old unresolved antagonism between British overlordship and Irish independence. And the struggle for socialism is subsumed under the struggle to 'liberate' Ireland.

One of the most important discussions on the national question in marxist theory occurred as a result of the conflict between Lenin and Rosa Luxemburg on the issue. In his work, *Critical Remarks on the National Question* and *The Right of Nations to Self-Determination*, which appeared in 1914, Lenin provides us with a series of clear methodological statements which are helpful in evaluating the development of the national question in

Ireland. First, Lenin is concerned to distinguish between two periods of capitalism, 'which differ radically from each other as far as the national movement is concerned.' These are the period of the decline of feudalism and absolutism and the rise of the bourgeois-democratic state, and the period of fully formed capitalist states in which there is a 'highly developed antagonism between the proletariat and the bourgeoisie.' It is in the former period that 'national movements for the first time become mass movements and in one way or another draw *all* classes of the population into politics . . .' In the second period there are no mass bourgeois-democratic movements, for 'developed capitalism, in bringing closer together nations that have already been fully drawn into commercial intercourse, and causing them to intermingle to an increasing degree, brings the antagonism between internationally united capital and the international working class movement into the forefront.'[13]

Lenin's first point, therefore, is that: 'There can be no question of the Marxists of any country drawing up their national programme without taking into account all these general historical and concrete state conditions.'[14] 'The categorical requirement of Marxist theory in investigating any social question is that it be examined within *definite* historical limits, and, if it refers to a particular country (e.g., the national programme for a given country), that account be taken of the specific features distinguishing that country from others in the same historical epoch.'[15] Second, Lenin emphasises that marxist theory must recognise the 'right to secession' in general, as a 'negative demand for recognition of the *right* to self-determination, without giving guarantees to any nation, and without undertaking to give *anything at the expense* of another nation.'[16] Thus, although the proletariat recognises the equality and equal rights of national states, it also 'values above all and places foremost the alliance of the proletarians of all nations, and assesses any national demand, any national separation, *from the angle* of the workers' class struggle.'[17] Finally, in any concrete situation, marxist theory demands that the analysis should proceed by way of studying the position of the various classes in that society on the question.

Nationalist ideology is being revived throughout the United Kingdom at this time, and it is particularly important to try and define the main characteristics of this period of capitalism as well as to analyse the relations between classes in specific cases. In the main body of this study many of the assumptions inherent in the traditional nationalist interpretation of Irish politics are critically reviewed in a historical perspective, and questions are raised about the continuing validity of the assumed general identity of nationalist and socialist objectives. In this Introduction, however, my intention is simply to draw attention to some of the main difficulties that this traditional interpretation encounters in understanding recent political developments in the Northern Ireland crisis, and to outline the way in which it nevertheless came to dominate socialists' interpretations of events.

The first problem concerns the nature of the 'British interest' in Ireland today. The anti-imperialist basis of the unity between socialist and nationalist aspirations, and the identification of British imperialism as the force which links the Northern Ireland problem to the age-old Irish question, depends on the assumption that Britain's interest in the control of Ireland has remained unaltered since the Act of Union in 1800. In the context of recent developments in Northern Ireland, however, British policy has revealed an ambiguity which demands a re-evaluation of this dimension. There is no evidence of a British commitment to the maintenance of partition, the defence of Unionist supremacy in the North, or the perpetuation of sectarian divisions within the working class. As Boserup points out, 'To British capital Ireland provides a supply of labour, a protected environment for ailing companies and a not unimportant export market. None of these would be jeopardised by Irish unity and Irish independence.'[18] Others have drawn attention to the tremendous burden which is carried by British capital in the form of state expenditure in the province, including subsidies to ailing industries and assistance in maintaining welfare services.'[19] Hence Britain's insistence on reforms in Northern Ireland, despite powerful opposition from Unionists, and her willingness to negotiate with nationalists of all descriptions, including the IRA.

It is indeed the case that the struggle for the Irish Republic manifestly failed to establish a genuinely independent Irish state, and to alter Ireland's economically dependent status. Connolly warned in 1897, 'If you remove the English army tomorrow and hoist the green flag over Dublin Castle, unless you set about the organisation of the socialist republic your efforts would be in vain. England would still rule you through her capitalists, through her landlords, through her financiers . . . '[20] This does not mean, however, that the issue of reunification and the struggle for socialism can be subsumed under the demand for national independence.

The dominance of the national question over the socialist one manifests itself concretely in the present conflict in Northern Ireland in the traditional republican framework within which opposition to the old Stormont system is organised. The radical alternative to the reformism of the civil rights movement is the republicanism of the IRA. However, this raises a second problem for the traditional perspective, which concerns the relationship between this 'national liberation' movement and the 'nation' it seeks to represent. Despite diffuse sympathy for the IRA in their role as defenders of the Catholics in the North, the people of the Republic have, for the most part, consistently rejected its broader objectives.[21]

The Irish Government's recent legislation to inhibit the activities of the IRA provoked little opposition in the South, and this must be explained partly by the absence of working class support for the organisation. If the IRA gained support during the late 1950s and 1960s, years which mark a veritable turning point in the history of the South as well as in Ulster, it is mostly because its traditional base, the petty-bourgeoisie, was directly threatened by the new economic policies of that period; policies which marked the end of the protectionist era in Ireland, and the reintegration of the country into the international capitalist economy. From an extremely economistic perspective it has even been argued that:

> The Irish working class no longer has anything to gain from an alliance with the nationalist petite bourgeoisie, because this bourgeoisie no longer has a role to play in the capitalist arena. Working class interests lie in an alliance with England, whether it be with capitalism and the English State, which alone are able to provide unemployment assistance and to furnish jobs in times of social peace, or with the English proletariat.[22]

The third problem that this traditional perspective encounters concerns the status of the one million Protestants in Northern Ireland whose unwavering opposition to reunification remains the major obstacle to nationalist aspirations. By characterising Unionist workers as unwitting tools of British imperialism whose consciousness of their true interests has been distorted by the distribution of petty privileges, the economic and political (non-ideological) aspects of their resistance to reunification can be ignored. The campaign to bring down Stormont, and with it the Unionist system of distributing patronage, then appears as a revolutionary step towards reunification in that it reveals to the Protestant workers their real interests. In a review of a recent book on Northern Ireland which 'stands self-consciously in the long tradition of Irish nationalist ideological polemic', Paul Bew asks the following very important question. This question is in his own words: [if] as the nationalist tradition in Irish Labour history has heavily implied, Orangeism is to be understood solely as the means by which the "master class" diverted the working class from its essential unity of class interest, how are we to explain the failure of major outbreaks of a relatively united proletarian militancy (the 1919 strike of the engineers and the very much more significant Out Door Relief riots of 1932) to shatter Orangeism?'[23]

In the event, the abolition of Stormont, and the subsequent fragmentation of the Unionist bloc provoked quite different responses from those predicted. The establishment of a Council of Ireland was supported by Britain and the reformist wing of the old Unionist government. It was the Ulster Workers' Council strike which brought the province to a standstill in May 1974 in protest against this provision, and which put an end to the new power-sharing Assembly, thus clearly illustrating the need for a systematic class analysis of Protestant politics.

During the 1960s there were attempts to reorientate the thinking of radical republicans. In 1962 the IRA was obliged to abandon the military campaign it had launched in 1956 to eject the British from Northern Ireland. Lack of support from the Catholic population in the North, and a very poor showing in the Dail elections of 1961 clearly indicated the need for some critical rethinking of traditional republican strategy. After this failure a section of the leadership began to emphasise the importance of being involved in the more mundane social issues, and sought to minimise the organisation's traditional military role. The IRA remained divided over these strategies, but a significant segment, based in Dublin, welcomed the 'reintroduction of radical socialist republicanism into the movement'[24] and devised a gradualist strategy for the organisation. This involved a campaign for reform within the six counties of Northern Ireland and the unification of the working class in the province as a prerequisite of a campaign towards a united socialist Ireland.[25] Following this strategy the IRA fully supported the civil rights movement as it developed in the late 1960s.

Within Northern Ireland it was the Young Socialist Alliance, based at the Queen's University of Belfast, which picked up the new challenge presented by the growing agitation for civil rights. People's Democracy was formed as a result of police behaviour at the second major civil rights demonstration, in Derry in October 1968. The violence with which the police broke up the march, and the nationwide publicity that resulted from television coverage of the event, turned the civil rights campaign into a mass movement. Its reformist demands for one man, one vote, and one family, one house, presented the Unionist Government with the most serious challenge of its fifty years of unbroken rule. The original objectives of People's Democracy were to 'enter into the Civil Rights movement in order to participate in the mobilisation of the Catholic working class, and to radicalise the civil rights demands themselves.'[26] The optimistic radicalism of People's Democracy represented a new element in Northern Ireland politics. It was only in 1960 that any significant number of Ulster's lower-middle and working class Catholics found it possible to obtain higher education through the provisions of the welfare state and the Butler Education Acts. The Young Socialists at Queen's University inherited the ideology of traditional republicanism, but they were also exposed to less parochial socialist perspectives, and to the internationalism of student politics.[27]

However, as the situation escalated into increasingly violent confrontations with the state, the absence of agreement over broader questions of strategy, and the party's lack of organisational strength became critical problems. Many of the theoretical and practical difficulties that People's Democracy encountered are openly discussed by its leading members in an article which appeared in *New Left Review* in 1969. On the question of Protestant working class politics, the discussion clearly reflects the limitations of the traditional republican perspective in its optimistic assessment of the chances of winning over the Protestant workers to a revolutionary republican programme. Eamonn McCann is alone in expressing serious doubts about this possibility, and an awareness of the real danger that, in Northern Ireland, the politics of confrontation might lead to sectarian conflict. But his appraisal does not stem from a coherent analysis of the status of Protestant workers in Ireland, but rather from an appreciation of the tenacity of Catholic sectarianism. 'The cry "get the Protestants" is still very much on the lips of the Catholic working class. Everyone applauds loudly when one says in a speech that we are not sectarian, we are fighting for the rights of all Irish workers, but really that's because they see this as a new way of getting at the Protestants.'[28]

Between 1969 and 1971, against a background of escalating violence and the growing involvement of the British Army, many socialists, especially those in People's Democracy, moved toward nationalist positions as a result of their anti-imperialist stand. The change was reflected in increased support for the militant nationalism of the Provisional wing of the IRA and its final breakaway from the Official movement. In his book *War and an Irish Town*, Eamonn McCann describes how the process occurred in Derry, where, 'notwithstanding the absence of organised Republican involvement in the rioting, Republican sentiment was growing, and most strongly among the rioting elements.'[29] With the arrival of the British Army McCann notes:

> The struggle "against injustice" became, in practice, a struggle against British forces — a pattern of play which matched perfectly the old Republican idea of the way things really were — and people were almost relieved gradually to discover that the guiltily discarded tradition on which the community was founded was, after all, meaningful and immediately relevant.[30]

As Marx wrote:

> The tradition of the dead generations weighs like a nightmare on the minds of the living. And, just when they appear to be engaged in the revolutionary transformation of themselves and their surroundings, in the creation of something which does not yet exist, precisely in such epochs of revolutionary crisis they timidly conjure up the spirits of the past to help them; they borrow their names, slogans and costumes so as to stage the new world-historical scene in this venerable disguise and borrowed language.[31]

So, in Derry, ' "We Shall Overcome" and "We Shall not be Moved" gave way to "The Soldier's Song" and "Kevin Barry".'[32]

In view of the multiple and complex forces at work in contemporary Irish politics, and the historically determined dominance of religious and nationalist interpretations of political struggles, it is not surprising that socialists outside Ireland have found it difficult to penetrate beneath the surface forms of conflict, and to present an alternative structural analysis. As the violent battle between the Provisional IRA and the British Army came to dominate day to day events in Northern Ireland after 1970, socialists' sympathy for the anti-imperialist stand of the former led to increased support for the traditional interpretation of Irish politics. However, it is clear that while there is indeed a direct historical continuity in Anglo-Irish conflict, the central aspect of which remains the struggle for genuine Irish independence, so also qualitatively new contradictions are involved. These contradictions are related to the general level of the development of capitalist forces of production in Europe and the world economy, and their penetration into Ireland. While marxist analyses have consistently emphasised the broader Anglo-Irish framework of relations in which the Northern Ireland question is located, they have, for the most part, failed to take account of the profound changes that have occurred in this context.

This book starts by examining the consequences of the defeat of the United Irishmen's rebellion in 1798, and the subsequent economic and political integration of Ireland into the United Kingdom under the Act of Union, 1800. An analysis of the uneven development of capitalism in Ireland during the nineteenth century, based on a particular combination of modes of production, provides the basis for a critical re-evaluation of the political struggles that developed towards the end of the century between the Nationalists in the South and the Unionists in the North-East. From this perspective the partition settlement, and the establishment of a separate parliament in the North-East appear not simply as the result of a plot to protect British imperial interests in Ireland, but rather as the political reflection of deep-seated economic divisions within Ireland; divisions which were nonetheless the result of the island's historic colonial status.

In this context the Northern Ireland question is attributed with a certain autonomy from the historic 'Irish question', and the study proceeds with a more detailed characterisation of the main features of Northern Irish society after partition. This involves a reappraisal of such fundamental questions as the relationship between the economic, political and ideological levels of this social formation, and the historical convergence of Unionism, Protestantism and Orangeism into a cohesive social system which depended on the total exclusion of Catholics.

During the 1950s and 1960s major structural changes occurred in the broader Anglo-Irish framework which directly and indirectly began to undermine the logic of partition and the consonance of interests upon which the Unionist State in the North was based. This study therefore attempts to analyse the forces which led to the decline of Northern Ireland's traditional industrial base, and the province's increasing dependence on outside investment and the provisions of Britain's welfare system, and examines the forces which caused the Republic to abandon its efforts to establish an independent national economy through protectionism, and its reintegration into the British market. These forces, associated with the increasing international centralisation of capital and control over the means of production, are the key to the political realignments which permitted a real rapprochement to take place between the British and Irish governments in the mid-1960s. They lie behind their over-riding concern with the need for stability in the region, and the subsequent development of an almost bi-partisan approach to the problems of reform in the North.

The central concern of this book is the attempt to identify the major contradictions which emerged from the interaction between the forces supporting an unreformed Orange state in the North and the pressures for change emanating from the broader Anglo-Irish economic and political environment. It is within this framework that the attempt is made to provide a consistent and coherent explanation of the actual political developments that have transformed Northern Ireland in recent years, and the particular forms that political struggles have taken. However, political struggles are never direct unmediated reflections of underlying economic contradictions, and any analysis of Protestant political relations demands an explicit recognition of what Althusser has called *'the relative autonomy of the superstructures and their specific effectivity.'*[33]

Finally, the object of any genuinely marxist study must be the development of a class analysis which attempts to elucidate the interests of the working class and its allies. This book is intended as a contribution to this task; a task which has proved so difficult in Northern Ireland.

IRISH NATIONALISM AND ULSTER UNIONISM

Irish politics have been inextricably linked to the course of British history since Henry II assumed the 'lordship of Ireland' in the twelfth century. The history of Irish political development is dominated on the one hand by Britain's successive attempts to subjugate the island through military conquest and reconquest, through colonisation and political integration, and on the other by the various attempts by the native Irish, and on occasion the settlers, to oppose this domination. The most striking feature of Britain's imperial plans for the subjugation of Ireland is their almost total failure, for 'Irish rejection of the English connection does not come at the end of the development of an imperial process; every element of that process is rejected, and at every stage.'[1] The form that this rejection took has varied over the centuries, but it is not until the late eighteenth century that it is realistic to speak of Irish 'nationalism', and even then this must be modified by the understanding that Ireland and the Irish were not 'politically modern'. For, as Patrick O'Farrell has argued, 'the net result of English policy in Ireland, achieved in those sixteenth and seventeenth centuries when English assertive energy was great and self-doubts few, was to effect a work of destruction. What was destroyed was the loose social and political forms of the old Gaelic Ireland. In their place the English attempted to erect the centralised political forms of modern England. The substitute had no roots in the soil: it had to be propped up by the English until the Irish could learn to accept and use it.'[2]

The first challenge to British rule in Ireland that assumed the form of a struggle for 'national' independence occurred at the end of the eighteenth century, when a section of the Protestant settler community in the North-East produced 'the most ambitious attempt yet made in Ireland to separate religion from politics, and to unite all Irishmen in a purpose at once liberal and patriotic.'[3] The radical proposals of the Society of United Irishmen developed from earlier moderate demands for some degree of self-government which were voiced by the English and Scots Protestant colonial ascendancy in the latter half of the eighteenth century. These demands were classically colonial, directly comparable to those of the American colonies, and led, in 1782, to the granting of a limited degree of political autonomy in the form of Grattan's Parliament.

The impetus behind the radicalisation of these demands and the development of a struggle for national independence came from the descendants of the Scots Presbyterian colonists who had settled in Ulster in large numbers at the beginning of the seventeenth century. By the second half of the eighteenth century there was a rising Presbyterian bourgeoisie in the North-East, which naturally resented Britain's interference in Irish trade and manufacture, and was bitterly opposed to the civil disabilities imposed on protestant dissenters under the anti-popery bill of 1704. This bill not only deprived Roman Catholics of economic and political power in Ireland, but also demanded a sacramental test which prevented Presbyterians from holding public office, for example in the municipal corporations. For these reasons, despite the passing, in 1780, of a bill which relieved Irish dissenters from this sacramental test, Northern Presbyterians responded sympathetically to the aims and ideology of the French Revolution. In 1791 the Society of United Irishmen was established in Belfast with the aim of bringing about a radical reform of the Dublin Parliament which was firmly controlled by the great landowners. The strength of the movement was to lie in a democratic alliance between Roman Catholics and Protestants, built out of the Society's commitment to complete religious equality in Ireland, and the demand for equal representation of all the people of Ireland.

Failing to gain any substantive reforms through political pressure, the United Irishmen led an armed uprising against Britain in 1798. The rebellion was savagely repressed and, in 1801, under the Act of Union, Ireland was deprived of even its formal political autonomy in the form of the Dublin Parliament, and, like Scotland a century earlier, was merged with England in the 'United Kingdom of Great Britain and Ireland'.

This chapter is concerned primarily with the transformation of the economic and social base of the Irish struggle for national independence that occurred in the years following the Union with Britain, and particularly with the increasingly severe conflict that developed within Ireland between those seeking to preserve the Union and those seeking its repeal. For, by the end of the nineteenth century, the Protestants of Ulster, birthplace of radical Irish republicanism, had become intransigent defenders of the Union with Britain, implacably opposed to the growing demand for repeal expressed by the Dublin-based Catholic nationalists. The nationalist movement of the nineteenth century lost sight of the secular radicalism of the United Irishmen, and during the second half of the century came increasingly under the influence of the Catholic Church.

The United Irishmen's rebellion should be seen in the context of a wider pattern of national uprisings which affected not only the settled colonies of America, but also most of Europe. Lenin characterised the phenomenon thus:

> Throughout the world, the period of the final victory of capitalism over feudalism has been linked up with national movements. For the complete victory of commodity production, the bourgeoisie

must capture the home market, and there must be politically united territories whose population speak a single language, with all the obstacles to the development of that language and to its consolidation in literature eliminated. Therein is the economic foundation of national movement.[4]

The failure of Ireland's first 'national' uprising, and the subsequent loss of all economic and political autonomy, meant that during the crucial epoch of industrialisation and national consolidation in the nineteenth century, the island's development was totally subordinated to the needs and interests of British capitalism. This period saw the further development of the structural dependence that has continued to dominate Anglo-Irish relations in the twentieth century.

Ireland's dependence did not result in uniform national impoverishment. On the contrary, it created the conditions for the emergence of severe contradictions *within* Ireland, reflecting the uneven development of the forces of production. The possibility of national unity was progressively undermined by the emergence of two centres of capital in Ireland, and of two divergent modes of production. The eventual partition of the island in 1920, and the establishment of a Unionist Government in the North, and a Nationalist Government in the South, must be analysed in this concrete historical framework.

THE UNITED IRISHMEN'S REBELLION

During the last decade of the eighteenth century Ireland became increasingly ungovernable, for the political relations of power and authority which had been established after William of Orange defeated James II in 1690, were being challenged from all sides.

James II had turned to Irish Catholics for support in his attempt to restore Roman Catholicism in England, but was finally defeated on Irish soil by William's Protestant army and by the tenacious resistance of the Protestant settlers of the North-East. The settlement which followed William's victory strengthened English domination over the island, and firmly established Protestant supremacy within Ireland, for 'the bulk of the Catholic army passed into the service of France, and the great confiscations that followed the Revolution completed the ruin of the old race. When the eighteenth century dawned, the great majority of the former leaders of the people were either sunk in abject poverty or scattered as exiles over Europe; the last spasm of resistance had ceased, and the long period of unbroken Protestant ascendancy had begun.'[5] The ascendancy was intended to be a colonial garrison in Ireland, and the existence of religious differences prevented its being absorbed into native Irish society. However, by the second half of the eighteenth century many Protestant settlers had begun to develop a spirit of independence; the germ of a new

Irish nationalism.

The Protestant ascendancy in Ireland was made secure in a variety of ways. To begin with, the confiscations which followed the war reduced Catholic land ownership to a new low: to about one-fifteenth of the total land in Ireland. The great bulk of it now belonged to English landlords, as a result of the successive confiscations under James I, Cromwell and William III. Furthermore, the anti-popery laws of 1704 made it illegal for land to pass into Catholic hands, and placed a thirty-one year limit on any lease of land. These same laws also excluded Catholics from parliament, from the army, the militia and the civil service, and from municipal corporations and the legal profession. The object of the penal code was not religious persecution, but rather it was to deprive Catholics of all political power in Ireland. As a result of these restrictions, which bore most heavily upon the Catholic gentry, political leadership passed into the hands of the clergy. The tremendous political influence wielded by the Catholic Church in modern Ireland has its roots in the historic elimination of alternative avenues for Catholic political participation in Irish politics. The Irish Parliament in Dublin was therefore an exclusively Protestant affair, indeed an exclusively Anglican affair, for Protestant dissenters were also excluded by the imposition of the sacramental test.

In Ulster there were large numbers of Presbyterian colonists, many of them engaged in small-scale independent commodity-farming and weaving. The linen industry was well established amongst the colonists of Ulster by the end of the seventeenth century, and continued to expand throughout the eighteenth. It was the growing class of urban entrepreneurs, together with the more substantial tenant farmers and independent artisans in the North-East who had most to gain by a reform of the Dublin Parliament and a measure of 'national' independence.

During the seventeenth and eighteenth centuries, Ireland's economic development was deliberately retarded and distorted by England's colonial policies. Growth in any branch of trade or manufacture which presented a threat to English economic expansion was promptly curtailed. In 1663 the most prosperous element in the Irish economy, the export of live cattle to England, was severely restricted by the English Parliament. The jealousy of English cattle breeders which stimulated this restriction led to the total prohibition of cattle imports from Ireland three years later. In 1679 Ireland's trade with other colonies was interrupted by the Navigation Acts which required that, 'with a very few specified exceptions, no European articles could be imported into the English colonies except from England, in ships built in England and chiefly manned by English sailors. With a very few specified exceptions, no articles could be brought from the colonies to Europe without being first unladen in England.'[6] The Irish wool industry was destroyed in 1699 to prevent competition with English wool, and to keep Ireland as a market for that wool. In 1710 it was the brewing, and in 1747 the glass-manufacturing industries that were restricted.

Irish agriculture, the backbone of the economy, was inefficiently organised and highly vulnerable to fluctuations in the price of agricultural commodities on foreign markets, and to changes in the pattern of demand. The Dublin Parliament had no executive power to oppose English intervention into Irish trade and manufacture, for in 1720 the constitutional dependence of the Irish Parliament on the British Parliament had been reaffirmed by an act commonly known as the 'Sixth of George I'. Indeed, the Dublin Parliament had little interest in such questions since it was dominated by English landlords whose sole interest was the extraction of rent from their tenants.

These externally imposed restrictions hampered and distorted the development of the Irish economy as a whole, but during the second half of the eighteenth century progress in some sectors led to the emergence of an independent class of indigenous manufacturers and traders, whose interests were in direct conflict with England's mercantilist policies. Ireland still enjoyed a limited but profitable share of colonial trade, and between the 1730s and the 1760s the value of this colonial trade more than doubled. Trade with Britain and Europe also expanded during this period. More important, though, was the development of the linen industry in Ulster, 'the only Irish industry that did not threaten the prosperity of any Englishman.'[7] The export of cattle products such as beef, butter, tallow and hides was also expanding profitably, and the Irish ports made great profits from the provisioning of ships. In addition, the clandestine export of wool to France contributed to Irish overseas trade.

It was the American War of Independence which provided the necessary external stimulus for the political mobilisation of this growing class of traders and manufacturers. The parallel between the position of the American colonies and the position of Ireland was obvious. Sympathy for the American cause was particularly strong in Ulster, for during the previous fifty years thousands of Protestants had emigrated to America. Some were driven out by depressions in the linen industry, and others were Presbyterians seeking to escape the legal disabilities under which they suffered in Ireland. Britain's heavy military involvement in the war with America left Ireland extremely vulnerable, so that when France joined the war there was no force available in Ireland either to keep the peace on the domestic front or to repel a foreign invasion. In Lecky's words 'The desire for national independence was growing stronger and stronger in Ireland. The wretched condition of the finances, the corrupt disposal of patronage, the refusal of the English Parliament to grant that commercial liberty which was essential to Irish prosperity, and, above all, the example of America, had strengthened incalculably the old spirit of Swift and Molyneux.'[8]

In 1772 two important events occurred as a result of these developments. First, an important part of the Popery Act of 1704 which related to land was repealed, allowing Catholics in Ireland to take leases for life or a fixed term up to 999 years, and to inherit and bequeath land on the same terms as Protestants. This reform was sponsored by the 'patriots' in the Dublin Parliament; those members who were particularly insistent on the constitutional rights of Ireland and critical of English encroachments. This group of Protestants recognised the growing economic power of Catholic merchants and traders, and, after many years of relative social peace in Ireland wished to conciliate the Catholic population in order to promote the campaign for legislative independence. Second, sincerely fearing a French invasion, and finding the government utterly unable to form a militia, the Irish gentry organised the people into defence associations, and the Volunteers were born. On being told that a French invasion of Belfast was imminent, 'the people at once flew to arms. A sudden enthusiasm, such as occurs two or three times in the history of a nation, seems to have passed through all classes. All along the coast associations for self-defence were formed under the direction of the leading gentry.'[9] The Volunteers were a Protestant body since the laws forbidding Catholics to possess arms were still in force, but there was widespread Catholic support and the Volunteers became increasingly liberal in their attitude toward the relaxation of the rest of the penal code.

It was inevitable that the Volunteer movement should come to adopt increasingly political objectives, for though these Irish Protestants were determined to defend their country as part of the British Empire, they also insisted upon the abolition of trade restrictions. The desire for self-government was spreading through the country, and events in America did much to convince them that only through self-government could they maintain their commerical liberty in the face of the great commerical jealousy of English industries, and prevent taxation without representation. Agreements were made to use only goods manufactured domestically, and to abstain from buying English goods until the commercial restrictions were removed.

The Volunteers met with some success in their demands for free trade, for as J.C. Beckett points out, 'the cutting off of colonial trade had made the Irish market much more important to British merchants and manufacturers; and so Ireland must be enabled to buy more British goods. In short, the prosperity of Ireland now seemed as likely to be advantageous to Great Britain as formerly it had seemed to threaten her.'[10] In 1782 the British Government, in the face of large scale Volunteer mobilisation over the demand for legislative independence, repealed the 'Sixth of George I', and established the sole right of the Irish Parliament to legislate for Ireland. Ministerial power, however, remained firmly in the hands of the Lord Lieutenant and his Chief Secretary who were both Englishmen, appointed and instructed by English Ministers, and changed with each succeeding administration.

In the 1780s, Ireland entered on a period of comparative prosperity, based on an expansion of manufactures, both old and new. The linen and cotton industries expanded dramatically, though mostly within the confines of the North-East of the island; brewing and the wool industry also developed strongly. Of great importance was the growth of population and a quite widespread rise in the standard of living, which meant that the home market was expanding. Under these circumstances the Protestant manufacturing classes in Ulster became increasingly interested in the question of national legislation to protect Irish industry, and began to agitate for a reform of the Irish Parliament that would give them real political power. In a pamphlet published in 1791, Theobald Wolfe Tone reviled Grattan's Parliament for sacrificing Irish interests to the protection of English monopolies and English political interests. Their new demands, however, met with little success.

It was the French Revolution which provided the political impetus behind the setting up of the Society of United Irishmen in 1791, and the spread of ideas about revolutionary republicanism in Ireland. The emphasis on religious equality created the ideological basis of a democratic alliance between Catholics and Protestants, and gave Britain just cause for alarm. 'The idea of an "Irish nation", indifferent to religious rivalries, rooted in history, but enlightened by the Revolution, takes its rise in the Belfast of the late eighteenth century.'[11] The story of the United Irishmen's ill-fated uprising has been told many times, and it is not my intention to repeat it here. Rather, my aim is to draw attention to the complexity of Ireland's social formation in this period, and to the nature of the obstacles in the path of national unity that are of particular significance for the development of political struggles in the nineteenth century.

The driving force behind the United Irish movement was the Protestant manufacturing class in Belfast. Outside the urban centres the movement was strongest among fairly substantial tenant farmers and independent artisans who 'attacked the privileged position of the landlord and the Episcopal State Church and the taxes of the central government. They advocated the end of landowners' domination of local government, the abolition of tithes, Church tax and hearth money, and also of excise taxes, State pensions and sinecures.'[12] It was only in the province of Ulster that England's policy of establishing control through 'plantation' had any success, with significant numbers of English and particularly Scots Presbyterian settlers taking over the land. The remaining three provinces of Ireland were still overwhelmingly dependent on agriculture, with political and economic power firmly in the hands of the great English landlords. The United Irishmen could expect the support of an important section of the Catholic middle class for, although by the end of the century much of the original penal code had been relaxed, Catholics were still branded as inferior by being excluded from Parliament. The United Irishmen were committed not only to Parliamentary reform but to Catholic emancipation, and a number of active Catholics in the towns turned to rebellion faced with the refusal of emancipation.

It was through the Defender movement, however, that the great mass of poorer Roman Catholics joined the ranks of the disaffected. Defenderism originated among the Catholic peasants and weavers in Ulster who were organised in bands or 'vengeance groups' for mutual protection and religious rioting. By 1793 Defenderism had become linked with an older tradition of agrarian terrorism and had taken up the long-standing grievances of the Catholic peasantry, such as the levying of tithes and extortionate rents. In this way the organisation spread into neighbouring counties where the poorer population was exclusively Catholic, and where there was no religious animosity. The great mass of impoverished Catholic cottiers and small farmers had little interest in the reform of Parliament or even in Catholic emancipation, but the levying of tithes by the Established Episcopalian Church had been the cause of passionate agrarian outrages throughout the eighteenth century. The United Irishmen were committed to the complete abolition of religious establishments, as in France. Lecky concludes that by 1797 'the tithe grievance was now the chief political bond between the Presbyterians of the North and the Catholics of the South; and the fact that the French had begun their Revolution by abolishing tithes, was one of the chief motives put forward for welcoming a French invasion.'[13]

The great landlords who still dominated the Dublin Parliament vigorously opposed the campaign to enfranchise the middle classes, and the emancipation of Catholics, for their position in Ireland was directly threatened by the increasingly revolutionary republicanism of the United Irishmen. The Protestant ruling class in Ireland had been granted huge tracts of land through military conquest and confiscation, and their ability to hold that land and extract the maximum rent from it depended on the continuous backing of British force in the repression of rebellion and agrarian unrest.

The radicals of Belfast also met with resistance from certain elements in the Protestant tenantry and growing numbers of Protestant journeymen weavers. By the second half of the eighteenth century linen manufacture had become almost universal in Southern and mid-Ulster, and in Armagh particularly this expansion was accompanied by a rapid and significant decline in small-scale agricultural commodity production. This process led to the virtual eradication in this area of independent weavers, artisans and small farmers, and the growth of an essentially proletarian class of weaver employees. The declining status and loss of independence felt by this emergent class did not, however, make for class conflict. Peter Gibbon has shown that the 'pace of local industrial and peasant differentiation was sufficiently rapid to succeed in removing most sources of social and political independence from the countryside, while at the same time it was sufficiently slow to prevent the new class of employers assuming strategic positions.'[14] The appearance of this new mode of production in fact reinforced the hegemony of the landlord class in these areas, as Gibbon explains:

> .. it ensured that landlords, who stood largely outside the linen trade,
> would find themselves cast in the role of tribune, of potential cham-
> pions and courts of appeal to a population suffering for the first
> time the vicissitudes of submission to free market relations. This
> tendency was supported by the structural difficulties standing in the
> way of new proletarians developing their own leadership constituted
> by the fragmentation of centres of production.[15]

The Protestant proletariat expressed their resentment of this decline in
their fortunes not through class antagonism, but through a renewed
determination to defend their status within the Protestant ascendancy.
They demanded the preservation of traditional barriers to Catholic social
mobility, and the maintenance of Protestant privilege within the labour
market. 'The general tendency in the linen trade's recruitment patterns
until the 1770s was to conscript labour almost solely from the Protestant
population. As far as the weavers of Armagh were concerned, this constituted a recognition by the new industry of the traditional obligations to
loyalties which many landlords had recognised before.'[16] For a historical
justification of their stand they turned inevitably to the memory of 1690,
when William of Orange had defeated James II at the Battle of the Boyne,
thus establishing the victory of Protestantism over Catholicism in Ireland.
The exclusively Protestant Orange Order which appeared in 1795 played
a central role in the intimidation of Catholic weavers. Large numbers of
Catholic families were driven out of Armagh, and mill-owners or linen
manufacturers who employed Catholics were also attacked.

The persistence of Orangeism and this clear hierarchical division within
the industrial working class as it has developed over the last 200 years
raises important theoretical questions, for it cannot be explained simply by
reference to strategies of the ruling class, as a product of the ruling class's
ideological hegemony. The persistence of Orangeism as the relatively
autonomous expression of Protestant working class interest within this
social formation necessitates a consideration of what Louis Althusser has
called 'the *accumulation of effective determinations* (deriving from the
superstructures and from special national and international circumstances)
on the determination in the last instance by the economic.'[17] The significance of Gibbon's analysis of the origins of Orangeism derives from his
recognition of the relatively independent role of political and ideological
structures in creating a religiously stratified working class. This is clearly
revealed in his discussion of the 'frontier' culture that existed in Armagh, and
of the key role played by the intervention of the State apparatus in the
clash between the Orange Order and the United Irishmen, 'in order to
secure the services of one party against the other.'[18]

The ruling class in Ireland, and the British armed forces were not slow
to appreciate the counter-revolutionary significance of Orangeism, and
members of the Irish Parliament saw the advantage of reviving religious
animosities in order to defend the Protestant ascendancy. When an armed

uprising appeared imminent the Orange society was quickly taken up by men of rank and property, for as a magistrate in Dungannon observed: 'As for the Orangemen, we have a rather difficult card to play; they must not be entirely discountenanced — on the contrary, we must in a certain degree uphold them, for with all their licentiousness, on them we must rely for the preservation of our lives and properties, should critical times occur.'[19] The growth of the Orange Order outside Armagh was based on the sanction and encouragement of the State, with its need for allies in the struggle against the United Irishmen.

The spread of Orangeism inevitably provoked an increase in sectarian violence in Ulster, and encouraged the alliance between the United Irishmen and the Defenders, between the Protestant manufacturing class and the Catholic peasantry. In their attempts to win over the Defender groups to the cause of rebellion, the United Irishmen argued that Catholics would never be safe from the Orangemen until the existing regime had been completely overthrown. A large body of Defenders responded positively, but 'they were moved mainly by local grievances: neither the objects that they fought for nor their conduct of the war reflected the spirit of the United Irishmen, with whom they were connected by accidents of time and circumstances, rather than by any real community of ideas.'[20]

The armed uprising led by the United Irishmen finally began in May 1798 under the most inauspicious circumstances. On the eve of the rebellion most of the important leaders were arrested since the government had been kept well informed about the progress of the conspiracy by a network of spies. Wolfe Tone was in France, unable to mobilise an invasionary force to assist the rebellion. Martial law had been declared in disturbed districts before the rebellion broke out, and the army was sent in to disarm the populace. The quartering of an ill-disciplined army upon these areas inevitably led to military outrages and sectarian abuse, and extreme violence accompanied the search for arms. When the rebellion finally began there was fierce fighting, accompanied by indiscriminate executions and destruction of property on the part of the government forces, and inevitable sectarian attacks by Catholic rebels who began to suspect all Protestants of being Orangemen. After six weeks the rebellion was broken, and most of the rebel leaders were caught, tried and executed.

By the end of the eighteenth century there was no middle ground in Irish politics. The hope of liberty, equality and fraternity was banished by a year of terror and repression, and Ireland was left bitterly divided.

IRELAND UNDER THE ACT OF UNION

Britain's interest in establishing a legislative union between the two kingdoms was primarily political and strategic. Pitt's main concern was the danger of a French invasion and the need to protect Britain's strategic interests, for a disaffected and rebellious Ireland was a danger to British security. In the longer-run Pitt saw that the Union with England would permit the pacification of Ireland by enabling Catholic Emancipation, a reform which the Protestant Dublin Parliament refused. The Protestant ascendancy in Ireland, was, for the most part, very reluctant to abandon its 500 year old parliament. But in 1799 Ireland was politically bankrupt; the rebellion had revealed such deep-seated divisions within Ireland that even those who opposed the Union could not agree among themselves on any alternative remedy. So, in 1801 Ireland gave up its parliament in exchange for representation at Westminster.

The Act provided that the king's subjects in the United Kingdom of Great Britain and Ireland should be entitled to the same privileges in all matters of commerce, and that there should be free trade between the two islands. England was now entering a period of unrivalled industrial expansion and the ideology of laissez-faire was ascendant over traditional mercantilism. In both England and Ireland advocates of the Union seem to have been genuinely convinced that it would make Ireland prosperous through contact with the wealthy and expanding economy of Britain, and that prosperity would provide the basis of a stable political order. England's policy of defending the Protestant ascendancy in Ireland through military repression was to be wound up in favour of granting Catholic Emancipation, thus laying the foundation of unity between the Protestant and Catholic upper classes as defenders of the established order.

In the event, the Union heralded a century of industrial decline for most of Ireland, famine and pauperisation for most Irish peasants, and continuous political unrest. Agrarian disturbances necessitated the continuation of martial law, and for more than thirty years the country was almost continuously administered under special coercive legislation. Furthermore, Pitt's failure to implement his promise of Catholic Emancipation did little to encourage the Roman Catholic hierarchy in their support for the new order, and left a legacy of resentment and distrust that spread through the whole Catholic population. Yet, despite these ample grounds for grievance, no national movement emerged to take up the cause of the United Irishmen, the cause of Irish independence from Britain. One of the chief characteristics of Irish political history in the nineteenth century is the growing disunity within the island: between landlords, manufacturing classes and peasants, between Catholics and Protestants, and between the elected representatives and the populace.

Between 1801 and 1829 the only issue that gave any measure of unity or continuity to Irish political life was that of Catholic Emancipation. The struggle for Emancipation was concentrated at Westminster for twenty years and carried on by Protestant champions, until in the 1820s Daniel O'Connell turned it into a truly popular cause by mobilising the broad mass of Catholics in Ireland. In the years that followed his victory over Emancipation, O'Connell declared himself in favour of the repeal of the Union. However, he did little actively to prosecute this objective, and repeal in itself meant no more than the restoration to Ireland of the constitutional status she had enjoyed between 1782 and 1800. The Roman Catholic bishops and middle classes, as Beckett pointed out, 'had fought for Emancipation as a means of gaining political power and a share of public appointments; and now they wanted to enjoy the fruits of victory, not plunge into another agitation that could only alienate the very people to whom they must look for advancement.'[21]

It was not until the 1880s, under Charles Stewart Parnell's leadership, that the Irish Parliamentary Party made Home Rule its primary political objective, and even then its professed aim was to achieve limited autonomy within a federal system, to be established by an act of the British Parliament. The dramatic electoral success of the Home Rulers in the majority of Irish constituencies, which resulted from this campaign, was overshadowed, however, by their total failure in Ulster. The Union with Britain had radically transformed the economic and social basis of Irish nationalism by depriving it of the support of the most industrialised region in the country.

THE INDUSTRIALISATION OF THE NORTH-EAST

At the beginning of the nineteenth century it looked as though Ireland was on the verge of an industrial revolution.

> Irish farmers were producing more and more cereals, meat and dairy produce, for which they were getting extremely good prices. Landlords and tenants alike, throughout the country, were enjoying a higher standard of living and all social classes but the poorest could afford consumer goods that had previously been beyond their reach. The demand for these goods was opening up opportunities for commerce and industry, and there was no lack of labour to man the workshops, factories, warehouses and shops, because Ireland's population was rising rapidly.[22]

By the end of the nineteenth century, however, the only part of Ireland to have become fully industrialised was Belfast and the surrounding area. Outside the North-East, industry had contracted dramatically.

The legislative union of 1801 was followed by complete economic integration, with the abolition of Ireland's last tariff barriers by 1821. However, the tremendous pace of development in England was rapidly concentrating industry in areas where coal and iron ore were available and which had ready access to markets, with the result that industrial undertakings in less favoured regions such as Ireland were becoming increasingly uncompetitive. The development of an efficient transport system based on steam navigation and railways further strengthened the ascendancy of the great industrial districts. 'Few Irish manufacturers, left to their own resources, could hope to stand against the competition of the more highly-developed industries of Great Britain, to which they were now exposed.'[23] Furthermore, capital was also being drained out of Ireland throughout the greater part of the century, in the form of rent, for absenteeism amongst the landlord class had increased after the Union. This loss of capital was not compensated for by any steady inflow from British investment, for 'British capitalists knew little about Ireland, save that it was poor, and frequently disturbed; they saw no prospect either of a quick return, or of substantial profits to compensate for delay and the risk of loss; and the capital that might have transformed the economic life of Ireland went elsewhere.'[24]

Only in Ulster did free trade with Britain lead to industrial expansion and prosperity. Even prior to the Union we may detect the seeds of uneven development, for the cornerstone of Ulster's advanced industrial development in the nineteenth century was the linen industry which developed on the basis of widespread small-scale manufacture amongst Ulster tenant farmers in the eighteenth century. In contrast to the remaining three provinces of Ireland, the transition to a market economy in Ulster was soundly based on the emergence of a tenant farmer class, actively engaged in simple commodity production. The ability and willingness of Ulster tenant farmers to diversify into linen manufacture has traditionally been explained by reference to the supposedly advantageous tenurial system that prevailed in the North-East, known as 'tenant right' or the 'Ulster custom'.[25] According to this view the Ulster tenant enjoyed relative security of tenure, did not suffer from rack-renting, and if he left his farm was entitled to be paid the full value of any improvements he might have made. The significance of the custom, it has been argued, lay in the fact that it permitted and encouraged the accumulation of capital on a small scale. Thus C. Gill, in his book on the rise of the linen industry in Ireland, points out that 'the small capital of a thrifty peasant could be used in acquiring a loom, building a weaving shed, or buying raw material. The profits of manufacture in turn could be invested in land, or in hiring additional workers.'[26] There is, however, as Solow has pointed out, no empirical evidence to support this view.[27]

In his important recent work Gibbon has produced an analysis of the causes of uneven development in Ireland which begins with the fact of two different forms of colonisation in the seventeenth century.

> Most of the land which changed hands in the south during the first half of the seventeenth century was acquired by wealthy English adventurers and Crown creditors. This first generation of southern colonial landlords tended to acquire large tracts of land unconditionally, and to use their not inconsiderable resources to stock them with livestock. So great were these estates that most of their owners also found it profitable or convenient to sub-let to lesser tenants.[28]

In the North-East, however, confiscated lands were entrusted to

'undertakers' who were required to bring over English and Scots settlers
to 'colonise' the province. The colonists who settled in Ulster during the
seventeenth century came from areas of small-scale independent commodity
farming and weaving. Many brought with them their small capital savings
and basic skills in linen manufacture, while the Flemish and Huguenot
colonies of the 1690s provided more advanced techniques.[29]

The settlers who came to Ulster were numerous enough to ensure that
the average size of farm available to them was small, and, in any case, few
of them had sufficient capital to be able to invest in large-scale farming.

> It was in these circumstances that northern colons sought to
> diversify their farming operations and — probably precipitated by
> a relative depression in prices after 1650 — to combine them with
> textile production. Local agriculture in itself made little contri-
> bution to the latter's growth either by providing ready-made
> stocks of free labour or by allowing the accumulation of capital
> through any purportedly advantageous tenurial system (the 'Ulster
> custom', so called). The crucial input in the process was the
> relation between the low *level* and high *generality* of colon
> capitalisation, which followed specifically from the character
> of the petty commodity-producing agriculture which the
> immigrants brought with them.[30]

Outside the province of Ulster the policy of colonisation never got off the
ground, and the overwhelming majority of tenants were native Irish
peasants. Factors in the failure of the linen industry to establish itself here
were the lack of skilled weavers, the lack of capital to invest in manufacture,
and a growing dependence on specialised agricultural production. The
success of the linen industry in Ulster provoked an increase in population
in the eighteenth century, which in turn encouraged the further subdivision of agricultural land. However, since weavers were able to pay
higher rents than farmers, relations between landlord and tenant improved,
in contrast to their deterioration in the South.

As well as being endowed with a widespread, if primitive, marketing
infrastructure at the time of the Union, the Belfast area had abundant
water power and a good harbour. It was, moreover, linked with the rest
of Ulster by the Lagan valley, which provided a communicating corridor
with other parts of Ulster for collecting homespun linen yarn and linen
web. Even in the eighteenth century linen was a sizeable and valuable
export, despite the fact that it was largely supplementary to framing, and
was organised on an old-fashioned basis. The transition to machine production did not occur on a significant scale until the 1830s, and it was the
introduction of the cotton industry to Ireland that first caused Belfast to
begin to develop into a sizeable industrial city. During the 1780s production
of cotton became centralised around Belfast, since many of the techniques
required for its marketing and manufacture were established features of the
linen industry. The manufacture of cotton was technologically more
advanced, however, and promised high profit rates. The raw material was

imported, and entrepreneurs were quick to see the possibilities in spinning cotton by machine. Control of production rapidly concentrated in the hands of the industrialists, who attracted large numbers of workers to Belfast, and around this manufacturing process there sprang up an enginee-ring industry based on the maintenance of the cotton machines. The prosperity of the cotton industry did not last, because of a series of depressions which followed the Napoleonic Wars, and severe competition from Lancashire. However, the long term importance of the cotton industry was that it provided the model for the reorganisation of the linen industry, which, unhampered by lack of home demand and able to exploit export markets to the full, developed vigorously. Gibbon notes that 'in 1846 there were 1,000 factory hands in the city. In 1859 techniques of factory weaving became widespread, decimating the extensive remains of rural domestic production, and by 1875 incorporating 60,000 factory hands into the trade.'[31]

During the first half of the nineteenth century Belfast's population increased five-fold, reaching 100,000 by 1850. Then, in the 1850s Belfast acquired its second major industry, iron ship-building. As long as ships were made from timber it was difficult to compete with American and Canadian ship-builders. However, once it became cheaper to build ships from iron, Belfast's position was ideal. It had the essential combination of available land and deep water, and an enterprising Harbour Commission which had the foresight to carry out extensive alterations to develop the harbour. By the end of the nineteenth century, Belfast's Harland and Wolff and Workman shipyards ranked among the giants of British ship-building, responsible for about a quarter of the total United Kingdom tonnage between them. [32]

On the basis of the needs of the linen and ship-building industries a host of smaller industrial concerns sprang up, making spinning machines, scutching and hackling equipment, steam engines and ropes. In this climate of expansion, local capital was reinvested, supplemented by Scottish and English capital. 'In fact concentration and centralisation of capital became a dominant economic trend in Ulster by the last years of the nineteenth century.'[33] Before the First World War, Belfast had a population approach-ing 400,000, and it was one of the more prosperous cities of the British Isles, where wages were keeping pace with those in English cities, and there was little unemployment.[34] Already in 1891 its population had outstripped that of Dublin.

One further cause of the dramatic growth of Ulster's economy was its access to British and foreign markets, and its integration into the British economy on an equal basis. The Irish economy could not provide the framework for an autonomous centre of capitalist development in the nineteenth century, with its small home market and its vulnerability to British competition. Even in the eighteenth century the linen industry relied on the English market, and foreign markets were absolutely vital for its expansion in the nineteenth century. The shipbuilding industry, which in 1886 employed 5,000 men and by 1915 employed a quarter of the male labour force, was inevitably an export industry, and goods required by the industry that were not produced in Belfast itself were all imported. The industrialisation of the North-East occurred independently of any economic development in the rest of Ireland, and had little impact on the agricultural South beyond offering employment in Belfast as an alternative to emigration.

It was this pattern of grossly uneven development in Ireland that lay behind Ulster's increasing isolation from the mainstream of Irish political development in the nineteenth century, the resurgence of Irish nationalism. Unionism was the natural political reaction of a province which had benefited so dramatically from the Union with Britain.

IRISH AGRICULTURE AND THE LAND QUESTION

In stark contrast to the economic progress enjoyed by Ulster in the nineteenth century, the rest of Ireland suffered industrial decline and agrarian disaster. Various explanations have been given for this uneven development, from the unequal distribution of entrepreneurial talents as between Belfast and Dublin[35] to the inefficiency of Southern Irish agriculture. The causes are obviously complex, but Gibbon has provided an important starting point by drawing attention to Ireland's two distinct experiences of colonisation. Outside Ulster 'colonisation took the form not of a large-scale independent colon immigration but of the transfer of land — generally in large quantities — to wealthy colonists.'[36] Associated with this pattern of land-ownership was a 'relatively high level of agricultural specialisation'. This specialisation was increasingly influenced by the demands of the British market.

Gibbon also notes that 'the predominantly agrarian character of the southern economy became more pronounced as time passed. It was, as much as anything, a product of the increasing integration of the British and Irish economies during the eighteenth and early nineteenth centuries.'[37] The abolition of Ireland's protectionist barriers and exposure to British competition had profound repercussions. E.R.R. Green concludes:

> This meant that the Irish economy was now forced back onto those kinds of activity for which it was endowed by nature or in which it had developed some special skill. There was precious little of the latter other than the linen industry. It was a matter, then, of concentrating on the production of foodstuffs to satisfy the English market.[38]

England's enormous demands assured Ireland in normal times of a monopoly over the grain market, and between 1800 and 1830 trade in grain and provisions flourished. The majority of Irish tenants, however, saw little corresponding improvement in their condition for, as F.S.L. Lyons has pointed out, the tenure system imposed by the colonists, 'as it had operated since the upheavals of the seventeenth century, had substituted a rent economy for the old familial economy and had thus opened the way for an individualistic scramble for land which, in the relatively favourable circumstances of the late eighteenth and early nineteenth centuries, had made possible the upsurge of population.'[39] The tremendous increase in population, accompanied by high rates of subdivision in peasant holdings led to the highly inefficient use of resources and to rural underemployment on a massive scale.

The poverty and insecurity of the mass of Irish peasants was greatly exacerbated by the development of a trend away from labour-intensive tillage toward pasture, reflecting a change in British demand for Irish agricultural products. The pattern emerged in the 1830s, and the rapid transformation of Irish agriculture that had occurred by the 1840s is described by Marx in a letter to Engels:

> The system of 1801-46, with its rack-rents and middlemen collapsed in 1846 . . . The repeal of the Corn Laws, partly the result of or at any rate hastened by the Irish famine, deprived Ireland of its *monopoly* of England's corn supply in normal times. Wool and meat became the slogan, hence conversion of tillage into pasture. Hence from then onwards systematic consolidation of farms.[40]

The clearing of the peasants from the land required for pasture was facilitated by the great famine, in which the vulnerability of a great mass of peasants was cruelly revealed. Between 1845-49 one million Irishmen died of hunger or disease, and more than one million emigrated, out of a total population of just over seven million. Paradoxically, land became scarcer rather than more plentiful for those who survived, for there was continuous consolidation of land to make room for cattle and sheep. In the process of this transformation, a large number of English landlords went to the wall, for the famine deprived them of their rents and the capital necessary to invest in improvements. Under the Encumbered Estates Act of 1849, 3,000 estates were sold, passing mainly into the hands of a new Catholic middle class, eager to invest in the land for reasons of prestige and security.[41]

The new agricultural policies meant prosperity for the surviving landowners, but brought little comfort to the vast majority of Irish peasants who still had no right to fair rents or fixity of tenure. The successful consolidation of agricultural land into large farms is reflected in the dramatic fall that occurred in the number of small plots. Holdings of under five acres fell from nearly 182,000 in 1845 to 88,000 in 1851, and farms between five and fifteen acres also began to disappear. Despite the fact that population declined sharply after the famine, evictions were on the increase. Marx notes that between 1855-66, 1,032,694 Irishmen were replaced on the land by 996,877 head of livestock.[42] In 1867 he wrote to

Engels that the Irish Lord Viceroy, Lord Abercorn ' "cleared" his estate in the last few weeks by forcibly evicting thousands of people. Among them were prosperous tenants, whose improvements and investments were thus confiscated.'[43] A similar transformation, from tillage to grazing, was occurring in British agriculture, but in Britain there was expanding manufacture to absorb the labour that was displaced in the process. The Irish countryman, if he could not make a living on the land, had no recourse but to emigrate.

From the time of the great famine until Gladstone's first Home Rule Bill in 1886, the issue of land reform occupied a central position in Irish politics. The Young Ireland movement of 1842-48, dedicated to the revival of a distinctive Irish revolutionary nationalism, believed that 'a secure and independent agricultrual peasantry is the only base on which a people ever rises or ever can be raised; or on which a nation can safely rest.'[44] And the peasantry of Ireland was at this time in great distress. The insecurity, poverty, and real threat of starvation faced by many tenants in this period were revealed in continuing agrarian 'outrages'. The threatened small-holders and agricultural labourers in the South of Ireland also gave considerable support to the disruptive activities of the Fenian Brotherhood, an oathbound secret society founded in 1858 whose aim was to overthrow by force British rule in Ireland. However, the Brotherhood's main supporters were Irish emigrants in North America, and they had no real programme for reform. The struggling tenants found a far more immediately effective method of combatting the landlords in banding together in the Land League which was set up in 1879, under the leadership of the radical, Michael Davitt. The League's objectives were a reduction in rents, state aid for tenants to buy out the land they worked on, and an end to evictions. Davitt's belief in the possibility of establishing a revolutionary movement on a national scale was increased by an economic crisis in the Irish economy, stemming from falling agricultural prices and a series of bad harvests. Lyons concludes:

> that the land question was the engine which would draw the national question in its train was partially glimpsed by the tenant-right agitation of the 1850s and then brilliantly vindicated in the Land War which, between 1879 and 1882, laid the foundations for the ultimate revolution in land tenure whereby over the next thirty years the tenant was enabled to become the owner of the farm he worked.[45]

In the event, the movement's radicalism was undermined by its own success in winning reforms from Westminster, and by its partial co-option into Parnell's parliamentary campaign for Home Rule. Between 1881 and 1903 the Westminster Parliament passed a series of acts by which the tenant farmers of Ireland gradually obtained possession of the land. The growing influence of the Irish rural bourgeoisie, and a tremendous increase in the numbers of small peasant proprietors were key factors in severing the land question from the national question. The agrarian revolution which Marx, along with revolutionary Irish nationalists, had hoped would be the lever for Irish independence was thus accomplished by the British State.

At the end of the nineteenth century there were two divergent modes of production in Ireland: in the North, machine industry; in the South, extensive commercial farming. Gibbon summarises the main distinctions between 'the north. . . with barely a fifth of its employed population outside production [and] the south with almost a third.' The industrial workforce of both regions was also internally differentiated between employees in specific occupations and general labourers, without regular employment. General labourers constituted 34.5% of the labour force in the South, but only 19.2% in the six Northern counties. 'Accordingly it must be reckoned that the lumpenproletariat occupied a more central place in the southern than in the northern social structure, and that this in turn reflected the existence in the North (and the absence from the south) of the type of machine industry requiring a large and stable work force.' Furthermore, in Dublin in 1881, '12.3 per cent of the employed population were free professionals, in Belfast 6.3 per cent. Likewise, while 19.1 per cent of the Dublin work force were in domestic service, the Belfast figure was only 13.3 per cent.'[46]

The existence of two regional economies within Ireland is the key factor in explaining the emergence of two divergent, major political movements in the nineteenth century: Nationalism and Unionism.

NATIONALIST POLITICS

From its rise under O'Connell, after the granting of Catholic Emancipation in 1829, to its rout by Sinn Fein in the 1918 general election, the Irish Parliamentary Party did little to prosecute the cause of real Irish independence, or even to remedy the grievances of the majority of Irish citizens. Yet the Party did not lack influence at Westminster, often holding the balance of seats between the Conservatives and the Liberals. In the 1850s they adopted the title, 'the Irish Brigade', and began to work in unison. However, Marx noted in 1854 that:

> With all this power of Cabinet-making, the Brigade have never prevented any infamies against their own country nor any injustice to the English people. The period of their greatest power was at the time of O'Connell, from 1834-1841. To what account was it turned? The Irish agitation was never anything but a cry for the Whigs against the Tories, in order to extort places for the Whigs . . . It is time for the Irish people to put off their dumb hatred of the English and call their own representatives to an account of their wrongs.[47]

In 1880 Parnell brought new life and unity to the Irish Party with the demand for Home Rule. The Party's interests were not those of the manufacturing classes, nor those of the peasants, despite a formal alliance between Parnell and the Land League. The influence of the Parliamentary Party at Westminster depended in great part on the support of a powerful mass movement at home, but there was little genuine commitment to the peasant's cause within the Party. In fact the leaders of the Home Rule movement were particularly concerned to control and divert the revolutionary forces which had been mobilised in the country by the Land League and by the Feinians. Landlord influence declined after the Party's dramatic electoral success in 1885, but its ranks were swelled by members of the substantial business class and of the professions. Despite a growth in the farming and shop-keeping membership, Lyons concludes that 'it seems not unfair to suggest that the political and social attitudes of the bulk of the members were distinctly conservative. So, at any rate, it seemed to those excellent judges of conservatism, the Irish hierarchy.'[48] Few of the Parnellites wanted to see any radical economic or social change in Ireland, and most looked to the restoration of the Dublin Parliament as a source of political patronage. Liam de Paor, suggests that:

> The most significant indication, however, that revolution had been contained, and the independence movement successfully diverted into a relatively 'safe' struggle for power within a basically unchanged colonial system, was the winning over, from an initially suspicious attitude, of the Irish Catholic bishops to a qualified support for the nationalist movement.[49]

Parnell's alliance with the Catholic Church did little to allay the suspicions of Protestant Ulster, for from the late 1880s Catholic Ireland underwent a dramatic religious revival which combined 'militant ascetic Catholicism with aggressive emotional nationalism'.[50] The moderate Irish Party was in fact subsequently swept aside by a new tide of uncompromising nationalism which combined religious and cultural revivalism with an economic plan that posed a far more direct threat to the industrial interests of Ulster. However, it was during the period of the Irish Party's alliance with the Liberals at Westminster, in their parliamentary campaign for limited political autonomy, that Ulster's links with the Conservative Party were consolidated, and the foundations of a powerful alliance laid in the mobilisation of the Orange Order to oppose the Nationalist cause.

In the general election of 1918 the Irish Home Rule Party was overwhelmingly defeated by Sinn Fein candidates, whose aim was to secure international recognition of Ireland as an independent Irish Republic. Instead of taking up their seats at Westminster, they proclaimed themselves an independent Irish parliament: Dail Eireann. They had the backing of the Irish Republican Army, formed out of the Fenian Brotherhood. From the point of view of Ulster, Sinn Fein's republicanism was crucially different from the Home Rule which Parnell had envisaged, for it posed a direct threat to Northern industry. Sinn Fein's economic policy was designed to create the conditions whereby an independent Irish manufacturing class could come into existence. The keystone of the policy was protection from foreign competition. Tariff barriers, however, were anathema to the regional economy of Ulster, whose advanced industrial development depended on free access to British and foreign markets.

Little interest was shown in the industrial sector of the Irish economy outside Ulster until after 1880. By then the years of agricultural prosperity which followed the great famine had come to an end, and intense competition from abroad had shown up the deficiencies of farming practice in Ireland.

> The report of the select committee of 1885 on industries in Ireland really marks the beginning of industrial revival if only by drawing attention to a truly alarming state of affairs. Irishmen had become more or less reconciled to the loss of handicrafts and the disappearance of local breweries, tanneries, rope-walks and the like, but now the basic agricultural life of the country and the trades dependent upon it were also threatened.[51]

In 1898 Arthur Griffith founded the *United Irishmen*, a weekly paper in which he preached the doctrine later to be known as 'Sinn Fein' — 'Ourselves'. His aim was to make Ireland an industrial nation through policies of economic self-reliance and protectionism, and his source of inspiration was the German economist Friedrich List and his book *The National System of Protection*. Griffith was also convinced that Ireland must be politically free before it could be economically prosperous. He rejected, however, the paths of violent revolution or parliamentary action, advocating instead a policy of non-cooperation like that adopted by the Hungarian nationalists.

At the beginning of this century the class profile of Southern Ireland was beginning to change in such a way as to provide a growing audience for Griffith's ideas. Under the provisions of the Wyndham Act (1903), the last of Westminster's land reform Bills, 270,000 Irish tenants were able to buy up their holdings in the space of six years, thus creating a vast new class of peasant proprietors. This development stimulated the growth of Catholic trading and manufacturing classes, who had a common interest in finding ways of protecting and expanding their activities. In 1905 the political party, Sinn Fein, was established to organise militant nationalist sentiment and to articulate the new economic policies. In his pamphlet, 'The Sinn Fein Policy' Griffith states: 'A nation cannot promote and further its civilisation and its social progress equally as well by exchanging agricultural products for manufactured goods as by establishing a manufacturing power of its own.' Therefore, 'If a manufacturer cannot produce as cheaply as an English or other foreigner only because his foreign competitor has better resources at his disposal, then it is the first duty of the Irish Nation to afford protection for that manufacturer.'

This economic nationalism was accompanied by a Gaelic revival: a movement led by Irish intellectuals to restore Gaelic culture, history and language to its rightful place in Irish life. In the early 1900s the Gaelic League, which had been founded in 1893, succeeded in establishing Irish teaching in school hours, Irish qualifications for teachers in the Gaeltacht and Irish as a subject in the new National University. In sport and literature as well, this cultural nationalism asserted itself with the rejection of all that was English in origin. The inevitable fusion of nationalist cultural and economic forces gave rise to the idea of an 'Irish Ireland', ' " Ireland not free only but Gaelic as well; not Gaelic only but free as well" — an Ireland, in short, in which the Ulster Protestant could hardly be expected to feel at home.'[52]

In 1913 these nationalists were becoming increasingly militant, angered by the slow progress of the Liberal Government's latest Home Rule Bill (1912), and by the sight of the Ulster Volunteer Force openly training in the North. By the end of 1913 the Irish Republican Brotherhood had launched a volunteer movement similar to that in the North. When the First World War broke out, the Irish Parliamentary Party agreed to the postponement of Home Rule measures, and pledged their support for the British cause. But the Party had lost its pre-eminent position in Irish politics. 'Its power base was so secure for so long among the expanding middle class of peasant proprietors and aspiring tenants that it failed to make any really serious efforts to broaden its appeal. For a nationalist party it allowed its base to become too narrow.'[53]

The most militant nationalists regarded the war as an opportunity to snatch full independence from Britain. The Irish Republican Brotherhood who were the real advocates of violent revolution in Ireland never sought to recruit on a mass scale, but acted as a revolutionary secret society. The IRB, with the support of James Connolly's tiny socialist militia, planned an armed uprising in 1916. I do not intend to retell the story of the Easter Rising here. The rebels' one week stand in Dublin, the violence with which it was suppressed, and the subsequent execution of fifteen of the insurrection's leaders, including the wounded Connolly, assured for these events a central place in the developing national consciousness. However, it is important to note that the rising did not in fact have the support of 'nationalist' Ireland. Irish manufacturing workers and farmers benefited considerably from the boost that the war gave to the economy, and at least 100,000 Catholics from Ireland joined the British Army. In other words anti-British feeling was not at its strongest. Nonetheless, in the period between the rising and the general election of 1918, public opinion moved away from the Parliamentary Party to support the heirs of the rising, the developing republican movement. Sinn Fein and the IRB found themselves in the centre of the Irish political stage, and the attempt by the British Government, in 1918, to introduce conscription in Ireland gave Sinn Fein the opportunity to take political leadership. In the general election held in December 1918 Sinn Fein swept the board, winning 73 out of a total of 105 Irish seats.

The nationalist movement which led to the establishment of the twenty-six county Irish Free State in 1921 was not the direct descendant of the

United Irishmen. There is no simple continuity in Ireland's struggle for independence between Wolfe Tone, Charles Stewart Parnell and Arthur Griffith. The rebellion of 1798 formed part of the 'epoch of bourgeois democratic revolutions in Western Europe', which, according to Lenin, 'embraces a fairly definite period, approximately between 1789 and 1871. This was precisely the period of national movements and the creation of national states.'[54] In this context, the emergence of a national bourgeoisie, and its struggle for independence, was bound up with a particular phase in the development of capitalism, and its victory over feudalism. The national State was the framework within which the most progressive capitalist relations of production might be established, permitting the unhampered expansion of productive forces on the basis of control of the home market. The nationalist struggle of Sinn Fein reflected the desire of the small-scale Catholic manufacturers in the South to create an autonomous centre of capitalist development in Ireland. But, by the beginning of this century, this no longer coincided either with the interests of the most advanced industrial sector in Ireland, or with those of the North-East's urban proletariat. Economic integration with Britain had resulted in the creation of two centres of capital in Ireland, with divergent interests; large-scale Irish manufacturing and farming was totally dependent on Britain and her imperial markets. The secession of the six North-Eastern counties from the Irish Free State was a direct reflection of this contradiction within Ireland.

The conflict of interest was not limited, however, to a simple North-South dichotomy, but became an increasingly divisive force within Sinn Fein in the South. Sinn Fein's social base was greatly widened by the failure of the rising and the collapse of the Parliamentary Party, and the coalition of nationalist interests that it led was open to the real danger of internal class conflict. The civil war which followed the signing of the Anglo-Irish Treaty in 1922 clearly revealed the class structure of the nationalist movement, and the divergent interests it had united.[55] The civil war was not fought out between those who accepted and those who rejected partition. The argument between Treatyites and anti-Treatyites was about the precise nature of the future relationship between the twenty-six county Free State and Great Britain. Under the Treaty the Free State was granted Dominion status within the Commonwealth.

> The Cumann na nGael Party — the pro-Treaty faction of Sinn Fein which formed the first Independent 26-County government — represented large farmers and commercial businessmen who wished as far as it was possible, to minimize economic friction with Britain and to obtain for themselves as comfortable a position as they could within a colonial situation. Many, like Kevin O'Higgins, were fearful of the effect of high tariffs on existing Anglo-Irish trade. Mr de Valera's minority faction (representing small manufacturing capitalists) held to the original Sinn Fein policy of protectionism and represented those who wanted to wage an economic war against

British domination and thereby quickly to build their own Irish industrial structure.[56]

The Labour Party and the trade unions adopted an official position of neutrality in the civil war, on the grounds that their fight was now against capitalism, regardless of whether the government took the form of a Free State or a Republic. In fact they were regarded as a *de facto* pro-treaty party.

During the 1930s, when de Valera's new party, Fianna Fail, had defeated Cumman na nGael, the Republicans set about implementing the original Sinn Fein policy. The history of the Irish Republic shows clearly the impossibility of building an autonomous centre of capitalist development in Ireland; of realising Griffith's dream of a prosperous, independent, industrial Irish economy. Sinn Fein's national revolution could not establish new social and productive relations. The agrarian revolution had been carried out by the British Government at the turn of the century, and industrial capitalism was implanted in the North. Rather, the independence of the South reinforced its agrarian backwardness. Unemployment increased, with a quarter of a million people emigrating during the first ten years of independence; and capital continued to flow out of Ireland in search of more profitable resting places. Furthermore, de Valera's drive towards 'self-sufficiency' in the thirties necessitated internal repression and reaction, for Irish capital was fighting for its survival, and could not withstand militant attacks from labour.

The ideological picture in this period is as dismal as the economic one. The Unionist claim that Home Rule would mean Rome Rule seemed clearly substantiated by growing links between the Government and the Catholic Church. Denominational education remained, and in 1935 the import and sale of contraceptives was banned. Finally, de Valera's Government accorded the Catholic Church a 'special place' in the new constitution of 1937, which was drawn up 'in the name of the Most Holy Trinity from whom all authority derives.' National unity in the South was further reinforced by constant attention to the Gaelic past, and increasing emphasis on the teaching of the Irish language in schools. By the end of the 1930s the economic, ideological and political forces dividing North from South left little grounds for cooperation or even communication.

UNIONIST POLITICS

By 1830 the chief literary organ of Ulster Liberalism was the unromantic *Northern Whig*, which supported Catholic Emancipation, parliamentary reform, the repeal of the Corn Laws, and denounced rack-renting landlords. But it took the Union for granted, and attacked O'Connell for advocating its repeal. In other words, Ulster Liberalism had lost its outstanding characteristic, the insistence on maintaining Ireland's national independence, and had become indistinguishable from English Liberalism. The material basis of the North-East's conversion from republicanism to support for the Union was described earlier. However, as Gibbon has stated, there are important questions to be answered concerning the form that the Unionist movement took; questions 'of the origins of its pronouncedly Conservative leadership and outlook, of its use of Protestantism as its major symbol, of its integration of the lower orders.'[57]

The political repercussions stemming from the industrialisation of the North-East were not confined to the simple conversion of Republicans into Unionists. After the granting of Catholic Emancipation and the passing of the 1832 Reform Bill, the Liberal Party suffered a dramatic set-back in Belfast, which had no parallel in other urban centres in Britain. Many Conservatives were bitterly opposed to these reforms, and they became even more concerned when the liberals promised support for O'Connell's civil rights proposals, which were combined with a threat to the House of Lords and a movement for the repeal of the Union. Faced with this challenge the Conservatives began to agitate successfully in Ireland against the Liberals, and between 1833 and 1874 they managed to hold about three-quarters of the parliamentary seats in Ulster. After 1850 the Liberals never succeeded in winning the support of a majority of the urban bourgeoisie, while rural Liberalism was overwhelmingly dependent on the Catholic vote, and in these seats the rise of Home Rule in the 1880s meant the total eclipse of the Liberal Party in Ireland.

The rise of Conservatism in Belfast was accompanied by a vigorous campaign against the Presbyterian tradition of religious tolerance.[58] The Protestant Crusade was started by a group of ultra-Tories, led by six Irish peers who saw the political potential of using the cry of 'no-popery' to mobilise support for the defence of the Union and of the House of Lords. All these peers were officials in the Orange Order which provided a meeting ground for members of the Church, the professions, the business community and the gentry. By the 1830s popular Orangeism had already developed its familiar myths:

> ... the plantation, the wilderness settled with bible and sword, the massacres of 1641 and the martydom of the settlers by the treacherous and barbarous uprising of the natives; the threat to 'freedom, religion and laws' caused by the accession of the popish James II, the glorious revolution which overthrew him, the sufferings, endurance, valour and triumph of the cause and Derry, Enniskillen, Aughrim, and the Boyne.[59]

In 1834 the link between Protestant fundamentalism and Conservatism was firmly established, when Henry Cooke, a Presbyterian minister, began his campaign to get the Presbyterians to join with the Established (Anglican) Church and the Tories to combat the impact of Catholic Emancipation. Cooke's bigoted and inflammatory speeches and sermons in Belfast provoked violent confrontations between Catholic and Protestant workers.[60]

Liberals and Radicals at Westminster succeeded in restricting the public activities of the Orange Order, for its ability to provoke violence and disorder led it into disrepute, and it lost the support previously given it by the middle and upper classes. It did not emerge as a significant political force until the 1880s when it was taken up again by 'men of property' during the campaign against Home Rule. The spirit of Orangeism, however, thrived under the 'new reformation' in Belfast, as preachers vied with each other to denounce the anti-Christ pope. The first sectarian riots began in the decade after the famine, which drove large numbers of half-starved Catholics into Belfast in search of employment, and crowded them into segregated ghettos in Belfast. Orangeism was imported into Belfast with the urbanisation of Protestant mill-workers in areas such as Sandy Row, and this section of the Protestant working class was particularly prone to sectarian rioting in the 1850s and 60s.[61]

In the general election of 1885 the Liberals failed to win a single seat in Ulster, and control of the Unionist cause was placed firmly in the hands of the Conservatives. (Outside Ulster the Conservatives had no success, however, in the face of the Home Rulers.) Parnell's success in winning over the Roman Catholic hierarchy in the South to his cause, and the appearance of a Catholic religious revival, lent credence to the Conservative claim that 'Home Rule is Rome Rule'. Furthermore the breakdown in law and order in the South and West which had followed the radical Land League's campaign against evictions had frightened many Liberals into the Conservative camp. The Conservatives were also aided by the active intervention of the Orange Order which used its influence to promote candidates who were firm on the retention of the Union. Indeed the strength and cohesion of the Unionist cause in Ulster lay in this alliance between Irish Conservatism and Orangeism. In 1886, under the shadow of Gladstone's first Home Rule Bill, the Conservatives remembered the significance of the 'Orange card' in the defeat of the United Irishmen, and saw in the Orange Lodges the basis of a political machine. The Order retained its proletarian base, but was progressively taken over by a steady stream of applicants from the business and professional classes, who joined up just as the landlords had in the 1790s.

It is important to note, however, that Orangeism was not simply absorbed into Unionism, to be manipulated by the Conservative leadership. Class and economic rivalries, between landlords and tenant farmers and between capitalists and industrial workers, threatened the unity of the movement. In Belfast there were industrial clashes 'resulting from the blossoming of a working-class consciousness and resulting in independent political activity on the part of the Protestant working classes.'[62] At the beginning of this century this was manifested in the activities of the Independent Orange Order which roundly attacked the traditional Order and the Unionist movement as enemies of Protestant working people.[63] This 'class' militancy was, however, generally accompanied by the most aggressive Protestantism and tended to degenerate into sectarianism in the face of the polarising Home Rule issue.

By 1905, when the Ulster Unionist Party was formally established, the Orange Order had been transformed into a respectable and powerful, religious and political organisation. Beckett points out that the 'tradition of fraternal equality between members tended to blur class distinctions, and helped to reconcile the protestant proletariat to the leadership of landlords and wealthy businessmen.'[64] In 1912 the Order's system of local lodges provided a ready-made framework for the recruitment and training of the Ulster Volunteer Force. In 1913 a fund was established to compensate members of the UVF and their dependents for any loss or disability they might suffer in the service of Ulster, and by January 1914 the fund stood at well over a million pounds. In this way the business community of Belfast underwrote the UVF.

The Protestant proletariat had a clear material interest in the preservation of the Union, particularly the more skilled elements who, at the beginning of this century, were earning wages well above their counterparts in Dublin. In the 1880s the Conservative leaders began to focus on this shared material interest and to develop the ideology of social imperialism in their attempt to build up a united Unionist movement by the integration of bourgeoisie and proletariat. Gibbon concludes that

> If the logic was not clear, the message was. Home Rule signalled not
> only economic disaster but also the interruption of the extension
> of social reforms to the working class, reforms 'guaranteed' by the
> participation of Ireland in the empire . . . The Ulsterman, by virtue
> of his imperial citizenship, shared the most advanced privileges and
> liberties in the world; the threat of home rule was threat to them,
> just as in classical social-imperialist ideology the threat of socialism
> occupied a similar position.[65]

Furthermore, as Buckland has pointed out, the Home Rule crises of the 1880s and 1920s coincided with economic crises which curbed the independence of the Protestant working-class, and encouraged it to accept the leadership of the employers in the Unionist movement.[66]

The fact that appeals to 'loyalism' and 'unionism' were used as weapons by the bourgeoisie against radical elements of the proletariat, particularly in putting down the general strike that occurred in 1919, does not negate the fact that the proletariat had an interest of its own in refusing separation from Britain. However, the formal co-option of the Orange Order into the Unionist Party meant that the defence of the Union became inextricably linked with the defence of Protestantism. While this greatly strengthened the solidarity of the Unionist movement in Ulster, it also presented the conservative business classes with a powerful ideological weapon in their struggle to retain the 'loyalty' of working-class Protestants once a Unionist government had been established in Northern Ireland. The danger of defection from the Unionist Party was met with the familiar claim that it provided a Protestant parliament for the Protestant people.

PARTITION

Ever since the failure of the Irish nationalist movement to secure independence for all the thirty-two counties of Ireland, students of Irish nationalism have tended to adopt the view that partition was an arbitrary political compromise, imposed by Britain in an attempt to protect the privileges of a small land-owning and bourgeois Protestant elite, and British imperial interests, both strategic and economic. Thus, T.A. Jackson, in *Ireland Her Own:*

> It is cardinal to remember that what passed for a "spontaneous" resistance of "Ulster" to the "menace" of Home Rule was (1) not spontaneous but deliberately worked up . . . (2) did not originate in Ulster but in the inner councils of the English Tory-plutocracy . . . and was aimed at no "menace" (since the Home Rule Bill contained none) but at preserving the privileged position of a minority-caste in Ireland.[67]

Within this perspective the Protestant proletariat were duped into betraying their own real interests;

> What calls for comment is the fact that the proletarian masses of Belfast and the industrial North-East were still blinded by sectarianism sufficiently to react as desired to the "No Popery" bogey, set up to terrify them by the Orange agents of the Tory conspiracy.[68]

The analysis developed in this chapter has attempted to show that, on the contrary, if the North chose 'loyalty' to Britain, it was not simply because it had been subjected ideologically or militarily to British imperialism, but rather because all social classes, including the proletariat had some interest in remaining within the United Kingdom. Cutting themselves off from the British market would have spelled economic disadvantage for all. The defenders of the Union in Ulster were not simply a small parasitic class of alien landlords. The leader of the Unionist revolt, Edward Carson, was indeed a Tory whose prime concern was to defend the integrity of the British Empire but, as Beckett notes, 'the man who most fully embodied their fears, their prejudices, their arrogance, their courage, and their stubborn self-regard was one of themselves — James Craig, member for East Down, and a typical representative of the wealthy middle class that controlled the economic and political life of the province.'[69]

On the question of Britain's strategic and political interests, it is indeed the case that Randolph Churchill and other Conservative British statesmen such as Bonar Law, called on Ulster to stand fast, not for Ulster's sake, but for the integrity of the Empire. Such sentiments found concrete expression in the actions of a group of army officers based at the Curragh camp in Ireland, who in 1914 handed in their resignations rather than face the prospect of being asked to 'coerce' Ulster. Prior to the First World War, the Unionist cause had many supporters among Tories, army officers and landlords in England, and these supporters presented a defiant opposition to the English Parliament. However these elements were not the dominant force in British politics when the third Home Rule Bill was presented in 1912, and they were forced to reconsider their support for Ulster as the war dragged on and an Irish settlement became essential to victory. By the end of the First World War there was a general consensus at Westminster of the desirability of some form of Home Rule for Ireland. Boyce in his study of Conservative opinion on this issue concludes that

> British conservatives had in 1886 taken up the cause of Ulster, not merely for Ulster's sake, but for the sake of the United Kingdom and of the empire; and by 1921 most of them were convinced that these causes could best be served, not, as in 1886, by Ulster unionist resistance, but, on the contrary by the Northern Ireland government taking part in an agreement with Sinn Fein that would settle the Irish question and keep Ireland in the British Commonwealth.[70]

In his book, *The Irish Crisis*, C. Desmond Greaves, who is sympathetic to Jackson's analysis, argues specifically that the nightmare of capitalist politicians at Westminster was the junction of British socialism with Irish republicanism, and that 'partition was aimed at stifling a revolution that was in progress in Ireland and raising an insurmountable barrier in the path of another.'[71] However, although it is undoubtedly the case that, as Connolly warned, partition shattered 'all hopes of uniting the workers, irrespective of religion or old political battle cries', it was not this aim that motivated British policy. In view of the unrevolutionary character of the Irish nationalist movement at this time, Westminster's persistant attempts to effect a compromise between the two communities in Ireland, in order to establish an all-Ireland political structure, seem to have been made in good faith. Certainly British capitalism had no need to partition Ireland in order to protect its interests, for it was really not an essential source of raw materials, nor a vital market for British goods. British capitalists had little to fear from the protectionism that might follow independence, for the bourgeois national 'revolution' in the South could not alter the fundamental relations of economic dependence and subordination established during the nineteenth century.

> The history of the Republic shows the impossibility of building an autonomous centre of capitalist development in Ireland. Even more, it shows that imperialism is not some outsider which one need only boot out by armed force in order to be master at home. Imperialism is only a system of *private* international exchange in which finished products of different organic composition are exchanged at their market value, a system which results in the domination of one country over another, or of one region over another.[72]

British imperialism in Ireland is no longer essentially a military economic force blocking the development of dominated regions, a characteristic long attributed to it. By 1919 the British Government strongly opposed the exclusion of Ulster from Home Rule, for the retention of British authority in any part of Ireland was seen by both Conservatives and Liberals, as a political liability rather than a strategic or economic advantage. This is why Gladstone was willing to grant Home Rule as early as 1886, and why opposition to Home Rule was not led by British capital but by Ulster Protestants. 'It was Ulster, not Britain which insisted on the Union, and it was only reluctantly (at first) that Ulster accepted a separate legislature at Stormont, which was forced on it by Westminster.'[73]

2

A PROTESTANT STATE
FOR A PROTESTANT PEOPLE

By the end of the nineteenth century, controlling power in the Unionist movement had passed out of the hands of the great landowners and into those of the manufacturers of Belfast, the Presbyterian bourgeoisie. The Unionist movement in the South was mainly a landlord movement, and the impetus behind it was greatly reduced by the land purchase legislation which culminated in the Land Acts of 1903 and 1909. These Acts gave considerable protection to the gentry's economic interests by allowing them to sell out on very favourable terms. In 1905, the issue of devolution for Ireland provoked a crisis, and an Ulster Unionist Council was set up to strengthen and link up the main Unionist organisations in the North. From then on Ulster Unionism became increasingly more articulate and intransigent than Irish Unionism, until by 1913 Carson had recognised the probable necessity of abandoning the Southern Unionists and making a stand for the six North-Eastern counties.[1] Within the Ulster Council the alliance between Conservatism and Orangeism was formalised, with the Order having the power to nominate one quarter of the delegates to the Council.

By 1920 the challenge of labour in industrialised countries had brought forward the capitalists everywhere as the natural defenders of the established order. 'So it was that the Northern Presbyterians came to take the leadership in the struggle, nominally against nationalism alone, but also in fact against a possible growth of the Labour movement.'[2] The manufacturers of the North had not wanted a parliament of their own, but once established, it presented them with a means of preserving and protecting the interests of Ulster capital, not just against the threat of reunification under the Southern Government, but also against the danger of conflict with their own workers.

The Government of Ireland Act (1920) provided for the establishment of two parliaments in the country, permitting the Irish Free State to become a self-governing dominion with 'the community of nations known as the British Empire', and creating a provincial government for the six North-Eastern counties at Stormont. The Act was not designed to create a permanent partition of Ireland, and provided for its eventual reunification.

Although at the beginning there are to be two parliaments and two governments in Ireland, the Act contemplates and affords every

48

facility for Union between North and South, and empowers the two parliaments by mutual agreement to terminate partition and to set up one parliament and one government for the whole of Ireland.

The agreement of Northern Ireland was not forthcoming, and the Council of Ireland provided for in the Act never functioned. It was formally dissolved in 1926, once it was apparent that no boundary changes were going to result from the findings of the Boundary Commission. In 1949, when the Irish Free State finally became the Republic of Ireland and ceased to belong to the British Commonwealth, Westminster's Ireland Act (1949) gave a specific guarantee of Northern Ireland's constitutional position:

It is hereby declared that Northern Ireland remains part of His Majesty's dominions and of the United Kingdom, and it is hereby affirmed that in no event will Northern Ireland or any part thereof cease to be part of His Majesty's dominions and of the United Kingdom without the consent of the Parliament of Northern Ireland.

Under Section 4(1) of the 1920 Act, the Stormont Parliament had power to pass laws for the 'peace, order and good government of Northern Ireland' subject only to certain specific limitations. These 'excepted matters' included war and peace, the armed forces, international treaties and external trade. There were also certain 'reserved matters' which it was originally intended to transfer to an all-Ireland parliament, but which reverted to Westminster's control. These included control over a number of important revenue-raising taxes such as income tax, excess profits duty, corporations profits tax and customs and excise duties. The Act created important anomalies in Northern Ireland's relationships with Westminster. First, Northern Ireland became a self-governing, self-financing 'region', with its revenues separated from the national accounts, but at the same time it lacked any real, independent power to raise revenue, and exert fiscal or monetary control over its economy. Second, although the Act ensured that 'the supreme authority of the Parliament of the United Kingdom shall remain unaffected and undiminished over all persons, matters and things in Northern Ireland and every part thereof', Westminster in fact studiously avoided the exertion of that authority, or even the expression of interest. As the Sunday Times Insight team pointed out, 'During all the Civil Rights campaign's long exposure of Ulster injustice, any parliamentary question at Westminster was turned aside on the grounds that "by convention" the "internal affairs" of Northern Ireland should not be discussed.'[3]

This chapter is concerned primarily with the way in which the leadership of the Unionist party, the Presbyterian bourgeoisie, was able to retain the 'loyalty' of the Protestant masses during almost fifty years of uninterrupted rule. The Unionist Government's familiar claim to have established a 'Protestant parliament' and a 'Protestant State' rested on surer foundations than the simple numerical superiority of Protestants over Catholics. The analysis of Protestant political unity raises important theoretical questions concerning the relative autonomy of political and ideological superstructures in determining the form of class struggles within the social formation. For, 'History "asserts itself" through the multiform world of the superstructures, from local tradition to international circumstance'[4], and in Northern Ireland both these dimensions have a particular and vital importance. The quasi-nationalist alliance of classes on which the Unionist party was originally based was, in part, a response to the external threat of Irish republicanism, and its internal cohesion was greatly increased by the coincidence of 'national' with religious identities. The Unionist movement which arose out of the uneven development of capitalism within Ireland is therefore ideologically specified by the interpenetration of political and religious nationalisms. The establishment of two separate states within Ireland did nothing to weaken this external threat as long as the Free State continued to claim sovereignty over Northern Ireland while moving in the direction of an increasingly protectionist, and officially Catholic, Republic.

Within Northern Ireland the existence of a large nationalist Catholic minority reinforced the link between Unionism and Protestantism, and political struggle in the province was dominated by the primacy of these constitutional-religious loyalties. These circumstances permitted the Ulster capitalists, the dominant economic class within the Protestant alliance, to establish political hegemony within the Unionist party. The absence of overt class conflict within the Unionist alliance was not, however, simply a 'survival' from the historic struggle against Irish nationalism. The displacement of class conflict into sectarianism depended on the decisive intervention of Orangeism as the relatively autonomous ideology of the Protestant working class. Orangeism was at once the economic ideology of the Protestant labour aristocracy, reproducing a clear hierarchical division within the working class, and a political ideology determining the obligations of the Unionist leadership to the Protestant community as a whole; the defence of the historical Protestant ascendancy.

The strength and cohesion of the Unionist movement, under the leadership of the capitalist class, was in turn reinforced by the creation of State apparatuses which institutionalised Protestant privilege in a variety of ways, and greatly increased the repressive powers of the Government. One of the first measures to be introduced by the Stormont Parliament was the Civil Authorities (Special Powers) Bill, which gave the Minister of Home Affairs the power 'in respect of persons, matters and things within the jurisdiction of the Government of Northern Ireland to take all such steps and issue all such orders as may be necessary for preserving the peace and maintaining order.' The Act included specific regulations to permit, for example, arrest without trial and the prohibition of inquests, as well as granting the Minister unlimited power to introduce any further regulations without consulting Parliament. Regulations to permit the outlawing of organisations, and indefinite internment without charge or trial followed swiftly. The Bill which was initially brought forward as a one-year emergency measure to cope with Catholic disaffection, and IRA violence in 1922, was continually renewed until 1933 when it was made permanent.

THE ECONOMY 1920-39

According to the 1926 Census, the population of the six counties of Northern Ireland was 1,256,561, amounting to 30% of the total population of Ireland.[5] Despite its advanced industrial development, Northern Ireland was still primarily an agricultural community, and in the inter-war years agriculture accounted for 25% of employment, compared with about 6% in the United Kingdom as a whole. The predominant form of agricultural organisation in the province was the small family farm, worked mainly by the farmer himself and members of his own family. The farms were equipped with little specialised machinery relative to those in Great Britain, and were therefore more labour intensive. 'Because of the organisation of the industry in small holdings (together with a shortage of industrial jobs) they have been able to carry on production in this manner largely by means of cheap family labour.'[6]

The form of industrial development in Northern Ireland was determined by its meagre natural resources, its remoteness from the rest of the British economy and the smallness of the provincial market for most specific finished goods. As described in the previous chapter, the basis of Ulster's rapid industrial expansion in the nineteenth century lay in the linen and ship-building industries, and the enterprises that sprang up to meet the needs of these two giants. The narrow base of the industrial structure meant that a high proportion of all workers employed in production were concentrated in a very few industries.

A further important characteristic of the industrial structure was that the staple industries depended on selling a large part of their output in markets outside the province. This was true not only of the larger manufacturing industries but of many of the smaller ones as well. It was also true, broadly speaking, of agriculture. The limited size of the provincial market meant that expansion was only possible in those manufactures on which the direct and indirect transport costs were relatively low, permitting them to compete successfully in markets in Great Britain and abroad.

Employment was not only concentrated in a handful of industries but was also geographically highly concentrated. The main centre was in Belfast and the industrial towns of the Lagan valley and the upper Bann. In 1927 almost 70% of industrial workers were located there, employed in the ship-building and marine, textile and other light engineering industries.[7] Outside these areas it was the traditional textile industries which provided the medium of industrial growth.

> One of the most interesting and important features of the location
> of industry . . . is the wide dispersion of the textile and clothing
> group of industries throughout the province and the preponderance
> of these industries, compared with other manufacturing industries,
> in almost all the areas in which manufacturing is highly developed,
> and in some in which it is not.[8]

From the 1935 Census of Production it is apparent that, just as in
agriculture, the unit of production in the manufacturing industries is
smaller in Northern Ireland than in the rest of the United Kingdom. In all
but five out of the thirty-four industries classified the average number of
workers per establishment is smaller in Northern Ireland, as is the average
paid-up capital per company.[9] However, even more striking than the
disparity in company size between Northern Ireland and Great Britain is
the contrast between public and private companies in each.

> In Northern Ireland the total amount of paid-up capital in private
> companies is greater than that in public companies: it is almost
> half as much again. In the United Kingdom, by contrast, it is
> barely more than half as great, accounting for only 36.3 per cent
> of the total compared with 63.7 per cent in public companies.[10]

The 'family firm' was the typical unit of production in the province, and
the local economy remained largely unaffected by the rise of monopoly
capital in the rest of the United Kingdom, and the general trend toward
concentration of capital in the advanced industrialised countries.

The narrow structural base of the Northern Ireland economy, its
inability to diversify, together with its dependence on the export market
meant that the province was highly vulnerable to recession. Employment
was liable at any time to suffer a heavy and permanent fall, whether
because of a decline in any one of the major industries by itself, or because
of factors causing a shrinkage in Britain's total export trade. These
characteristics of the economy help to explain the chronic state of
industrial depression in Northern Ireland throughout the 1920s and 1930s.
When the new government came into being in 1921 the province was
already feeling the full blast of the general slump which followed the
immediate post-war boom. 'Being associated with a relative over-production
of primary products in world trade, this slump affected Northern Ireland
with special severity.'[11] Unemployment rose from 18% in 1923 to 25%
in 1926. Between 1930 and 1939 unemployment never fell below 20%
and averaged about 25%. Income per head declined to little more than half
the average for the United Kingdom.[12]

Under conditions such as these the danger of working class defections
from the all-class Protestant alliance, upon which the Unionist Party was
built, became a major concern. To survive, Ulster capital needed a quiescent
labour force. Stormont had no regulatory powers over the provincial
economy, and indeed notions of central planning and State intervention in

the management of the economy were still viewed with suspicion at this time. However, an alternative formula for the defence of Ulster capital had been developed during the struggle against Home Rule, when the Orange Order had begun to preach 'corporatism', a holy alliance between owners and workers.

In 1919 the Belfast ship-yard workers went on strike for a forty-hour week, despite condemnation by the Orange Order. The strike spread to the power-stations, and then to factories all over Belfast. The strike was only partly successful, but it was followed by a year of major strikes and stoppages throughout the province. In January 1920 the Belfast Labour Party, which was based in the trade unions, put up twenty candidates in the municipal elections, thirteen of whom were elected. In July Carson discovered a 'Bolshevik-Sinn Fein Alliance', and at a public demonstration declared:

> What I say is this, the men who come forward posing as friends of Labour care no more about Labour than does the man in the moon. Their real object, and the real insidious object of their propaganda, is that they may mislead and bring about disunity among our own people, and in the end, before we know where we are, we may find ourselves in the same bondage and slavery as in the rest of Ireland in the south and west.[13]

Nine days after Carson's speech Protestant workers in one major ship-yard decided to expel all 'Sinn Feiners'; in other words all Catholics. In the same year, workers at another shipyard waived their claim for a forty-hour week, in the interests of 'good order', and engineering wages were actually cut without opposition from the workers. With the setting up of the Ulster Special Constabulary, recruited largely from the Orange Lodges and the Ulster Volunteer Force, sectarian violence increased, and expulsions spread to the other major firms in Belfast. During the first two years of the State's existence 10,000 workers were driven from their jobs.[14] They were not all Catholics. Protestant radicals were included in the purge. On the political level the effect of the sectarian war was disastrous for the Labour movement. At the elections for the first Northern Ireland parliament, held under proportional representation in May 1921, none of the four Independent Labour candidates for Belfast was elected.

Throughout the twenties and thirties, every labour-based challenge to Protestant unity met with a similar sectarian response both from the employers and Government officials. However, the point to be emphasised here is the ability of the Protestant bourgeoisie to reinforce the ideology of Orangeism through the distribution of concrete privileges. Control of the economy, through ownership of the important industrial enterprises, rested firmly in the hands of the Presbyterian capitalists, and the predominance of 'family firms' greatly facilitated the implementation of sectarian employment policies.

Catholics, who formed 33% of the population in 1926, presented a very different occupational profile to Protestants. The majority of Catholics were of Ulster origin, and as a result of historical disabilities were mainly small farmers, shop-keepers and unskilled labourers. The Protestant ascendancy, which was established under the 1691 settlement, set definite limits on Catholic social mobility, and maintained a system of structured social inequality, particularly in Ulster. Besides the Ulster Catholics there was a sizeable Catholic population which had been drawn from the South and West of Ireland into Belfast at the time of the great industrial expansion of the 1860s, the majority of whom were unskilled workers.[15] From the 1901 census figures, it may be shown that Catholics were 'under-represented in the professions, such as accountancy, and in middle class employment, such as in insurance and banks. Equally significant, they were under-represented in the skilled working class jobs and over-represented in domestic service.'[16] Catholics played some part in the commerical life of the province, but controlled none of the engineering and textile industries which were the major employers. Furthermore, given the structural limitations on the development of Northern Ireland's economy in this century, they had little opportunity to improve their status. On the basis of 1971 occupational data it has been shown that 'there is a marked tendency for Protestants to dominate the upper occupational classes while Catholics are found predominantly in the lower classes.'[17]

It was the Catholic population who suffered most from the economic effects of partition, in that it was particularly the border towns which were hurt by the loss of markets and trade connections with the South. It was in these areas that Catholic representation was strongest. For example, Derry had been a port serving the North-East of Ireland, with an industrial base in shirt-making. Partition isolated this historic town from its Southern markets, and was a factor in the town's progressive decline. However, it was not partition alone which was responsible for the decline of these areas, since overall lack of diversification had left most of the province extremely vulnerable to recession. In the inter-war years the sectarian division within the working class and consequent absence of labour militancy, meant that wages could be kept very low in an attempt to offset the declining productivity of Ulster capital. The cost of this arrangement was borne by the Catholic working class which endured disproportionate levels of unemployment.

THE ULSTER UNIONIST COUNCIL

The Ulster Unionist Council was created in 1905 to integrate and coordinate the various organisations in the province that supported the Union, the most important of which were the local Unionist constituency associations and the Orange Lodges. It was the body which represented the mass party in the country. With the establishment of an independent parliament at Stormont, the Council developed into an umbrella organisation, under which Unionists of all classes and depths of conviction were united for the purpose of maintaining Protestant power, and hence the Union. In 1929, after various reorganisations, it had a membership of 508. The local constituency associations accounted for 288 of the delegates, and the Orange Order for a further 128, allocated on a county basis according to membership. The remaining places were divided between various affiliated organisations such as the Junior Imperial League Divisional Council; Unionist MPs and their wives were ex-officio members.

The loose federal structure of the Ulster Unionist Council was intended to 'give the rank and file a greater voice, or at least the appearance of a greater voice, in the formulation of party policy'.[18] However, during the inter-war years the Unionist party showed no signs of attempting to develop a coherent political programme, or coordinate Unionist activities for any purpose beyond the continued defence of the status quo. The Unionist parties at Stormont and Westminster were not subject to any centralised discipline or control. Power was concentrated at the local level, in the individual constituency associations, which remained autonomous bodies, free to make their own rules and choose whether to affiliate to the Council. Candidate selection was a matter for each constituency association, and there was no uniform procedure. Much of the important political process in the province resided in the selection of the local candidate, who was then returned to office from a safe seat.

Discussions in the Council reflected the narrow concerns of the Unionist leadership, and were largely confined to three recurring themes: the constitutional issue, anti-socialism and anti-Catholicism. The constitutional issue, being the cornerstone of Party policy, was not debated regularly, although it figured in most speeches. Anti-socialism became an explicit concern with the establishment of the independent parliament, when the Nationalists were no longer a real threat, and there was danger of internal defections to the Labour Party. After the general election of 1925, the Council reported that:

> Owing to Unionist apathy, and also the eccentricities of Proportional Representation, three Socialists were returned to the Northern House of Commons . . . Your Committee have taken every opportunity . . . of countering the movement by exposing the fallacies and shams of Socialism, and the menace to society which it constitutes.[19]

The Council's anti-Catholicism was less explicit in the inter-war years, but was a persistent theme, nonetheless. For example, in 1924 the Annual Report records the following resolution, which officially sanctioned religious discrimination in employment: 'That in order to relieve the distress due to the continued depression in trade, it is the duty of the Council to do all in its power, by individual effort, to relieve the unemployment amongst the Loyalist population in Ulster.' Apart from generally echoing the Unionist leadership's pleas for unity, the Council performed an important informal role in the maintenance of Protestant solidarity. 'The constituent parts controlled every avenue through which patronage was dispensed; they were found everywhere that jobs, houses and contracts were within the gift of the Party, and these were given to the faithful.'[20]

CENTRAL GOVERNMENT

In the first general election for the Stormont Parliament in 1921, the Unionist Party had uniform success at the polls, returning forty out of the fifty-two members, with Sinn Fein and the Irish Nationalist Party returning six each. It has often been claimed that their strength was boosted by the gerrymandering of constituency boundaries. However, as Barritt and Carter point out it does not seem as though this had any great influence on representation at Stormont except in Londonderry and Tyrone.[21] As will be explained later, the significance of gerrymandering lay in the drawing up of local council constituencies. The fifty-two seats were at first divided among multi-member constituencies, elected by proportional representation, on a single transferable vote system. Four of the seats were reserved for the Queen's University constituency, and the picture was further qualified by the existence of the business vote. This gave an additional vote to those electors who occupied business premises with a rateable value of at least £10 in another constituency. Despite these anomalies it cannot be said that the central government electoral system materially weakened the position of the Nationalists. It deprived them of perhaps one extra seat, but as a permanent minority at Stormont this was of little significance. More importantly the electoral system favoured the property-owning classes.

Given the security of their permanent majority, the Unionists were happy to see the Nationalists abandon their policy of abstention in 1925, and trickle back into Stormont. Their presence could only reinforce Unionist solidarity. The real threat to the Unionist Government lay in the possibility of deviation among their own supporters. It was fear of this which led the Government to abolish proportional representation in parliamentary elections in 1929. This had no effect on Nationalist representation, but did prevent splinter-groups of Unionists from securing representation at Stormont. As early as 1926 the Belfast Trades and Labour Council protested strongly against the declared intention of the Government to abolish proportional representation, and the Labour Party was vociferous in its condemnation. The Government was not to be deterred, however, since in the 1925 general election the Unionist Party had lost eight seats. The Parliamentary Secretary to the Ministry of Home Affairs lost his seat to a representative of the 'Unbought Tenants', three seats went to the Labour Party, and four to Independent Unionists. The Party was also under pressure from Temperance Reformers, the Orange

Order and the churches for a measure of local option. A party calling themselves the 'Local Optionists' even put up candidates in the 1929 elections. In 1927, in divisions on the Intoxicating Liquor Bill, the Government's majority had fallen as low as eight at times. In defending his decision to abolish proportional representation the Prime Minister, Lord Craigavon, formerly Sir James Craig, said:

> What I hold is, if the Ulster people are ever going — and pray God they may not — into a Dublin parliament, I say let the people understand they are voting to go into a Dublin parliament and not go in by any trick of a complicated system of proportional representation.[22]

And

> What I want to get in this House and what I believe we will get very much better in this House under the old-fashioned plain and simple system, are men who are for the Union on the one hand, or who are against it and want to go into a Dublin parliament on the other.[23]

In effect he abolished proportional representation in order to preserve the traditional divisions in Ulster politics, upon which the stability of Unionist government depended.

Under these conditions the extraordinary continuity that prevailed in the inter-war years is not so surprising. With the abolition of proportional representation many candidates were returned from uncontested seats. In the 1933 election twenty-seven of the thirty-six Unionist members were returned unopposed. Furthermore, of the fifty-two members sitting in 1927, twenty-eight were still sitting in 1936, and twenty-one of them had been members since 1921. The same continuity prevailed at Cabinet level. Lord Craigavon was Prime Minister from the setting up of the State until his death in 1940. Only one member of his Cabinet had resigned by 1927, and three of his original five ministerial colleagues were still in office in 1936. The House of Commons met only three afternoons a week, and was in recess for substantial periods of time at Christmas, Easter and in the summer. Even ministerial office in the early years was a part-time occupation. Indeed, the large size of ministerial salaries occasioned widespread criticism even within the ranks of the Unionist Party.[24] Furthermore, the code of conduct laid down for Stormont MPs is more lenient than that which pertains at Westminster, and permits members to retain directorships, details of which are published at intervals. Also peers are allowed to sit in the House of Commons.

Given the continuity of representation there was little change in the class and occupational profile of the Government during the inter-war years. Nicholas Mansergh describes the Stormont Cabinet thus:

> The Cabinet is a Government of business men ornamented by a landed aristocracy. Since his accession to office, Lord Craigavon has had altogether seven Cabinet Ministers serving under his leadership. Of these, three were past Presidents of the Belfast Chamber of Commerce, one a partner in a large well-known firm of

solicitors, one an industrialist and director of companies, one a peer and one the titled owner of one of the largest estates in the North.[25]

The Government could in no sense be called 'representative', except of the business classes whose power rested on family ownership of capital in the handful of dominant industries that had emerged from the economic conditions of the nineteenth century.

The Unionist Party's economic policies, or lack of them, reflected the dominance of this class of local capitalists. They were based, as Mansergh describes, on 'the essential individualism of the Ulsterman. His sympathies lie, not with the ever-increasing social services of the modern State, but rather with the economic radicalism of English nineteenth century thought.'[26] The point is elaborated by J.W. Good, in *Irish Unionism:*

[Ulster's] main industries — textiles and ship-building — not only import their raw materials, but export their finished products, with the result that those who control these industries have, in their everyday life, no intimate relationship with the mass of their fellow-countrymen, and not unnaturally come to feel themselves in Ireland rather than of it. Economically, their outlook has not advanced beyond that of the later Victorians, and remains a curious blend of the arrogant individualism of the Manchester School combined with a belief . . . that the world will be saved only in so far as it places dictatorial powers in the hands of the 'business man' '.[27]

The main institution which served to bind the mass of the Protestant workers to the Unionist ruling-class was the Orange Order, which exerted a powerful integrating influence, both politically and ideologically. The Government was careful to preserve and emphasise its links with Orangeism. Thus, in 1932, at the height of the depression, when Protestant workers rioted in sympathy with Catholics, the Prime Minister, Lord Craigavon, sought to restore unity by appealing to this common tie. 'Ours is a Protestant government and I am an Orangeman,' he announced. And later, 'I have always said I am an Orangeman first and a politician and member of this parliament afterwards . . . all I boast is that we are a Protestant parliament and a Protestant State.'[28]

LOCAL GOVERNMENT

It was at the local level rather than at the central level that Protestant solidarity was most powerfully reinforced, through the close alliance between local business, the Unionist constituency associations, local government and the Orange Order. The central Government was more of an administrative or coordinating body than a controlling power. The Party's Glengall Street headquarters was a shoestring organisation, surviving on the capitation fees from the constituency associations, plus small-scale

handouts from the business community.[29] As described above, its interests
were limited to the protection of the status quo, and the defence of local
capital. Prime Minister Craig was particularly interested, however, in
conciliating local interests and local authorities. Patrick Buckland cites
from the diary of the permanent head of the Northern Ireland Ministry
of Finance to illustrate Craig's philosophy of government:

> The Prime Minister told me whatever happened he expected our
> Ministry to provide a surplus which would be available for our
> special local purposes. He believed in the policy of 'distributing
> bones' and thought that we ought to be able to arrange with the
> . . .[British Government] . . . that funds were available for the
> purpose. I replied that giving the bones to one set of dogs very
> often created trouble amongst those who did not get the bones,
> and that our Local Authorities had been so much spoilt in the
> past that it was very hard for us to get the [British] Treasury not
> to press for a substantial reduction in our expenditure.[30]

The strength of local government was symptomatic of a social formation in which large-scale State intervention into the distribution of
resources was absent, in which relations were based on patronage and
clientilism rather than the sorts of impersonal criteria characteristic of the
modern welfare state. In a situation of high unemployment, affecting
many Protestants as well as Catholics, and exacerbated by a growing stock
of inadequate housing, the local council, as a source of both jobs and
houses, became an important part of the political system. Furthermore,
the allocation of jobs in the private sector was also intimately connected
with local government, and in particular with individual Unionist
Associations. The significance of this was twofold. First, it permitted a
far more widespread and efficient policy of discrimination in employment,
and second, it provided a method of ensuring continued political support
for the Unionist Party among Protestants. In order to maintain a sectarian
political hierarchy it was necessary to distribute goods according to
sectarian criteria. The Nationalists held power in those areas where they
predominated, without threatening the stability of central government.
Furthermore, the gerrymandering of ward boundaries significantly reduced
the number of areas lost to Unionist control.

It is interesting to note that it is at the local level that the peculiarities
of Northern Ireland's franchise have their most powerful effect. Prior to
1969, as in parliamentary elections, there was plural voting, but the
franchise was also restricted. The vote was limited to rate-payers and their
wives, and was weighted in favour of property owners. Thus it was
necessary to qualify either as a resident occupier, or a general occupier.
A resident occupier was the owner or tenant of a dwelling-house with a
minimum valuation of £5. A general occupier was the owner or tenant of
land or premises (not a dwelling-house) of an annual valuation of at least
£10. In addition to this, limited companies had an extra vote for every
£10 of valuation, up to a maximum of six extra votes. This electoral system,

as well as favouring the business classes, disenfranchised a large section of the population. Thus in 1967 there were 933,723 people on the parliamentary electoral role, while there were only 694,483 people on the local election registers. It should be noted that the system not only penalised Catholics because of their generally lower class profile, but also many working class Protestants. When the Civil Rights movement emerged in the 1960s, the slogan 'one man, one vote', brought widespread support from Protestants for the reform programme.

The importance of local government in maintaining loyalist unity is reflected in the Government's decision to abolish proportional representation in local elections immediately after the setting up of the State. The electoral system was changed in 1922, just after the first local polls had resulted in a bias toward minority representation. After the delayed granting of Royal assent to the Local Government Bill, the seats had to be redistributed in the various electoral districts. The Government took this opportunity of redrawing electoral boundaries in such a way that new areas passed under Unionist control even in districts where the Nationalists enjoyed major voting strength. The change resulted in a rapid increase in the number of uncontested seats. It should be noted here that the first serious challenge to the legitimacy of the political regime in Northern Ireland came at the local level.

The Cameron Commission, set up to investigate the causes of the 'disturbances in Northern Ireland' accompanying the civil rights demonstrations in 1968, lists among the general causes of disorder:

> Complaints, again well documented, in some cases of deliberate manipulation of local government electoral boundaries and in others a refusal to apply for their necessary extension, in order to achieve and maintain Unionist control of local authorities and so to deny Catholics influence in local government proportionate to their numbers.[31]

The best example of the gerrymander was to be found in Londonderry, where Catholics formed 63% of the total city population, but were in a minority on the city council after 1922. This effect was achieved by the division of Derry into three wards: the South Ward, which is the largest with a population of 10,749, is largely Catholic, and returns two aldermen and six councillors, all of whom are Nationalist; the North Ward has a population of only 6,528, but also returns two aldermen and six councillors, all of whom are Unionist since 60% of the electorate is Protestant; finally the Waterside, with a population of 5,025, returns one alderman and three councillors, all of whom are also Unionist since Protestants are in the same majority here. Thus the large Nationalist vote is effectively concentrated in one ward, whilst slim Unionist majorities prevail in the other two. Many other cases of a similar nature are documented by Frank Gallagher in his book *The Indivisible Island.*[32] Local government powers in Northern Ireland were broadly similar to those in the rest of the United Kingdom, save that in the former they did not extend over the organisation of the police, or Civil Defence. Thus, councils were responsible for education, health and welfare, sanitation and housing etc., and a variety of public works, and could provide important channels of patronage. The data presented here relates mainly to the post-Second World War years, but the patterns which emerge are similar to those of the inter-war years.

Very few houses were built during the inter-war years, but between 1945 and 1969 176,000 went up, of which approximately 67,000 were built by local authorities.[33] Complaints about the distribution of council houses were one of the major features of the civil rights campaign, and the evidence of widespread discrimination is indisputable. For example in 1958, discussing seventy vacant houses in Dungannon, the local council decided that not one should go to a Catholic.[34] Discrimination in housing allocation was not simply a means of rewarding loyalists. It was also used by Unionist councils to prevent any population movements which might upset the prevailing electoral control of council wards. Thus, in Derry, where a significant number of houses have been built for Catholics, they have all been situated in the South Ward, where the Nationalist majority was absolute, and there could be no threat to Unionist representation.[35]

Discrimination in local council employment follows much the same patterns as in housing. The Cameron report notes that:

> We are satisfied that all these Unionist controlled councils have used and use their power to make appointments in a way which benefited Protestants. In the figures available for October 1968 only thirty per cent of Londonderry Corporation's administrative, clerical and technical employees were Catholics . .. In Dungannon Urban District Council none of the Council's administrative, clerical and technical employees was a Catholic . . . In Fermanagh among about seventy-five drivers of school buses, at most seven were Catholics.[36]

In areas such as Newry, where the Nationalist majority is absolute, council employees are all Catholic. However, the ability of Nationalists to 'look after their own' is greatly reduced by their overall under-representation at local government level. In addition, as was also pointed out in the Cameron Report, in areas such as Newry, Protestants do not have a 'serious unemployment problem', and are a very small minority, whereas Catholics often form a sizeable minority, affected with high levels of unemployment.[37] Discrimination in local government employment was the direct extension of a similar, officially sanctioned policy in the civil service. In 1925, the Minister of Agriculture, who was also the Imperial Grand Master of the Orange Institution, announced: 'I have 109 officials and as far as I know there are four Roman Catholics, three of them were civil servants turned over to me whom I had to take when we began.'[38] Barritt and Carter provide evidence of the effectiveness with which the policy was implemented in the civil service. In 1927 Protestants held

94% of posts, and those Catholics who were employed were concentrated at the bottom end of the scale. In 1959 the percentage was unchanged despite the enormous growth in absolute numbers.

It is important to note that it was not merely in the allocation of council jobs that discrimination was prevalent at the local level. The local Unionist Association was the institution through which discrimination by private employers was facilitated. During the 1930s when unemployment was running at 25%, the Minister of Agriculture, Sir Basil Brooke, the owner of a vast estate in Fermanagh who was later to become Prime Minister, made a series of notorious speeches on this subject. Thus, in 1933, he said:

> There are a great number of Protestants and Orangemen who employ Roman Catholics. I feel I can speak freely on this subject as I have not a Roman Catholic about my own place. . . I would appeal to loyalists, therefore, wherever possible, to employ good Protestant lads and lassies.

And, again in 1934: 'I recommend those people who are loyalists not to employ Roman Catholics, ninety-nine per cent of whom are disloyal'.[39]

In May 1961, in an address to the Unionist Labour Association, Mr Robert Babington is reported to have said that 'registers of unemployed loyalists should be kept by the Unionist Party, and employers invited to pick employees from them.'[40] Furthermore, during the 1961 Belfast Municipal elections, a pamphlet issued by the St Geoge's Ward Unionist Association proudly announced that its three candidates 'employ over 70 people, and have *never* employed a Roman Catholic.'[41] It is not difficult to implement discriminatory policies at the local level, where religion can be easily ascertained. However, the process was greatly facilitated by the widespread use of 'canvassing'. This meant that an applicant for a local authority job, for example, was given a list of councillors and committee members and was expected to visit them to plead his case. The significance of this lies not only in its relation to sectarian discrimination, but also in the fact that it is a clear example of the kind of clientilist relations that prevailed within the loyalist community. It is a method by which the Unionist elite can distribute patronage amongst favoured sections of the constituency, thus strengthening the loyalty of their supporters.

THE ORANGE ORDER

The marriage of the Unionist Party and the Orange Institution in the early days of the struggle against Home Rule has already been described. With the establishment of the Stormont parliament the Unionist leadership made no attempt to disassociate itself from this inherently sectarian organisation. On the contrary, the Order became a central organisational link in the Unionist political machine, and the ideology of Orangeism retained a dominant role in the social formation.

> In a situation where every Prime Minister of Northern Ireland had been an Orangeman, where 95% of all elected Unionist representatives in Parliament have been Orangemen, and where the Orange institution is officially represented in the major organs of the Unionist Party, it is clear the ethos of Orangeism permeates the Party.[42]

The Orange Order has become a vast, semi-secret society which in 1969 had a membership of 125-130,000 out of a total population of 1,512,000, drawing support from all sections of the Protestant community.[43] The majority joined for political motives, but the real strength of Orangeism lies in the combination of religion and politics; its identification of Unionism with Protestantism. M.W. Dewar describes it thus: 'The true Orangeman of today, deeply loyal to the British Crown and a faithful Protestant, is bound to support our Constitutional system which maintains the Protestant religion and preserves the Union between Great Britain and Northern Ireland.'[44]

It was at the local level that the Order's political involvement was most direct, and the Orange Hall commonly served as the meeting place for the local constituency association. It was in the Orange Hall that what is generally called the 'Unionist machine' worked, chiefly in the spheres of registering voters, selection of candidates, and the organisation of elections. The importance of registering voters to the Unionist Party stems from the days of the Home Rule struggle, when it was vital to know every person eligible to vote and his political sympathies. Strict watch was, and indeed still is, kept on voters, and it was the Orange Lodge which became largely responsible for this. The Orange Hall was also the place where most Unionist parliamentary candidates were selected, and some local Orange leaders were entitled to send official delegates to selection committees. In many cases the 'Orange vote' was decisive, as in those areas where each Lodge had the right to send two delegates per 100 voters on the Registers, so that representatives from constituency assocations could be outnumbered.

It is important not to overestimate the degree to which Orangeism was a tool in Unionist hands, a creation of the Protestant ruling class, and to recognise its relative autonomy in the social formation. Orangeism is indeed a potentially 'corporatist' ideology, as the following lines from an Orange song reveal:

> Against the altar and the throne
> the democrat may prate,
> But while I am an Orangeman,
> I'll stand for Church and State
> . . .
> Let not the poor man hate the rich,
> Nor rich on poor look down,
> But each join each true Protestant
> For God and for the Crown, etc.[45]

And it was to this source of loyalty that the Unionist leadership appealed in times of internal dissension. However, as Buckland notes, 'often Orangeism was a divisive influence, its exuberant sectarianism offending the susceptibilities of liberally inclined Unionists, and the very nature and structure of the Orange Order militated against sustained political action.'[46]

3

ECONOMIC DECLINE AND UNIONIST POLITICS, 1930-1963

The political structure within which Unionist hegemony was reproduced depended on continued sectarian polarisation for its survival. No serious economic or social programme, or anti-clerical movement could be permitted to divide the Protestant community; hence the abolition of proportional representation, and the tolerance of back-bench disagreements within the Unionist party. Although the Unionist Government succeeded in maintaining political unity for almost fifty years, it was continually confronted with the problem of containing internal conflicts, conflicts which reflected the development of a fundamental contradiction which went to the heart of the Unionist State. The key to this contradiction which, with the outbreak of the 'troubles' in 1969, finally destroyed Unionist hegemony in Northern Ireland, is to be found in the changing economic balance within Ireland and between Britain and Ireland. The continuing uneven development of capitalism, and the concentration and internationalisation which is characteristic of the rise of monopoly capital, led to the decline of Ulster's traditional industrial base and, after the Second World War, to the reintegration of the Southern economy into the wider British and European markets. By the mid-1960s the two regional economies in Ireland were reduced to similar dependent status within this larger economic framework, and a central factor in the historic conflict between Ulster Unionism and Irish Nationalism was eliminated. Within Northern Ireland these economic transformations threatened the consonance of interests on which the Unionist State had been established, by undermining the dominance of Ulster capital and creating divisions within the bourgeoisie, and by weakening its hegemony over the Protestant working class.

The vulnerability of Ulster's regional economy was already apparent in the 1920s and caused a series of important economic and political changes. First, the decline of the province's traditionally dominant industries led to increased dependence on foreign investment, and to the arrival of companies which owed no particular allegiance to the Unionist Party or to Protestantism. Second, the Government was unable to raise sufficient revenue to maintain welfare services and required growing subsidies from Britain for this purpose, as well as to assist ailing local industry. Third, there was increased recognition of the need for decisive State intervention to combat economic recession, and for centralised economic planning.

ECONOMIC DECLINE

At the time of partition the industrial development which had been the source of the province's economic growth in the nineteenth century was already threatened. The main problems were: (1) the predominance of agriculture, which was by far the biggest single industry in terms of the number of people employed and value of net output, (2) the lack of extractive industries, (3) the high concentration of industrial workers in the linen and ship-building industries, and (4) the dependence on exports, which amounted to 60-70% of the national product.

Chronic depression pervaded Northern Ireland during the twenties and thirties, with unemployment running at between 18% and 25%. The export trades and agriculture were both further weakened by the over-valuation of sterling, caused by the return to the gold standard in 1925 at the old rate of exchange. The Government's effort to maintain agricultural prices by restricting output had little success in making agriculture more profitable, or in arresting migration from rural areas. Furthermore, the province's lack of diversification meant that the contraction of the linen and ship-building industries were uncushioned blows. In fact the survival of the great Harland and Wolff shipyard was ensured during the inter-war years only by the Acts passed to empower the Minister of Finance to guarantee the repayment of loans raised for ship-building.

> The linen industry lost ground to cotton and man-made fibres, while it also suffered through the increasing protection operating in the world economy. With the decline in trade, the demand for ships fell — and the industry in the north declined correspondingly ... A survey of the Belfast working class in 1938-9 revealed that thirty-six per cent of those investigated were unable to afford sufficient food, clothing or fuel to maintain health or working capacity.[1]

The province's economic position was greatly improved by the change in the pattern of demand brought about by the Second World War. During the years 1941-42 industrial employment shot up by 20%. The increase was mainly due to a boom in building and construction for civil defence and war production, and greatly increased activity in engineering and shipbuilding. Farming, so long in the doldrums, benefited, along with farming in the rest of Britain, from all the general measures introduced by Westminster to secure the production of essential foods. After the war, employment contracted again, though it did not fall back to its pre-war levels. Various industries that had been engaged in war production continued to expand after the war. Thus, the aircraft industry, established in 1937, grew rapidly to become one of the largest employers in the province.

The increased buoyancy of the province's post-war economy was due in part to the relaxation of restrictions on world trade, and to the great expansion of demand in Britain as a whole, as well as to the political commitment to maintaining full employment. In addition the Provincial Government took more active steps to encourage investment. However, unemployment remained very high, running at about 8% until 1960, approximately four times the British average and higher than any other region in Britain. It should be noted here that these average figures disguise the fact that Catholics suffered from much higher rates of unemployment than Protestants. In 1961, for example, unemployment in the Catholic town of Newry was 17%, while in 1972, Catholic districts within Belfast had unemployment rates of twice the overall average.[2] These discrepancies were brought about partly by direct discrimination in hiring, and partly by the location of new industries in areas where the Protestant community was concentrated.

Employment generated by the new industries was not enough to compensate for the numbers being laid off in the traditional sectors. In the linen industry a very high percentage decline in employment occurred, with 31,000 being laid off between 1949 and 1967, amounting to 50% of those employed in the industry.[3] The decline in linen production came about, to some extent, as a result of competition from substitute synthetics and cheaper textiles from the Third World. Linen, being essentially a luxury good, was dependent on the export market, and was thus particularly sensitive to fluctuations in world trade and to international competition. Employment in ship-building was equally hard hit, declining by 42% between 1856 and 1965.[4] Between the end of the war and 1969 the total labour force was reduced from 23,000 to 9,200. The big decline occurred in 1961, when 8,000 men were made redundant by Harland and Wolff. This was largely as a result of the fall in world demand for new ships. In addition, shipbuilding is a highly competitive industry, and orders have to be won in international markets. Northern Ireland, in common with the rest of the United Kingdom, also experienced a continuous flow of labour out of agriculture. However, this loss of employment is more acute in Northern Ireland as agriculture occupies a relatively more important position as an employer of labour. Between 1949 and 1969 employment fell from 138,000 to 67,000; a decline of over 50%.[5]

Thus, agriculture, linen and shipbuilding have accounted for the loss of more than 120,000 jobs since 1949, presenting a formidable problem in a province where the total manufacturing employment was only 183,000 in 1969. The need for new investment on a more diversified basis was paramount. However, on the question of investment and the supply of capital in Northern Ireland, Cuthbert and Isles concluded in 1955 that 'while it is not possible to estimate the absolute amount of capital invested in production and trade, there is indirect evidence that it must be very substantially less, per head of population, than it is in Great Britain.'[6]

Furthermore, 'the analysis of estate-duty statistics shows that there is a remarkably strong tendency for people in Northern Ireland to invest their capital outside the province.'[7]

Industrial expansion was partly inhibited by the fact that the predominant form of business organisation was the private company, usually limited to family ownership. In 1955, 60% of all paid up capital was private, compared with 35% in the rest of Britain. The lack of public companies meant that the scope for industrial investment in the province was greatly reduced. Furthermore, the threat of high death duties restricted the expansion of private enterprises, since profits were often held as idle balances, as reserves to pay off duties in case of difficulty. Another negative aspect of this particular structure of ownership was that if a family firm was obliged or wished to sell out, it had to go to one of the large English finance companies, lock, stock and barrel, since it had no local access to the appropriate institutions of the capital market.

The economic foundations of Ulster's claim to political autonomy had begun to crumble even before the State of Northern Ireland was formally established. In 1966 real income in the province was 25% below the average in Britain, and showed little improvement in the following ten years; a stark contrast to the relative prosperity of the nineteenth century.

GOVERNMENT POLICY

In the inter-war years, ideas about economic planning were still somewhat primitive, and there was little interest in centralised control, or State intervention into the internal balance of the economy. However, as the depression hit the linen and ship-building industries, the Unionist Government began to appreciate the need for some State assistance. At first this took the form of the 'Loans Guarantee Acts', which empowered the Minister of Finance to guarantee the repayment of loans raised for the building of ships and other capital equipment. More important, though, than the Loan Acts were the 'New Industries (Development) Acts' of 1932 and 1937, which provided grants to new industries which would produce goods not then being manufactured in the province. These Acts were the first of a long series intended to encourage diversification and attract outside investment. The second of these Acts also provided for interest-free loans to existing local companies which sought to expand. In addition, local authorities were given power to exempt companies from rates at their own discretion.

Prior to the Second World War the situation was such that these measures had little real effect on the problems facing Northern Ireland's economy, despite the fact that some fifty firms took advantage of the assistance offered.[8] In the post-war context, however, when Government policies in the United Kingdom and elsewhere were reflecting the acceptance of increasing State intervention, particularly in the maintenance of full employment, there was growing interest in such measures among certain sections of the Protestant population. Between 1945 and 1953 Stormont introduced a series of 'Industries Development Acts', which empowered the Minister of Commerce to lease modern factory premises, and provide financial assistance to new industries, and to expanding old ones. The Ministry had very wide discretionary powers in these decisions, and it became clear that there was some division of opinion as to how this should be used. As the 1945 Act began to take effect, the Government found itself accused of neglecting the traditional industries while assisting new-comers, many of whom, it should be noted, offered improved wages and working conditions. The leaders of the linen industry had long been very influential within the Unionist Party and won themselves substantial aid from the 'Re-equipment of Industry Acts' of 1951 and 1953. They were provided with grants to meet one third of re-equipment and modern-isation costs.

It is remarkable that none of these acts carried a formal requirement to increase employment in the province. Northern Ireland was the only depressed region where capital grants were not tied to rigid employment conditions. These acts were followed by the 'Capital Grants to Industry Acts', 1954-62, which provided annual grants for expansion. Again no employment targets were set, and no specific schemes had to be under-taken. In the years covered by these Acts £31 million were spent. Furthermore, local authorities could still provide rates exemptions at their own discretion.

In addition to these steps taken by the Provincial Government, the province as a whole has been treated as a development area by the British Government, bringing further benefits in the form of tax concessions and regional employment premiums. The British Government is also the majority share-holder in Short Brothers, the aircraft manufacturers, and has provided big grants for the modernisation of the shipyards. Northern Ireland also benefited when, during the 1930s, the Westminster Govern-ment became increasingly involved in the agricultural question generally. In 1947 the 'Agriculture Act' established a system of guaranteed prices and markets for the United Kingdom as a whole. The net result of this has been that in mainland Britain subsidies represent about 50% of farmers' incomes, while in Northern Ireland they account for almost all the farmers' income.

Since 1945 legislation aimed at increasing employment had (up to 1969) brought about the creation of 69,000 jobs, at the enormous cost of £122,900,000.[9] In 1961, government sponsored industry employed some 22.5% of all manufacturing employees; by 1972 the corresponding figure was 44.9%.[10] It would seem reasonable to suggest that the linking of assistance to capital expenditure had the effect of creating a bias in favour of capital intensive industries. The cost of creating a job in the development regions of the United Kingdom between 1960 and 1968 was

£640, while in Northern Ireland it was £1,400.[11] In addition, some of these jobs have been short-lived, a reflection on the way in which the generous assistance available was abused by new firms whose stay in the province was very brief. For example, British Sound Reproducers, who were attracted to Londonderry in 1951 with free factory premises and seven years tax and rate relief, closed down in 1958. They reopened as Monarch Electric Ltd., only to close again in 1967 at a cost of some £700,000 and 1,000 jobs just when the period of tax and rate relief was coming to an end for the second time.[12] Thus, despite these measures, employment in Ulster's manufacturing industry continued to decline, from 206,000 people in 1950 to 166,000 in 1973. It was the tremendous expansion of employment in the service sector that helped to offset this decline.

More important, however, is the fact that little change has taken place in the structural base of the economy; rather, the change has been one of new specialisation within the traditional industries. Thus, partly because of its long textile tradition, Northern Ireland has become one of the major centres of the man-made fibre industry in the United Kingdom. The plants set up by such firms as British Enkalon, Monsanto, ICI and Courtaulds have all been assisted by the Northern Ireland Government. Not only has the cost of creating these jobs been high, but it has also tended to perpetuate the narrow structural base of the economy.[13] New industries have been, in the main, technologically advanced forms of traditional enterprises. On the whole the economy remains narrowly based, and thus exposed to the same economic dangers that have troubled Northern Ireland in the past: the possibility of fluctuations in world demand, or technical innovations in those industries on which the province depends. The dangers have in fact increased, since most of the new industries represent peripheral ventures by vast international companies whose capital is highly mobile.

The influx of foreign capital and the new wave of government assisted projects caused the Northern Ireland index of productivity to increase much more rapidly than that for Britain. However, Parker and Driver pointed out that:

> although representing a reorientation in the underlying direction of the economy in terms of the share of total production, employment created by the new projects has not challenged the relative importance of employment in the traditional industries. Although linen's absolute decline has been dramatic, it still represents some 56.9% of employment in the textile industry. The relative weight of man-made fibres in the NI economy is very clear in 1970. Thirteen firms produced more than half of the *output* of the entire industry. Yet the continued preponderance of *employment* in linen production is equally clear.[14]

Parker and Driver draw attention to this fact in order to illustrate the continued direct influence that the Unionist bourgeoisie can exert in employment discrimination. They also note that:

More important and enduring than discrimination directly practised by Unionist capital has been the indirect influence, through Stormont, on the location of industry. Although finance by the British state is crucial in encouraging capital to locate in the north, the precise location of an enterprise in the province has been dependent on the existing pattern of uneven development and on decisions taken by Stormont.[15]

Relatively few of the advance-built factories were in fact located in those towns with large Catholic majorities, such as Derry and Newry, where unemployment was highest. Most development has taken place in and around Belfast, and in the Protestant dominated Eastern towns such as Larne and Lurgan.[16] The unemployment situation would have been even worse had it not been for continuous migration out of the province, which between 1961 and 1966 accounted for an average annual loss of 7,000.[17] It is reasonable to assume that most of this was caused by economic necessity rather than choice. Furthermore, the location of most investment in the Belfast area has led to high rates of internal migration, from West to East.

THE WELFARE STATE

The depressed state of Northern Ireland's economy, and the Provincial Government's lack of powers to raise significant amounts of revenue, led to difficulties in maintaining adequate levels of public expenditure, and to increasing dependence on Westminster for financial assistance. Under the Government of Ireland Act (1920), 88% of Northern Ireland's revenue is raised by Westminster, as described in Chapter 2. From this sum deductions are made to cover the cost of operating the 'reserved services', such as the inland revenue, customs and excise departments, and the Post Office. A further deduction is made as a contribution to the armed services, defence and the National Debt. This is known as the 'imperial contribution'. The residuary share is then transferred back to the provincial exchequer to cover the cost of the 'transferred services'. It very soon became apparent that the imperial contribution had been set at too high a level if there was to be sufficient transferred revenue to maintain expenditure at the same level as in Great Britain. It was agreed that the imperial contribution should be made a residual figure, to be calculated after the necessary expenditures had been made in the province. Thus instead of the original fixed-sum contribution of approximately £8 million, it fluctuated from year to year. In the 1930s it fell as low as £10,000.

At the time of partition the Northern Ireland Government committed the province to maintaining parity with the United Kingdom in the provision of cash social services. However, the revenue raised locally was a small proportion of the total revenue raised from the province, and as the economic situation deteriorated it became obvious that, under the original arrangement, the burden of maintaining parity was too great. The 'Unemployment Insurance Agreement' of 1926 was a major factor, presenting an enormous drain on the province's funds. In the *Report of the Committee on Financial Relations between the State and Local Authorities*,[18] in 1931, it was decided that the costs facing ratepayers could not be increased, and that retrenchment should therefore be the policy, even if services then fell below United Kingdom levels. However, the British Government recognised the special problems of the area, and agreed to finance the deficit in Northern Ireland's unemployment fund. 1931 was the last year in which the province could pretend to both financial self-sufficiency and British standards of spending. Westminster exerted substantial pressure on Stormont to find new local sources of revenue, but finally recognised Northern Ireland's inability to finance services at British levels. In 1938 there came a specific guarantee, known as the Simon Declaration, that the British Exchequer would finance all cash social services which showed a deficit.

After the Second World War the range of the services provided by the State expanded dramatically as the British Labour Government began to implement the Beveridge Report, introducing a comprehensive National Health Service and social insurance scheme. Despite their hostility to welfare statism the Unionist Government were obliged to adopt these measures, and new social service agreements were signed in 1946 and 1948, under which Westminster was committed to subsidising the greatly increased costs. By 1968 the total amount of subsidies given to Northern Ireland came to over £100 million, of which £14 million went on the maintenance of parity in unemployment and sickness benefits, and £20 million in subsidies to agriculture.[19]

POLITICAL CONFLICT

In 1932 a group known as the Outdoor Relief Workers' Committee began to agitate on behalf of the unemployed workers, protesting at the Belfast Board of Guardians' refusal to give assistance to more than a handful of the applicants for Outdoor Relief (ODR). In order to qualify for a pitiful cash payment unemployed men had to do two and a half days'work per week on such ODR schemes as mending roads. With 28% unemployment many families faced starvation or the workhouse. The Unionist Government's response to the appalling economic conditions was to try and ensure that even if there was not much to go around, what there was went to Protestants. At the same time Unionist politicians were quick to suggest that the leaders of the agitation were communist republicans whose real aim was to destroy the State of Northern Ireland. Despite this the Protestant and Catholic workers maintained great solidarity and demonstrated their militancy through mass demonstrations and the successful ODR strike, which won them large increases in relief rates. Early in 1933 the predominantly Protestant railwaymen went on strike to oppose a 10% cut in wages that had been recommended by the Railway Wages Board. Two months later, after a protracted and violent struggle, they accepted cuts of 7½% and went back to work, but not without having clearly demonstrated their willingness and ability to engage in class conflict.

At the political level, however, this trade union consciousness made little impact, and the Labour Party failed to make any gains in the Belfast Corporation and Stormont elections held in 1933. This failure was, in part, the result of the ruling class policy of encouraging sectarian divisions within the working class. But the failure of these economic struggles to make any real impact on the divisive ideologies of the Belfast working class was also caused by the decisive intervention of Orangeism as a relatively autonomous force. In 1931 a section of the Protestant working class sought, through an organisation called the Ulster Protestant League, to 'urge all good Protestants not to employ Catholics, not to work with them, not to deal with them, and to accuse the government of softness in its dealings with what was regarded as the enemy within.'[29] In 1934 and 1935 there was sporadic sectarian rioting, with Protestant mobs attacking Catholic homes, and in June 1935 the Minister of Home Affairs banned all parades, including the great annual Orange march of July 12. The Orange Order defied the government ban, and its Grand Master announced: 'You may be perfectly certain that on the 12 July the Orangemen will be marching throughout Northern Ireland . . . I do not acknowledge the right of any government, Northern or Imperial, to impose conditions as to the celebration.'[21] The Government was forced to withdraw its ban, and the march went ahead. Three weeks of vicious sectarian rioting ensued, in which nine people were killed and hundreds of Catholics families were burnt out of their homes. The Orange militants, far from being satisfied, were incensed at the fact that more Protestants than Catholics had died during the riots. Bew notes that: 'This was attributed to Catholic influence within the police, and thus a campaign was sparked off against the government's alleged liberalism which included serious threats to found a "new" Unionist party — which would make the state more genuinely Protestant, purge Catholics from the police, etc.'[22]

The severity of the economic problems facing the province in the 1930s was such that the Unionist leadership also came under attack from a very different quarter. This time the challenge came from the more liberal sections of the middle class, whose interests transcended a limited concern with defending the privileges of a traditionally dominant political and economic elite. A Belfast businessman, W.J. Stewart, who was also a Unionist MP at Westminster, began to organise a group which wanted to see the Government play a more active role in such areas as aiding the unemployed and introducing reforms in agriculture. In the general election of 1938 Lord Craigavon found himself openly opposed by a section of his party which was critical of official policies on social and economic issues. Under the title 'Progressive Unionists' this section put forward twelve candidates at the election, mostly in constituencies where they felt that they might attract the usually unpolled Nationalist vote as well as that of disaffected Unionists. Their election manifesto focused on the problems of unemployment and inadequate housing for the low-paid, and promised to 'give a fair chance to the citizens of Northern Ireland to share in its Government.'[23] Such policies represented a radical break with orthodox Unionism's methods of winning political support.

The failure of the Progressive Unionists was caused, in part, by the intervention of external circumstances; by a renewed challenge from the forces of Irish nationalism. De Valera's more militantly republican stand in the 1930s enabled the Unionist leadership to fight the election on the traditional issue of defending partition. Under de Valera's leadership the Irish Free State became involved in an 'economic war' with Britain, in an attempt to protect the Southern economy behind high tariff barriers. Patrick Buckland has pointed out the importance of this development in its effects on the cohesion of the Ulster Unionist movement, in its contribution to the growth of a siege mentality in the North. 'The economic war between the Free State and British Governments seriously jeopardised one of the few real links between North and South. Exports from Northern Ireland to the Free State were drastically reduced or actually prohibited, the distributing trade, an important Belfast industry, being virtually destroyed as far as business in the Free State was concerned.'[24] Then, in 1937 de Valera introduced a new constitution for the Free State. McCann claims that 'the 1937 Constitution is crucial to any understanding of the political attitudes of both Catholics and Protestants in Northern Ireland: because, unlike the 1922 Constitution operated by Cumann na nGael, the 1937 one claims to be the Constitution for all Ireland, containing a blunt assertion of the Dublin government's right to legislate for the whole national territory.'[25] Furthermore, in Article 44 it enshrined the 'special position of the Holy Catholic Apostolic and Roman Church as the guardian of the faith professed by the great majority of citizens.'

Craigavon responded to this development by bringing forward the general election in the North, as a challenge to de Valera. And so 'the lines of the campaign had already been drawn and instead of housing, unemployment and the social services dominating debates, the Progressive Unionists found themselves involved in the inevitable discussion on Partition.'[26] Craigavon castigated the liberals as 'wreckers', and led the Unionist party to an overwhelming victory, increasing its majority by six seats and eliminating the Progressive challenge. As the *Sunday Times* commented:

A snap election on an unreal issue has given them complete victory. Their success merely demonstrates what was already known, namely that the great majority of the public of the Six Counties support Irish partition and wish to remain politically united to Great Britain. Whether it was worthwhile to advance the date of the election in order to prove what has been self-evident since Parnell's days is another matter.[27]

After the Second World War the Unionist Party embarked on the moderate programme of State aid to the economy described earlier. In its effects this policy further undermined the unity of Ulster's bourgeoisie, creating a division of interest between the representatives of local capital and those of British and foreign capital. In addition, it contributed to some weakening in the system of distributing patronage by which the elite retained power at the local level. Since the war large numbers of British and foreign companies have established enterprises in Northern Ireland, taking advantage of the generous inducements on offer, and a very quiescent labour force. Their arrival has done little to solve the major economic problems of the province, but it did cause changes in the province's social profile, creating a new middle class sector whose incomes and status were not related to the old Unionist oligarchy. Managers and technicians were hired by the huge parent companies, who had little concern for the peculiarities of Northern Ireland's political system, but rather placed great value on rationalisation and efficiency in the allocation of resources within the province. At the political level this group was concerned about the priorities that the Central Government employed in distributing the considerable resources which it now had at its disposal.

Given the small size of Northern Ireland's legislative body, a remarkable proportion of MPs held executive office, thus increasing the likelihood of 'undue influence' over the legislature. Ministries had considerable delegated powers to act on their own, and as described earlier, the Minister of Commerce had wide discretionary powers in the administration of investment grants. It was extremely difficult for the administration to be totally impartial in areas where influential business and political interests in the province were concerned. Thus conflicts arose about such questions as the neglect of traditional industries, or the location of new ones.

The question of centralised economic planning for the growth of the province's economy did not really make itself felt until the 1960s, when O'Neill became Prime Minister. However, during the forties and fifties those seeking to protect traditional local interests found themselves faced with growing pressure in favour of rationalisation and centralisation. It is interesting to note their response to the seemingly innocuous attempt by the House of Commons to bring the province into line with Britain concerning the gathering of records, through the 'Statistics of Trade Act'. Unionist back-benchers forced the Government to withdraw the Bill and revise it, since 'the Unionists concerned were unable to share even the

Conservative view of the requirements of economic oversight by the state.'[28] Conflicts arose over many issues as, for example, estate duty. Because of the large number of family-owned industrial and agricultural concerns, the Northern Ireland Government had introduced substantial concessions over estate duties in order to protect them. Westminster, while willing to provide a considerable sum in subsidies to the province, demanded that such concessions should be abolished in order to maximise revenues available within the province. The decline of the traditionally dominant industries, and the province's increasing dependence on outside investment also led to pressure for change at the local level. Conflicts occurred in local government under the discretionary powers vested in local authorities to grant rates exemption, and the question of how these were used. The arrival of British and foreign companies also began to undermine an important part of the Unionist system of distributing patronage in the shape of jobs. It is impossible to compile any reliable statistics on job discrimination, but the following categories are proposed by Barritt and Carter.[29] Complete discrimination in all posts would appear to be the natural pattern in many small enterprises, and in the larger ones which have expanded from local origins. This would apply particularly to family-owned firms. At the other end of the scale, mixing throughout occurs in firms which are controlled by outside interests, and which employ English managers and personnel officers.

The expansion of foreign investment meant that Catholics now had more access to managerial occupations, which in turn contributed to the growth of a reformist Catholic middle class, later to play an important role in the civil rights movement. And it contributed to the break up of the 'canvassing' technique of job allocation, thus reducing the ability of the Unionist elite to distribute patronage amongst favoured loyalist sections of the community. It is important not to exaggerate the extent to which new firms adopted non-discriminatory employment policies, for many un-doubtedly found it easier to adopt whichever pattern prevailed in the area in which they were located. However, they had no vested interest of their own in maintaining sectarian employment patterns, and placed a greater emphasis on the mobility of labour, and efficient resource allocation.

In their *Evidence to the Review Body on Local Government in Northern Ireland*, the provincial branch of the Confederation of British Industry clearly defined the areas in which their interests were in conflict with the Unionist machine. 'The government must be guided by the fact that, in the increasing complexity and sophistication of modern life, expertise and efficiency are of paramount importance, notwithstanding the necessity to reflect local loyalties in the pattern of administration.' In their remarks on the question of council housing, they called for allocation criteria that directly challenged traditional methods. 'It is, we consider, essential that everything possible is done to facilitate the mobility of labour, so that new industry, in particular, can be assured that labour can be made available to it, if it does not already exist in the required location.' The Confederation support the suggestion that a Central Housing Authority should be established, but it is concerned about how local interests might affect its functioning. 'It is therefore suggested that some form of Local Appeal Body might be established. . . Any such organisation, however, would require precise terms of reference and clearly defined powers to avoid frivolous and spurious representations to it. It should also be seen to be clearly non-political and non-sectarian in composition.' The theme of minimising local power is taken up again in the section on the size and number of authorities. The Confederation recommends large reductions in numbers, since the right sort of people will not wish to participate 'if the issues concerned are likely to be discussed at "parish pump" level with its concomitant vested interests. We feel there is a danger of over-emphasising local and parochial issues by making areas too small, and therefore too many, and by paying too much attention to the view of existing local authorities.'

The growth of the Welfare State did not contribute directly to the destabilisation of the social formation, for its operation could be largely controlled at the local level, with such institutions as hospitals and schools remaining in the control of the separate religious communities. It did lead, however, to some growth in central administrative offices, and by 1970 the rationalisation and centralisation of the social services was one aspect of the growing demand for the reorganisation of local government. More importantly, the Welfare State was responsible for the increasing integration of the Catholic community into the Six County State.

First, welfare legislation for Northern Ireland strengthened partition by maintaining the gap in living standards between the Six Counties and the Republic. In the 1950s and early 1960s the Republic lagged far behind Northern Ireland in the social services and benefits it could provide. Liam de Paor points out that:

> Nationalists in the North, who remained opposed to the maintenance of the partition of Ireland, must nevertheless now think twice before they would make any move which might bring them into the social and political system of the Republic, and so deprive them of the health, education, and welfare services they became accustomed to in the post-war period. [30]

Second, the provisions of the Butler Education Acts led to a fundamental change in the social profile of the Catholic population, by greatly increasing the number of young people who went on to higher education. By 1960 lower middle and working class Catholics found it possible to obtain further education through the new system of grants and allowances. In 1968 one group made its presence felt at The Queen's University, Belfast, with the formation of People's Democracy. They were dissatisfied with the reformist nature of the civil rights movement, and, whilst rejecting traditional republicanism, adopted a far more radical attitude toward economic and social questions. Others who were critical of old-style Nationalist politics sought to change the framework of Northern Ireland's politics in different ways; through the civil rights movement or, later, through the reformist parliamentary politics of the Social Democratic and Labour Party. The Catholic community's increasing participation in the economic and political life of the province meant that the constitutional question and the border issue inevitably began to assume less exaggerated proportions, despite the continued attempts by certain sections of the loyalist community to emphasise them.

The decline of Ulster's regional economy and its increasing integration into a world economy dominated by monopoly capital created severe strains within Unionism; strains which were already apparent in the 1930s. However, class struggle during the depression years was successfully contained within traditional sectarian political boundaries by the intervention of Orangeism, the dominant ideology within the Protestant working class. Furthermore, the solidarity of the Protestant Unionist alliance was reinforced during this period by the renewed external threat of Irish Nationalism. Although Unionism was thus able to contain class conflict and pressure for reform, it could not eliminate them. In the years following the Second World War the hegemony of Ulster's bourgeoisie was further weakened by economic and social changes over which it had little control. These changes did not provoke any further labour-based challenge to the conservatism of the Unionist regime, but they strengthened the liberal middle class opposition to those aspects of Unionism which were inhibiting the expansion of capitalist production in the province.

> The growth of state sponsored industry had given sustenance to a Unionist middle-class impatient with traditional loyalism. This section of the Unionist bloc was willing to concede to Catholics a measure of reform which breached traditional but anachronistic divisions . . . It was merely trying to fortify the rule of the larger Unionist capital, by removing some of the more minor discriminations which protected the Unionist petty-bourgeoisie, smaller Unionist capital and preserved the trivial but important privileges of Protestant workers.[31]

4

THE PROMISE OF REFORM

During the 1960s, under the leadership of Terence O'Neill, the Unionist Parliamentary Party found itself devoting an increasing amount of time to questions of economic and social reform. At the central government level, at least, the traditional preoccupation with loyalist unity and the constitutional issue seemed to have been superseded by an active concern with setting up 'development' programmes. Indeed, political activity at a variety of levels showed signs of breaking out of the loyalist versus republican deadlock. O'Neill's tentative modernisation plans were welcomed by a growing Catholic middle class which rejected traditional Nationalist aspirations and wished to participate in Ulster's 'reconstruction'. As the reformist movement gathered momentum within Northern Ireland it became linked with the issue of dismantling some of the overtly sectarian institutions in the province, and the granting of Catholic civil rights. Externally, the omens could not have been more favourable, for by the early 1960s the Republic was emerging from its early political and economic isolationism and adopting an increasingly tolerant attitude toward the existence of a separate State in the North. The establishment of political contacts between the two States in Ireland was a reflection of the fact that the forces of international capitalism were eroding the historic economic basis of partition.

These changes were not uniformly welcomed, however, by the Unionist Party at large. The major conflicts and tensions that came to the surface in the mid-sixties arose out of divisions within the loyalist community, between those backing O'Neill and those who strenuously opposed his conciliatory overtures to the Catholic minority and to the Government of the Republic. As the pressure for reform increased, O'Neill inevitably came into conflict with those elements of the Unionist alliance which sought to preserve their traditional privileges: the local bourgeoisie and the Protestant labour aristocracy.

THE ECONOMY

In 1957 a mammoth economic survey of Northern Ireland, commissioned by the Ministry of Commerce, was finally published.[1] It painted a gloomy picture of the state of the economy, and provided little ground for optimism. For this reason, the Government had in fact suppressed its publication for two years. It was followed in 1962 by the *Report of the Joint Working Party on the Economy of Northern Ireland*, commonly known as the Hall Report.[2] Its findings were equally unpromising:

> In our analysis of the economic situation we reached the conclusion . . . that, since the region was far from self-sufficient, additional employment could only be created either by increased exports or by increased subventions from Great Britain. Public works must depend on the latter though these may be offset by savings in unemployment benefit and assistance payments. They may strengthen the economy and enable it to export more, but most of them are a very indirect means of doing this. The case for an increase in public works on general economic grounds does not, therefore, seem strong.

The Report added that 'further steps should be taken to find employment opportunities outside Northern Ireland and to induce unemployed workers to avail themselves of them.' The popular view of the Hall Report was that it was useless, offering nothing better than emigration as a cure for unemployment.

In 1961 the province underwent a recession which hit hard at the already declining traditional industries, many of which, like the shipyards, were traditionally Protestant labour strongholds. The labour force in the shipyards was being steadily whittled away as a result of progressive rationalisation, and on top of this 8,000 were laid off by Harland & Wolff in 1961. Furthermore, the aircraft industry was jeopardised by the non-interventionist policy of the Conservative Government at Westminster. In the same year the old established Forth River Mills in Belfast paid off their entire workforce, and others followed.

After years of quiescence the Trade Union movement began to stir. Because of the movement's connections with the Republic, through its affiliation to the Irish Congress of Trade Unions, the Unionist Government under Lord Brookeborough had refused to give it due recognition. In 1960 the Northern Irish committee of the ICTU published recommendations which included cooperation with the Republic, and a programme of public works. In 1962 the unemployed organised a march to Stormont, and the trade unionists began to stump the six counties for a policy of increased employment. In February 1963 unemployment had reached 9.5%, and the following month a delegation of trade unionists, eighty-strong, flew to London, paraded in the West End and lobbied Parliament. In the Stormont election held in May 1962 the Northern Ireland Labour Party put up fourteen candidates, its most serious challenge since 1945. The party polled its highest total ever, holding the four seats they had won in 1958 with greatly increased majorities. Furthermore the Unionists lost two seats to left-wing republicans. One of these was Gerry Fitt, later to become leader of the Social Democratic and Labour Party, who must have attracted a substantial Protestant vote in winning his Belfast seat. For the first time the Unionists failed to poll a majority of votes in Belfast. It was becoming increasingly clear that the longstanding loyalist unity, which had so effectively taken precedence over any class antagonism, was in danger.

THE UNIONIST RESPONSE

Lord Brookeborough, who had been Prime Minister since 1943, was well-known for his intolerance of Catholics, and, in publicly encouraging discrimination in employment, he had constantly emphasised their disloyalty. He asserted that: 'Catholics are out to destroy Ulster with all their might and power. They want to nullify the Protestant vote, take all they can out of Ulster and then see it go to hell.'[3] Brookeborough had presided over a Cabinet which had shown great unwillingness to adopt constructive policies on any major issue facing the province. He regarded planning as a socialist menace.[4] Indeed, the casualness that had surrounded the conduct of parliamentary affairs in Northern Ireland is epitomised in his career. Under Brookeborough the Premiership was largely ceremonial; during the fifties the Prime Minister had spent a whole winter in Australia and New Zealand, going each way by ship. In his autobiography O'Neill can find only this to say about his predecessor: 'He was good company and a good raconteur and those who met him imagined that he was relaxing away from his desk. What they didn't realise was that there was no desk.'[5]

Early in 1963 a Unionist backbencher, Desmond Boal, voted with the Northern Ireland Labour Party on a censure motion on unemployment. Boal represented the solidly working class Shankill area in Belfast, and demanded Brookeborough's resignation. Ten more backbenchers joined him in this demand, and in March Brookborough resigned. The election of Terence O'Neill as his successor marked a new departure, for not only did he prosecute the cause of economic reform, but he also extended an olive branch to the Catholic community. O'Neill had been Finance Minister in the previous Government, and was deeply concerned about the province's economic problems. As the first important public figure openly to ally himself with the forces of reform and modernisation, he brought an air of optimism to the affairs of Northern Ireland. His new Minister of Commerce was Brian Faulkner who had made a name for himself as a hard-liner while Minister of Home Affairs under Brookeborough. More significant was the fact that he had the interests of the business community at heart, having been director of his father's clothing manufacturing firm. Faulkner was personally responsible for a massive Government initiative to stem the economic decline of the province and encourage new investment, the cost of which was met mainly by the British Exchequer.

O'Neill's first act was to commission an economic 'plan'. The Wilson Plan, published in 1965, called for 'an environment more favourable to the sustained expansion of output and employment.'[6] Targets were set for new house building programmes, and in three sets of employment areas: 30,000 new jobs in manufacturing industry, 5,000 in the construction industry, with the assistance of a programme of public investment, and 30,000 jobs in the service industries. Professor Wilson's economic plan was complemented by a major exercise in physical planning, the *Belfast Regional Survey and Plan: Recommendations and Conclusions*.[7] This document, commonly known as the Matthew Plan, was aimed at solving the problems of a heavy back-log of slum clearance, and an inadequate supply of land for redevelopment. It recommended that the Government should take direct responsibility for planning and development, and create a central authority which could co-ordinate work.

O'Neill's Government accepted both plans, though not without opposition from within the ranks of its own party. Local authorities were reluctant to lose their planning powers, for the reasons described in Chapter 2, and managed to hold on to them even after a Ministry of Development was established in 1965. O'Neill's interest in efficient central administration and state-aided economic development frequently brought him into conflict with local Unionist interests, for over the years the Unionist machine had developed interests of its own. As Eammon McCann points out:

> It had been created to serve a single class, but the people who operated it at local level had a vested interest in it for its own sake. They derived social prestige, local power and, in many cases, a degree of economic prosperity from being involved with it. They were not ready to give that up for vague reasons to do with trade figures.[8]

In August 1964 O'Neill gave official recognition to the Northern Committee of the Irish Congress of Trade Unions. Government plans to attract new investment to the province depended on good labour relations and the active cooperation of the Trade Union movement. O'Neill also made it clear that he was concerned to improve relations between the two communities in the North, and between Northern Ireland and the Republic. In the latter case the motives were connected with the changing economic relations between Britain and the Republic, and their united application to join the European Economic Community. O'Neill's desire to shed the traditionally sectarian image of the Unionist Party inevitably opened the question of Catholic membership. It was implicit in his new policies that the Unionist Party should welcome Catholic recruits, though it was not an idea that he dared prosecute actively. The lack of central party discipline, and the local autonomy within the party structure meant that power to accept or reject new applicants rested with the local constituency associations, most of which still held an uncompromising attitude towards Catholics. In the event, little was attempted publicly, and still less achieved.

The reformist section of the Unionist ruling class failed to establish dominance within the party, and in particular it failed to undermine the Unionists' traditional control over the subsidisation and location of industry. Although the Wilson report recommended that new industries be located in Derry, Government action systematically favoured areas with largely Protestant populations.

> Cautious investment from public as well as private sources has meant that eastern towns smaller than some in the west of the province have received more factories. Thus Lurgan with a population of 18,000 and only twenty-one miles from Belfast has attracted 13 new factories, while the city of Londonderry, or Derry, with a population of 55,000 but more than seventy miles from Belfast has attracted only 7 factories — two of which were vacant in 1968.[9]

Michael Farrell described the 'final insult' of O'Neill's new planning strategy, which came with the Lockwood Report at the end of 1964.

> It recommended a second university for Northern Ireland, but again not in Derry, the second largest centre of population, where there was already an old-established University College. The university was to go to Coleraine. There was a big protest campaign in Derry backed even by liberal Unionists, and it came out that hard-liners in the Derry Unionist Party had lobbied against their own city because investment and development would swell the already growing Catholic majority to such a size that no gerrymandering could keep the city in Unionist hands. The government endorsed the Lockwood decision.[10]

However, despite the distorted pattern of economic development which resulted from the intervention of these political factors, O'Neill's economic strategy made a considerable short-term impact. The structural base of the economy remained narrow and therefore vulnerable, but the Government succeeded in attracting a large number of international firms, and the province became a major centre of the artificial fibre industry. The *Northern Ireland Economic Report* for 1969 which reviewed the progress that had been made under the Wilson Plan, noted that: 'In manufacturing industry a total of almost 29,000 new jobs had been created by the end of 1969 compared with the target of 30,000.' By the mid-1960s the growth sectors in the Northern Irish economy were no longer owned by Ulster capital and no longer controlled by the local bourgeoisie. The new patterns of ownership affected both production and distribution. 'Locally owned distributors and retailers were hit by the operations of British Home Stores (from 1965), Boots (from 1966), Marks and Spencer (from 1967), and the expanded activities of the Mace and Spar chains (since 1968).'[11]

O'Neill's main political task was to convince sufficient numbers of Unionist voters that the benefits of these changes outweighed some loss of local autonomy and certain traditional Protestant privileges.

THE BROADER ANGLO-IRISH FRAMEWORK

The uncompromising basis of the Orange State was being weakened by the increasing importance of issues which cut across traditional sectarian loyalties. The decline of the province's regional economy, and its growing dependence on foreign investment and the provisions of Britain's Welfare State had altered the internal balance of forces in Northern Irish society, and made it increasingly difficult for the Unionist Party to contain within itself the divergent interests of the Protestant community. Northern Ireland's political autonomy could no longer disguise the fundamental fact of its peripheral status in the broader British and European economic communities. The underlying forces at work within the province were not endogenous, nor peculiar to Northern Ireland, but were part of basic changes in the economic structure of the capitalist world, associated with the rise of international corporations, monopoly capital and the Welfare State. These changes were not only altering political relations within the province, but were also transforming the broader structure of Anglo-Irish relations, in the direction of increased economic integration and political cooperation. This development had inevitable repercussions for relations between the Republic and Northern Ireland, and created pressure for some kind of rapprochement.

In the late 1930s the two states in Ireland stood in hostile opposition to each other, on economic, political and ideological issues. The attempt by the Progressive Unionists to liberalise some aspects of orthodox Unionism foundered on the over-riding concern with partition. In the economic sphere the conflicting policies of the two States continued to appear to be the relevant response to the situation in which each found itself until the 1950s. Thus, the industries of the North were dependent on a free trade policy with Britain, while the diversification of industry in the South demanded the shield of a protective tariff. Since the Six Counties were an integral part of the British economy, these tariffs necessarily formed a barrier between North and South.

In order to appreciate the altered external circumstances in which O'Neill made his attempt to liberalise traditional Unionism, it is necessary to examine the transformation that occurred in the 1960s in the Republic's economic relations with Britain, and consequently in its political relations with Northern Ireland.

FROM FREE STATE TO REPUBLIC

The setting up of the twenty-six county Irish Free State, and the signing of the Anglo-Irish Treaty in 1921 provoked a civil war in the South that lasted until April 1923. The causes of the division within Sinn Fein, and the victory of the pro-Treaty faction, were discussed earlier. The first independent Government of the twenty-six counties was formed by the Cumman na nGael party, which represented the interests of the large farmers and commercial businessmen, who desired, as far as possible, to minimize economic friction with Britain. They were supported by the majority of people in the country not so much because there was widespread enthusiasm for the Treaty, but because the people were weary of the war and the Treatyites offered them peace.

During the 1920s the Irish Free State remained an essentially free-trading country, despite the imposition of a limited number of tariffs. The Cumman na nGael party, which held power until 1932, was guided by principles of economic orthodoxy, and was accordingly cynical about the overall efficacy of tariffs and fearful for their effects on existing Anglo-Irish trade. These views were supported by the big farmers, who were an importance force in the country.

> At that time of the 1920s, it must be remembered, over fifty per cent of the working population were engaged in agriculture . . . The greater part of the national income came from agriculture. Obviously then, the first thing for a government to do was to make agriculture prosperous. Once it was prosperous then the benefits would filter through to everyone else in the country to the small industrialists, the shop-keeper, the professions. [12]

However, it was clear that farmers could only be prosperous if they were able to export, given the small size of the home market. To export meant to sell in the British market where at that time there were no tariffs against any country. The competition was therefore stiff.

On the domestic front the Government concentrated on such post-war reconstruction as the rebuilding of roads and railways. In addition, by 1928 three major public works schemes had been initiated: the Carlow sugar beet factory, the drainage of the River Barrow, and above all the Shannon electricity scheme, which enabled a cheap native supply of power to be transmitted throughout the sparse Irish population. The economic problems facing the country, however, remained acute. The separate status of Northern Ireland meant that the South had lost 40% of its taxable capacity, and the bulk of its industry. Massive rationalisation was required in agriculture in order for it to remain sufficiently competitive, and export earnings were constantly falling behind the level necessary to finance industrial imports. Furthermore, without protection, local industries stood little chance of survival against their ever-growing capital intensive rivals in Britain and Europe. Under these conditions, both capital and labour had strong incentives to leave the country. By the late 1920s it was clear that the bourgeoisie of the twenty-six counties who had preferred the settlement to a struggle were becoming dissatisfied with the results of their bargain. The full protectionist case advanced slowly as long as world prosperity lasted, but with the spread of the great depression it gained momentum. After 1929, the world economic crisis, limiting international trade and dealing a blow to the Irish sugar beet and grain industries, created conditions for the rise to power of the Republicans of Fianna Fail, de Valera's new party. Fianna Fail came to power in 1932, capitalising on widespread disillusion with the economic effects of the 'revolution'. Its platform was essentially populist, supporting and supported by the small farmers and small business people. It also cultivated, with considerable success, the working class vote. Its policies were the original policies of Arthur Griffith: 'self-sufficiency, capitalism tempered by a particularist nationalism, a dismantling of the emblems of subjection but a willingness scarcely less than that of their predecessors to be involved in the colonial system.'[13] The basis of Fianna Fail's economic policy was protection and import substitution.

Fianna Fail had not lost sight of its origins in the anti-Treatyite faction of Sinn Fein. It opposed and repudiated the Treaty settlement of 1921 with Britain, and proceeded by various means to dismantle it, abolishing the Oath of Allegiance to the English crown for members of the Irish Parliament, and refusing to pay the Land Annuities. These were the instalments by which, under the terms of the final financial agreement with Britain in the 1920s, Irish farmers, through the Free State Government, repaid to the British exchequer the capital cost of buying out the landlords. In retaliation for the withholding of the annuity payments, the British Government imposed tariffs on food and animal imports from Ireland. The 'economic war' had begun. Fianna Fail had in fact already begun to implement its policy of high tariffs on the importation of finished goods; their first budget contained forty-three new duties.[14] More than 1,000 items were affected by 1936, and between 1932 and 1939 the *ad valorem* tariff level rose from 9% to 35%, amongst the highest in the world.[15] It was generally accepted that new industries would only flourish by processing or assembling imported raw materials, for only here and there could native sources of supply be developed, and then very slowly and at considerable expense. But, if the raw materials had to be brought in, they had to be paid for, and this demanded increased exports. Hampered by these internal and external restrictions, the nationalist bourgeoisie struggled to establish Ireland's economic independence, but the limits to this growth, based as it was on a very small home market, were soon reached. In 1938 Fianna Fail signed an extensive trade agreement with Britain, permitting the import of iron, steel, metal goods, machinery and chemicals. This signalled the effective end of economic hostilities, and the failure of the attempt to establish an autonomous centre of capitalist accumulation in Ireland.

Moves to assert the political sovereignty of the Irish Free State, on the other hand, continued unabated. In 1937 the new constitution was drafted as part of the policy of repudiating the settlement of 1921. On the ideological level Buckland suggests that 'a constricting combination of Catholicism and nationalism caused southern society to stagnate, revelling in the traditional sanctity and loveliness of Irish society, protecting such myths as the holy and noble peasant by the clerically-supported censorship of literature.'[16]

In September 1939 de Valera proclaimed Irish neutrality in the Second World War. However, unlike the situation during the First World War, this did not mean the adoption of a policy of 'England's difficulty, Ireland's opportunity'. Irish neutrality was essentially benevolent toward Britain, particularly in the matter of trade relations. As a result of the war the production of foodstuffs became geared more than ever to the needs of the British market. It was not until after the end of the war that the South once again made a play for the North. During the negotiations that accompanied the setting up of NATO, 'official pronouncements while carefully avoiding commitment, managed to convey that if England wanted to do away with Irish neutrality the transference of the excepted powers in the Six Counties to Dublin would suffice for the necessary response.'[17] Britain declined to trade, and in the spring of 1949 the Republic was accordingly declared, and it withdrew from the Commonwealth. Westminster's 1949 Ireland Act which formalised the new relationship with the Republic also gave additional guarantees for the status of Northern Ireland by stating that 'in no event will Northern Ireland or any part thereof cease to be part of the United Kingdom without the consent of the Parliament of Northern Ireland.'

ANGLO-IRISH RAPPROCHEMENT

The economic situation in which the new Republic found itself is common to most 'developing' countries. Lack of diversification and dependence on one major sector in the economy is generally the result of historic colonial relations. The struggle for political independence cannot, in itself, alter the structure of economic dependence, and the dominance of the metropolitan countries is usually maintained through the establishment of 'neo-colonial' economic relationships.

First, capital, in as much as it is formed locally, tends to migrate to the metropolis, or other advanced capital markets, since the attempts to establish a local industrial base do not provide such a profitable outlet for capital investment. Thus the foreign investments of the substantial rentier class in the Republic were constantly increasing. Second, attempts to build up a diversified national economy can have little success without complete tariff protection from the vast capital-intensive corporations of the 20th century. Yet, such withdrawal from the international free-trade community is not possible for a country which depends on exporting to the international market in order to sustain output in its major productive sector. Third, there is a general tendency, under these conditions, for industrial development to be encouraged in any form, and for large international corporations to seek access to such protected markets through the establishment of subsidiaries behind the tariff barrier, or through the buying up of existing local enterprises. In their analysis of the Republican epoch, Rumpf and Hepburn note that 'twenty years after de Valera first assumed the direction of the country's affairs, economic ties between the two old enemies were so strong that a firm of American experts, called in to analyse the Irish economy, came to the conclusion that the country's dependence on Britain was so strong as to be incompatible with the status of political sovereignty.'[18]

The difficulties facing the Republic in the early fifties were exacerbated by the necessity of increasing agricultural productivity through the consolidation of small-holdings and the mechanisation of farming. Under pressure of a price system against which the Government gave no protection, the small farmers lost their grip on the soil. Between 1955 and 1960, with the withdrawal of Government price maintenance and some agricultural subsidies, 28,786 small-holdings disappeared.[19] The mid-20th century witnessed land clearances as decisive as those of the mid-19th, and again there was no industrial expansion capable of absorbing the new labour surplus. The annual rate of emigration between 1946 and 1951 was given as 8.2 per thousand of the population. Between 1951 and 1956 it was 13.4, rising to 14.8 by 1960. It is estimated that 408,766 persons emigrated in the decade 1951-61.[20]

In the 1950s it was becoming increasingly apparent that the Republic's attempts to build up an independent, national, industrialised economy within the context of an international free enterprise system were unlikely to have much success. On all sides the economic situation was deteriorating. In 1947 the excess of imports over exports stood at £91,823,000; more than four times the largest inter-war deficit.[21] The deficit was still increasing in 1955. In that year a number of import controls were imposed, and in subsequent years the foreign reserves were slowly built up. However, a major element on the credit side was derived from the growing influx of foreign capital.

In 1954 the first tentative steps were taken to encourage foreign investment in industry, though at this stage foreign capital was more of a temporary stop-gap in the economy. However, in 1958 the Fianna Fail Government published a report drawn up by T.K. Whitaker, entitled *Economic Development*, which, in a detailed analysis of the country's predicament, emphasised the need for productive capital investment, and the desirability of attracting it from abroad. The report which demanded a radical reversal of all previous policies, was adopted by the Government as the basis of their Programme for Economic Expansion.

> Foreign capital, already wooed by the coalition government in
> 1956 and more systematically by the Industrial Development
> (Encouragement of External Investment) Act of 1958, would be
> further enticed by tax concessions and other facilities. And not
> only that, protection for protection's sake would no longer be
> tolerated. The Programme took it for granted that before long
> Ireland would be participating in some form of European Common
> Market and that to aim at self-sufficiency in the old style was
> simply not realistic.[22]

The opening of the Irish market to foreign investment attracted mainly
British firms, but, aided by the flow of American dollars to Europe, the
Government succeeded in establishing a trade and currency relationship
with the USA. This in turn led to further investment from that quarter.
In addition the Programme expected agriculture to become more export
oriented, with grassland to be developed at the expense of tillage.

By the early 1960s, from being a temporary stop-gap, foreign capital
had become the financial keystone of the economy. In 1961 capital
exports roughly balanced capital imports. In 1962 the excess of capital
imports stood at £13 million, rising to £22 million in 1963, and £41
million in 1965.[23] Between 1958 and 1968 GNP rose by over 4% per
annum, and capital formation as a percentage of GNP rose from 13% to
22% over the same period. The economy of the South began to boom,
with industrial employment growing from 257,000 in 1961 to 328,000
in 1971.[24] As Parker and Driver have shown:

> The key to understanding these developments lies in the role
> played by the State in the economy. State involvement both
> in terms of direct grants to foreign capital and in terms of
> providing an infrastructure of communication, training,
> advisory services etc., increased dramatically in the 60s. — The
> ratio of State expenditure (current and capital) to GNP rose
> from 27% in 58/9 to 42% in 72/3. — To finance this and service
> the rising national debt necessitated massive taxation increases
> and further borrowing.[25]

These new domestic policies were accompanied by new directives in
foreign policy, including the decision to join GATT in 1960. In August
1961 both Britain and the Republic applied to join the EEC. The case
for the Republic's entry was made with frankness by Professor Joseph
Johnston in his book, *Why Ireland Needs the Common Market*.[26] He
argued that agricultural production in the Republic was underprivileged
compared with that in Britain and Northern Ireland, and operated at a
relatively low cost. The disparity arose from the policy of agricultural
price supports maintained in Britain over the preceding decade. The result,
he argued, had been to increase British agricultural production to 70%
above its pre-war level. Within the EEC however, it would be necessary
to scale British agriculture down, thus giving low cost producers the chance
to produce for an expanding export market. The alternative, he feared,
was the prospect of a 15% tariff being imposed on agricultural exports to

Britain, which would mean the loss of the market altogether, and not merely unfavourable terms.

Despite de Gaulle's veto in 1963, discussions continued on the question of developing Anglo-Irish relations in the context of EEC membership, with the result that in 1965 the Fianna Fail Government negotiated a Free Trade Agreement with Britain, to come into effect in 1966. The Agreement provided for the dismantling of all tariff barriers between the two countries, and in economic terms, the restoration of the Union.

CONVERGENCE BETWEEN NORTH AND SOUTH

By the mid- 1960s both the Unionist and Republican Governments in Ireland had abandoned their attempts to protect local capital, and had adopted policies of actively encouraging foreign investment. In addition, Northern Ireland was now increasingly dependent on subventions from Westminster. In the context of possible co-membership of the EEC, it was becoming apparent that the economic structure of Ireland had been transformed in such a way as to greatly reduce the significance of the barrier between North and South. Discussions in the Republic on joining the EEC raised the point that the dismantling of British agricultural price supports would remove one reason why the Six County farmers should prefer the British to a Dublin connection. Furthermore, the abolition of tariffs would greatly weaken the case for continued political hostilities.

It was clearly in the interests of the British and other foreign companies which were taking over an ever-increasing share of capital holdings in Ireland, both North and South, to see the integration of the two markets. The economic decline in the North, and British capital's reorientation away from the Empire and towards Europe encouraged new perceptions of Anglo-Irish relations, and greater responsiveness to the development of Southern Irish capitalism. Furthermore, British Governments, both Conservative and Labour, recognised Northern Ireland as a financial burden on British capital, and wanted to see it transferred onto the shoulders of the EEC.

In the Republic the question of partition was now seen in a different light. Lysaght notes that:

> With bourgeois internationalism went national quietism. This was especially notable on the outstanding issue of political Nationalism, partition. Whereas in the first half of the twentieth century, Irish Nationalist opinion had unthinkingly alienated the north-eastern Protestants, it began, in the second half, to try equally unthinkingly, to conciliate them.[27]

Indeed, the history of the Republic since the late 1950s has been shaped by policies that contrast directly with those executed over the previous thirty-five years. In 1959 de Valera, who had led the anti-Treaty faction at the time of the Irish civil war, retired from politics to become President of Ireland. The cultural traditions of the old Gaelic nation, which had been so important to de Valera, and the republicanism of Arthur Griffith were slowly being jettisoned. Fianna Fail began to attract the support of the business community as well as the traditional votes of small farmers and rural workers. The leadership of the party passed into the hands of Mr Sean Lemass in 1959, who, like O'Neill in the North, was the spokesman for the 'New Deal' forces in the South.

In 1963, in a speech which made explicit the new outlook of the Dublin Government, Mr Lemass announced that:

> We recognise that the Government and Parliament there [in Northern Ireland] exist with the support of the majority of the people of the Six County area — artificial though that area is. We see it functioning within its powers and we are prepared to stand over the proposal that they should continue to function within those powers, within an all-Ireland constitution for so long as it is desired to have them.[28]

The way was now open for the establishment of direct political contacts between North and South, and in January 1965 Lemass travelled to Belfast for discussions with O'Neill on possible areas of future cooperation. It was the first such meeting since 1925.

The direct effect of this meeting on the internal politics of Northern Ireland is described by O'Neill in his autobiography:

> There was one immediate tangible result from my meeting with Mr Lemass. The leader of the Nationalist Party, Eddie McAteer, went down to Dublin to see Mr Lemass. As a result of that meeting the Nationalist Party, for the first time in Northern Ireland's history, decided to form themselves into an official opposition party, which obviously made for an improved working of Parliament.[29]

In October of the same year O'Neill called a general election in which his reformist policies received widespread support. He himself celebrated the results thus: 'Co-operation between North and South is now publicly endorsed, and today when a militant Protestant housewife fries an egg she may well be doing it on Catholic power generated in the South and distributed in the North as a result of that first O'Neill-Lemass meeting.'[30]

THE CATHOLIC COMMUNITY AND CIVIL RIGHTS

It was inevitable that these developments should become linked to the question of Catholic civil rights in the North. As McCann points out: 'If, as economics demanded, there was to be a rapprochement between Protestant business in the North and Catholic business in the South something would have to be done about the way Northern Catholics were being treated by their Protestant rulers.'[31] The traditional justification for discriminatory policies, that Catholics were disloyal and a threat to the

State, was becoming increasingly untenable, for in the early 1960s changes began to occur within the Catholic community concerning attitudes toward participation in the political life of the province. These changes were connected with a decline in the support for traditional republicanism, both north and south of the border, and the growth of a Catholic middle class which wanted to play a more active role in politics.

In February 1962 the IRA formally ended their border campaign, issuing a statement that pointed to lack of support from the Catholic population in the North as a major factor in its failure. The campaign had been launched in December 1956, against a background of disillusionment with the British Labour movement, frustration with growing Unionist intransigeance, and despair of parliamentary politics. The formal declaration of war announced that: 'Resistance to British Rule in occupied Ireland has now entered a decisive stage. Early today Northern units of the Irish Republican Army attacked key British installations.'[32] The raids of the late fifties avoided attacking civilians, and were mainly made across the border and directed at various installations such as bridges, police barracks and customs posts. Nevertheless, the campaign succeeded in strengthening Unionist solidarity, by raising the familiar issue of the republican threat.

The IRA at this time had no clear political programme, and the campaign was a purely military one for which it was difficult to maintain longer-term support. However, its failure had important repercussions within the republican movement, as a result of which the organisation virtually abandoned its traditional military role for several years. The IRA was not directly involved in the growth of the civil rights movement and the sectarian violence that accompanied it, although it agreed to co-operate with the programme of non-violent demonstrations. J.B. Bell suggests that 'It would be fair to say that the civil rights movement had far more influence on the IRA than the reverse.'[33]

In December 1962 Gerry Fitt, the Republican Labour MP at Stormont, proposed that in view of the cessation of hostilities, there should be a general amnesty for republicans interned under the Special Powers Act. Stormont rejected the suggestion at first, but under growing pressure from the trade union movement and the Belfast Trades Council, the amnesty was granted in March 1963. By this time the dominant force within the minority community was already the civil rights oriented Catholic middle class.

Ever since the setting up of the Northern Irish State the main parliamentary opposition party had been the Nationalist Party, the northern wing of the old Irish Parliamentary Party. The party was strongly clericalist in character, and was linked with the sectarian Ancient Order of Hibernians. When, in 1918, Sinn Fein routed the Irish Parliamentary Party in the South, the Nationalists held on to their position in the North, and have always collaborated to some extent in the Northern parliamentary system. 'The party has maintained such strength as it had largely through local Tammany-

Hall-style organisations and local politics and through its association with opposition at local level to the Orange Order, itself largely sectarian in character.'[34] The party had never accepted, however, the role of official opposition at Stormont, thus avoiding recognition of the Northern Ireland constitution. They held nine or ten seats on average, but the attendance of their MPs was intermittent since they had no hope of exercising any influence over affairs at Stormont.

In the early 1960s there was some rethinking within the party, prompted in part by the formation of a new Catholic movement called National Unity. Essentially, this was an organisation of middle class Catholics, and reflected the desire of business men and professional people to play a more positive role in the province. The movement was orientated more to Belfast, while the strength of the Nationalists lay in the rural and border areas. In 1964, in response to the changing environment, the Nationalist Party produced, for the first time, a substantial statement of party policy that covered a wide range of issues. In February 1965, the party agreed to adopt the role of official opposition at Stormont, and in the following year the party held the first of a series of annual conferences.

The Nationalists, however, were being rapidly overtaken by the growing support for a civil rights campaign. In the early 1960s dissatisfaction with Brookeborough's response to the problems of high unemployment and economic stagnation provoked renewed criticism of discrimination in employment and the allocation of council housing. In April 1963 the Northern Ireland Labour Party conference passed resolutions calling for the establishment of a tribunal to examine cases of alleged discrimination, the introduction of a points system in the allocation of houses, and the awarding of employment on the basis of merit alone. There was some support for these demands from the Protestant working class, for the Unionist political system systematically enforced traditional relations of clientage between worker and employer, and between worker and the Government, not necessarily to the benefit of the former. Loyalty to the Unionist Party, despite conflicting class interests, was a central factor in obtaining either housing or employment. In the summer of 1963 the question of housing was taken up by Mrs McCluskey, the wife of a doctor in Dungannon, who was incensed by the refusal of the Protestant dominated council to rehouse Catholics in empty post-war utility homes. The 'Homeless Citizens' League' was founded, a demonstration organised, and the houses were won for the Catholics. By January 1964 the McCluskey's had organised a group of professional people in the three western counties into the 'Campaign for Social Justice'. Its aim was to collect and publicise information concerning cases of injustice in Northern Ireland, and over the next few years it established close links with back-bench Labour MPs at Westminster.

In March 1965 the National Council for Civil Liberties invited representatives from all parties to a conference in London, at which grounds were established for seeking an official enquiry, and organising a pressure group at Westminster. Later in the year the 'Campaign for Democracy in Ulster' was launched, with sixty-four supporters at Westminster. Optimism spread when the Labour Government was returned with an increased majority, for the Conservative Party's formal links with the Unionist Party had previously inhibited the reopening of any aspect of the 'Irish Question'. In May 1965 the Belfast Trades Council held a conference in Belfast on the issue of civil liberties. Despite the fact that the majority of the eighty delegates were Protestant, resolutions calling for an end to discrimination were passed. However, neither of the major political parties at Stormont, the Unionists and Nationalists, made any response to this sort of challenge. It was a Liberal MP from one of the University seats who finally raised the issue in February 1966, and introduced a Bill aimed at outlawing both racial and religious discrimination. It met with little support, though at the end of the year O'Neill did announce minor electoral reforms, including the abolition of the plural vote for Stormont elections, and the replacement of the four University seats with four in the county. The reforms were insignificant given the absence of proportional representation, and the particular importance of local government, where the bias in the franchise was far more pronounced.

The lack of response from the Unionist Government at this time was an indicator of the fundamental contradiction facing O'Neill. Despite the favourable external environment, and the moderate nature of Catholic aspirations, he still faced the problem of maintaining his position within the Unionist Party. Every Unionist MP at this time was a member of the Orange Order, and O'Neill's cabinet contained some of his most outspoken critics. In September 1966 his opponents in the Parliamentary Party conspired unsuccessfully to raise the demand for his resignation, thus clearly revealing the extent of the underlying conflicts of interest. Meanwhile, on the streets, the Reverend Ian Paisley was mobilising Protestant workers to defend their ancient privileges.

Faced with these rebuffs the civil rights organisers now attempted to draw together all those who were opposed to traditional Unionist domination, on the basis of demands for the extension to Northern Ireland of the civil rights enjoyed by citizens in the rest of the United Kingdom. An ad hoc committee was formed, which, in February 1967, founded the Northern Ireland Civil Rights Association. In April a constitution was agreed upon, modelled on the National Council for Civil Liberties, and an executive formed. It included trade unionists, members of the NILP, and even a moderate Unionist, but they were acting as individuals rather than as representatives of these organisations. NICRA was first brought onto the streets over the question of housing allocation in Dungannon. In July 1968 Austin Currie, a Nationalist MP at Stormont, occupied a council house in Dungannon which had been allocated to a Protestant girl of nineteen, in preference to many Catholic families who urgently needed rehousing. In August NICRA agreed to participate in a protest march, though with reservations about getting involved in this kind of political activity. Despite a counter-demonstration organised by Paisley's Ulster Protestant Volunteers, over 3,000 people marched peacefully into Dungannon.

In October the Derry Housing Committee followed the example of the Dungannon group by inviting NICRA to participate in a march in Derry. However, two days prior to the date chosen, William Craig, then Minister of Home Affairs and an uncompromising opponent of reform, issued restrictions on the march by banning all processions in the Waterside ward or within the city walls. The effect of this ban was to escalate tension. After lengthy discussions the organisers of the march decided to proceed regardless of the ban. The Cameron Commission noted that 'it guaranteed the attendance of a large number of citizens of Londonderry who actively resented what appeared to them to be a totally unwarranted interference by the Minister.'[35] There was widespread television coverage of the RUC dispersing the demonstrators with indiscriminate use of their batons and water cannon, and further publicity was ensured by the presence of three Westminster Labour MPs who had been invited as observers by Gerry Fitt.

Craig's action drove the civil rights movement into direct confrontation with the State. He succeeded in casting the demonstrators in the role of the Unionists' traditional enemy, disloyal Catholics. Yet it was precisely the Catholic bourgeoisie's moderate 'reformism' which threatened the vertical relations of patronage upon which the Orange State was built. There was no demand for Irish reunification, or 'power-sharing' and 'community government', only for equal access to resources such as jobs and houses. The demands of the civil rights movement were essentially a logical extension of O'Neill's tentative modernisation plans. What Craig's action, and that of the RUC, clearly revealed was that reform could not be achieved through agitation and piecemeal legislation; it demanded the break up of the Unionist alliance, and a total restructuring of the State apparatuses.

The atmosphere of confrontation, together with the outbreaks of sectarian violence which the marches provoked, immediately began to create tensions within the civil rights movement. On the one hand the middle class reformist element became increasingly cautious, intimidated by the scale of the reaction they had caused, while on the other, the radical elements became more explicitly militant. Signs of a split within the movement appeared shortly after the Derry march, when the Derry Citizen's Action Committee was formed to organise further demonstrations in the city. Among the leaders who emerged in Derry at this time were John Hume and Ivan Cooper, moderates whose views differed from other activists in that their aim was to apply steady pressure on the Government towards the yielding of reforms in the political and social system. Their views were opposed by McCann, who walked out of the Committee describing it as 'middle-aged, middle-class, and middle-of-the-road.'[36]

In November 1968, in consultation with the British Government, the Unionist Party finally agreed on the North's first reform programme, though much of it involved promises rather than action. The main points were: (1) that local authorities would be required in future to allocate houses on the basis of an agreed scheme such as a points system; (2) that the Central Government would get an ombudsman; (3) that a Government appointed development commission would replace the Londonderry Corporation; (4) that consideration would be given to a review of the local government franchise; and (5) that the Special Powers Act, in so far as it conflicted with international standards would be withdrawn 'as soon as the Northern Ireland government considers this can be done without hazard.' In response to these promises NICRA agreed to call a halt on further demonstrations. The more radical elements in the civil rights movement, however, now organised within People's Democracy, decided to go ahead with their plans for a march from Belfast to Derry at the beginning of the New Year, in support of the demand 'one man, one vote.' The demonstrators were ambushed at Burntollet by about 200 loyalists, armed with iron bars and coshes. 'From eye-witness accounts and the mass of press photographs taken in the hours that followed, about 100 of these 200 men were subsequently identified as being members of the Ulster Special Constabulary — the B Specials.'[37] That night the RUC raided the Catholic Bogside area of Derry, and as the Cameron Commission reported, 'a number of policemen were guilty of misconduct which involved assault and battery, malicious damage to property, to streets. . . giving reasonable cause for apprehension of personal injury among other innocent inhabitants, and the use of provocative sectarian and political slogans.'[38]

The demand for immediate action on the granting of civil rights brought out into the open the contradiction at the heart of O'Neill's 'new' Unionism. How could reforms which were agreed upon at Cabinet level be implemented in a society where the Government's agents, the police, were manifestly opposed to such reforms, and were seen to act in collusion with the opponents of all that O'Neill stood for?

With the backing of the Westminster and Dublin Governments, and the support of the Catholic middle class, it was now necessary for O'Neill to confront his opponents in the Unionist Party and attempt to consolidate his position as leader.

THE NEW ASSEMBLY
AND SUNNINGDALE

Between 1969 and 1974 many intense political struggles developed in Northern Ireland. These years witnessed a proliferation of political parties, pressure groups and paramilitary organisations, and an escalating confrontation between the British Army and the IRA. The central contradictions of the period were determined by the rise of monopoly capital, its penetration into Ireland, and the collision of these new material productive forces with the existing relations of production; relations that were dominated by the political and ideological alliance between local non-monopoly capital and the Protestant labour aristocracy. The transformation of Northern Ireland's social formation involved severe dislocations at all levels, and the reflection of the underlying contradiction in actual political struggles was, as Boserup has noted, 'an extremely complex and mediated one.'[1]   Northern Ireland is not simply a region within the British State. It is a social formation with its own state apparatuses, through which the reproduction of social relations can be controlled thereby increasing the autonomy of local non-monopoly capital as a social force.[2] The challenge to the hegemony of Ulster capital produced a major political crisis, as the rise of monopoly capital in Ireland, both North and South, threatened to cut across all the historically opposed class alliances, creating fundamentally new areas of conflict and collaboration.

The analysis of the increasingly complex political struggles presented here focuses on the suspension of Stormont and the establishment of a reconstituted, 'reformed' Northern Ireland Assembly in 1973, and the Sunningdale Agreement on a Council of Ireland. The polarisation of forces around this attempt to solve the Northern Ireland 'problem' provides a locus from which it is possible to investigate those class forces which were mobilised in support of reform, on the one hand, and those which succeeded in preventing it, on the other.

THE BREAK-UP OF UNIONISM

In December 1968, shortly after the first package of reforms had been introduced, O'Neill made his now famous television broadcast to the people of Northern Ireland.[3] He began his speech with the warning that, 'Ulster stands at the crossroads.' In asking for support for the reform programme, O'Neill outlined the alternatives quite explicitly:

> As I saw it, if we were not prepared to face up to our problems, we would have to meet mounting pressure both internally, from those who were seeking change, and externally from British public and parliamentary opinion, which had been deeply disturbed by the events in Londonderry.

In referring to the link with Britain, it was the practical aspects rather than the traditional symbolic ones that O'Neill emphasised:

> I make no apology for the financial and economic support we have received from Britain. As part of the United Kingdom, we have always considered this to be our right. But we cannot be a part of the United Kingdom merely when it suits us. And those who talk so glibly about acts of impoverished defiance do not know or do not care what is at stake. Your job, if you are a worker at Short's or Harland & Wolff; your subsidies if you are a farmer; your pension, if you are retired — all these aspects of our life, and many others, depend on support from Britain. Is a freedom to pursue the un-Christian path of communal strife and sectarian bitterness really more important to you than all the benefits of the British Welfare State?

The choice could hardly be put more clearly. Furthermore, O'Neill was quite blunt about Westminster's intentions, pointing out that 'Mr Wilson made it absolutely clear to us that if we did not face up to our problems the Westminster Parliament might well decide to act over our heads.'

The first package of reforms which O'Neill was defending was neither radical nor far-reaching, in the sense that it did little to tackle the real problems facing the minority. Its great significance lies in the effect it had on traditional relations within the broader Unionist political machine. The Unionist Cabinet had agreed to Westminster's demands, but the reforms threatened to undermine the basis of traditional Unionist solidarity by challenging the power of the local party associations and local government. O'Neill might be able to control the Cabinet, but the Unionist Party as a whole was a large and cumbersome organisation. Many MPs were sensitive to O'Neill's constantly repeated emphasis on the need to toe the British line. However, they were also extremely aware of the power of their own constituency associations. Most Unionist seats were safe seats in the sense that the Unionist candidate was usually returned unopposed. The real selection process occurred before the election, and the local association had the power to make things very difficult for an MP if he should desire to take an independent stand.

It was precisely at the local level that the reforms were most unwelcome. The distribution of council housing at local authority level in Unionist controlled areas was organised to ensure that houses were built and allocated in such a way as to maintain the local political balance. Furthermore, the power of individual councillors to hand out houses was a central element in the patronage system. It should be noted here that in April 1970 the Unionist Party annual conference voted 281 to 216 against the plans to establish a central housing authority which would take control of housing allocation away from local councils. The replacement of the gerrymandered elected council in Londonderry was a further challenge to the traditional workings of the Unionist machine. As a result, O'Neill could never count on being able to rally more than half of the wider party behind him. In such a situation the reform programme was adopted grudgingly, and the Catholic community were understandably unconvinced as to the commitment of the party to such measures.

O'Neill's 'Crossroads' speech appeared to consolidate his position, temporarily at least. Messages of support poured into his office from all over the province, and the Civil Rights Association issued a call for a period of truce without marches or demonstrations. The People's Democracy march, however, forced the issue out into the open again. An official Government enquiry was set up, under the leadership of Lord Cameron, to investigate the recent 'disturbances', and two of O'Neill's Cabinet opponents resigned in protest. There were renewed calls from within the party for his resignation, and in February 1969 O'Neill called a general election in an attempt to isolate his opponents in the Protestant camp. His platform was simple; a reformed Northern Ireland was the only Northern Ireland acceptable to the British Parliament. As Northern Ireland was dependent on subventions from the British exchequer, there could be no practical alternative to his policy of reform. Furthermore, this was the only way in which the Catholic community's growing hostility could be checked.

It was the first general election that was not dominated by the traditional conflict between Unionists and Nationalists, for both these groups were divided over the civil rights issue. O'Neill was forced to run 'independent' candidates against members of his own party, since many of the local Unionist Association selection committees chose to nominate anti-O'Neill candidates. In Catholic areas, civil rights oriented candidates ran as independents against the Nationalist Party. The majority of MPs who were returned to Parliament supported O'Neill, and three new Unionists, who were not, and never had been, Orangemen, were elected from middle class constituencies on the fringe of Belfast. However, while O'Neill still held his position inside the Unionist Party, he had completely failed to isolate his opponents. Of thirty-one uncontested Unionist seats, eleven were won on specifically anti-O'Neill platforms. Several others returned MPs who were ambiguous about their allegiance. All of O'Neill's most outspoken opponents inside the Parliamentary Party had been returned, and he himself had narrowly missed being unseated by Ian Paisley who ran as a Protestant Unionist. O'Neill could command the support of barely half of the traditional Unionist voters.

Two months later O'Neill succeeded in getting the Cabinet and the Parliamentary Party to accept 'one man one vote'. However, the issue provoked further defections, and within a week O'Neill resigned, knowing that the party demanded a new leader. His downfall was not caused by Catholic intransigeance or extremism. The IRA was an almost non-existent force in the Catholic community as yet, and the new MPs from the civil rights movement were more representative of Catholic aspirations. Nor did O'Neill resign because of complete lack of support from the Protestant community. He went because he could not carry the Unionist political machine with him, for that machine was built on just those forces of sectarianism and provincialism that he now sought to erase. O'Neill described his defeat with these words:

> The extreme back-benchers set about the job of bringing me down by extra-parliamentary methods, and to this end they decided to use the various groupings of the Unionist Party. There was a Standing Committee of between three and four hundred people and a much larger body called the Ulster Unionist Council nominally consisting of some nine hundred people, many of whom never attended . . . Obviously, or so it seemed to me, the Protestants had the better reasons for bringing about my departure from the political scene.[4]

It is interesting to note that, five years later, Faulkner finally resigned leadership of the Unionist Party when he too was defeated in the Ulster Unionist Council. He blamed his downfall on the undemocratic nature of the Council, and in particular on the high proportion of Orange Order delegates.[5]

O'Neill was replaced by his cousin, James Chichester-Clark, a man not known for any reformist zeal. Indeed he had resigned from the Cabinet over 'one man one vote'. It was under his premiership that the British Army was called in, in August 1969, when Orange demonstrations and loyalist rioting led to the destruction of Catholic housing and fatal sectarian confrontations in Derry and Belfast. However, during Chichester-Clark's brief reign the Unionist Party placed more reforming laws on the statute books than would have been dreamed of by any Unionist before him. Once the British Army were involved on such a massive scale in policing the province, the Unionist Party was even more vulnerable to Westminster's demands. On the 21st of August, Chichester-Clark announced the setting up of a commission under Lord Hunt, to enquire into the structure of the RUC and the Ulster Special Constabulary.[6] This was shortly followed by the establishment of the Scarman Tribunal to investigate the causes of the violence that led to British military intervention.[7]

The Hunt Report on the police, which was published in October, led to the disarming of the RUC and the disbanding of the B Specials. It also provoked violent and widespread opposition amongst the loyalist community by directly confronting Protestant workers with the reality of the 'new order'. Outbreaks of violent rioting were nothing new to Belfast, and on each occasion in the past the Unionist alliance had solved the problem by moving directly against the Catholic ghettos. To this end the B Specials had become a totally sectarian force, an Orange militia. When the Bogside rioting in August was at its peak, the B Specials had issued an ultimatum to the Prime Minister; if he would not call them in, they would mobilise themselves. In the event, Chichester-Clark was forced to call in the Specials, and the British Army as well. The Army replaced the former and took over the perimeter of the Bogside, to a rapturous welcome from its inhabitants who saw the removal of the RUC and the Specials as a massive defeat for the Unionist Government.

The point to be emphasised here is that such traditional repressive strategies were no longer possible given the British Government's support for the reform programme. Nor were they desirable or necessary from the point of view of the new reformist interests within the Unionist Party. However, loyalist unity had been built on just such sectarian local level organisations as the B Specials. The disillusionment and sense of betrayal felt by many sections of the Protestant community at the destruction of just those elements of social and political organisation which had symbolised and realised their traditional role in the Unionist alliance was hardly surprising.

Between June 1969 and March 1971 Chichester-Clark presided over all these dramatic changes, together with the setting up of the Community Relations Commission, and the Central Housing Executive. It was a period which witnessed a general and perceptible whittling away of the Unionist monopoly of power at grass-roots and even central level. However, as the reform programme progressed, it was accompanied by increasing violence on the streets. Since the rioting of August 1969 the RUC had been kept out of the Catholic ghettos, and the British Army had taken over the job of policing the 'peace line'. With the responsibility for the reform programme left in the hands of the Unionist Government it was inevitable that the Army would be used to bolster up its increasingly weak position. In July 1970 the British Army raided the Falls Road area in a search for arms, and, in response to the severe rioting that this provoked, imposed a thirty-six hour curfew on the area. This event marked the beginning of a new phase in the 'troubles', with the shattering of the Catholic community's faith in the British Army and Westminster's intentions. The Army seemed to have taken over where the B Specials had left off.

Chichester-Clark found himself facing mounting pressure from within his own party to do something about the security situation. Once again it was a question of how far the Unionist Party could in fact take the reform programme without destroying the basis of its own power within the province. It should be pointed out here that the British Government was totally unaware of the implications of the reforms that they were demanding. Reginald Maudling, the then British Home Secretary, knew little about Northern Ireland, and was widely supposed to care even less.

Westminster, guided by him, saw little urgency in the situation, and was preparing for a 'long slow haul'. The Army would be used to hold the warring populations apart while the Unionist Party got on with the political reforms. Westminster simply did not understand that every reform undermined the very existence of that party.

In the Spring of 1971, Chichester-Clark was becoming increasingly aware of his Government's inability to control the security situation in the province. He might be able to push the reform packages through his Cabinet, but he could not halt the violence on the streets. In March he resigned from the leadership of the party, with the following statement: 'I have decided to resign because I can see no other way of bringing home to all concerned the realities of the present constitutional, political and security situation.'[8]

Chichester-Clark's place was taken by Brian Faulkner, who was elected leader of the Unionist Party by a huge majority. Under his leadership the Government struggled on with a series of totally contradictory political initiatives which clearly illustrate the problem of the fundamental conflict within the party. On the one hand, Faulkner, widely known as a 'hard-liner' with strong right-wing connections, placed great emphasis on the problem of law and order, indicating that he saw this as the most important single question facing his Government. Loyalists were clamouring for stiff measures to be taken against the IRA who by now had re-emerged as a military force in the Catholic ghettos. The logical outcome of such an emphasis was the introduction of internment in August 1971, a measure designed to pacify loyalist feeling and regain control of the wider party. On the other hand, it was Faulkner who went some distance towards meeting Catholic demands for a share in policy-making. Three months after taking office he introduced a proposal to establish three new parliamentary committees to deal with social services, industrial development and environmental matters, and offered the chairmanship of two of them to the opposition, the newly formed Social Democratic and Labour Party.

It is in Faulker's relationship to the progressive business interests in the province that we may find the key to his reformism. Before entering politics he was a director of the clothing manufacturing business established by his father. In this respect his election to the leadership of the Unionist Party represented a real change from the aristocratic, land-owning classes from which his predecessors were chosen. It is in this class difference that his hostility to O'Neill lies, rather than in any disagreement about reform. In O'Neill's first Cabinet Faulkner had been Minister of Commerce, and in this position had been responsible for a massive initiative to revitalise the province's economy. Essentially, Faulkner continued along the path laid out by O'Neill and Chichester-Clark, deferring to pressure from Westminster over the reform programme, while attempting to hold together the Unionist alliance. In the latter respect Faulkner was in a stronger position than his two predecessors, in that his connections with the broader loyalist movement were strong. As Minister of Home Affairs from 1959, under Brookeborough, he was responsible for law and order at the time of the IRA border campaign. The effectiveness with which he quelled the campaign made him very popular amongst the local Unionist Associations, especially in those rural areas which bore the brunt of IRA activity. 'He did not shrink from invoking the Special Powers Act and interning many republican sympathisers until the campaign petered out about 1962.'[9]

Faulkner's reputation as a 'strong man' was enhanced by his opposition to O'Neill throughout the 1960s. In 1966 he was involved in a right-wing back-bench conspiracy to dislodge O'Neill. In January 1969 Faulkner resigned from O'Neill's Government because of the decision to appoint a Commission to enquire into the civil rights disturbances of October 1968, and made an appeal for 'strong government.' However, as the situation deteriorated Faulkner's connections with the province's modernising, reformist business community brought him increasingly into conflict with his traditional political associates. Only later, when the choice was forced upon him, did Faulkner reveal himself as an even more thorough-going supporter of reform than anyone had imagined. It was under his leadership that the unity of the Unionist Party was finally ruptured. In the Spring of 1971, however, his aim was to reunite the Unionist Party by the clever distribution of Government posts, balancing the divergent interests involved.

Faulkner, unlike some of his right-wing supporters, was well aware of the need for Westminster's continuing financial support, and of the province's dependence, for economic growth, on membership of the wider British market. For him there was no question of demanding a return to the *status quo ante*, in defiance of Westminster's wishes. Therefore, in order to mount an effective law and order campaign along traditional anti-IRA lines, it was necessary for the British Army to take over the role once played by the B Specials. There was to be no campaign against the loyalist terrorists, since the passage of the reform programme depended on stability within the Unionist Party.

It was this policy which was directly responsible for the withdrawal of the Catholic representatives from Stormont, only three months after Faulkner took office. In May, Faulkner had amazed the opposition with his statement on Army policy, in which he announced that: 'Any soldier seeing any person with a weapon or acting suspiciously may, depending on the circumstances, fire to warn or with effect without waiting for orders.'[10] On the 8th of July, two young Catholics were shot dead in Derry by the British Army in situations where it was far from clear whether they had in fact been involved in anything more serious than stone-throwing. In the face of Faulkner's refusal to set up an enquiry into these events, the SDLP had no option but to resign if they were to retain any credibility within the Catholic community.

Enough has been said on the nature of internment and the particular way in which it was introduced to establish the fact that it destroyed the possibility of continuing to integrate the Catholic population into the existing parliamentary system. It is not my intention here to trace out the spiral of events which followed the introduction of internment, culminating in 'Bloody Sunday', nor to investigate the reasons for the military failure of the operation.[11] Such accounts have appeared elsewhere, and tend to see the operation as a 'mistake', a political blunder which failed to appreciate the possibility of massive Catholic opposition; or as 'inefficient', a military strategy that failed on account of inadequate intelligence and its ham-fisted application. The point I wish to emphasise here is that its introduction was inevitable as long as Westminster was to rely on the Unionist Party to carry through the reform programme at the parliamentary level. The mobilisation of the B Specials and the introduction of internment were the traditional responses of Unionist Governments to problems of internal security, and played an integral part in the maintenance of the Orange State. The B Specials were now *hors de combat*, but the pressures within the Unionist Party to bring in internment were undiminished. Without a direct challenge to the foundations of the Unionist alliance, there was no alternative.

The total failure of the law and order campaign to re-establish the power and unity of the Unionist Party, and the violence and disorder that it provoked, finally shattered the last vestiges of solidarity within the Protestant community. In October 1971 Faulkner made a final unsuccessful effort to win back the Catholics, to Stormont at least, with the publication of his Green Paper on the future of parliamentary government in Northern Ireland, which reiterated his proposal for a committee system in the House of Commons. Without a far more radical realignment of political forces in the province, this was his last card. The British Army shot dead 13 civilians at a large anti-internment rally in Derry. The IRA retaliated with a massive bombing campaign, and 56 British soldiers were killed in the following two months.

Meanwhile Faulkner's reformist stand was now being directly challenged by the emergence of Vanguard, an umbrella organisation for traditional loyalist groups. It was led by William Craig, a notorious opponent of reform, and the Reverend Martin Smyth, county Grand Master of the Orange Order in Belfast. They organised a series of public rallies at which the dominant theme was the call for a return to pre-O'Neill Unionism, and the threat of loyalist military action to prevent the implementation of any reform which would permit the participation of republicans in government at Stormont. The question of whether the opponents of reform could capture control of the party was less significant than the fact that Protestant unity, the basis of the party's power and hegemony had been finally broken. The Unionist Party was manifestly unable to carry through the reforms without destroying itself.

In March 1972 Westminster suspended Stormont and imposed direct rule.

THE SOCIAL DEMOCRATIC AND LABOUR PARTY

While O'Neill, Chichester-Clark and Faulkner were struggling to maintain their position within the Unionist Party, the reformist Catholic middle class was attempting to win political leadership within the minority community. When O'Neill called a general election in April 1969, the leaders of the civil rights movement were presented with an opportunity to challenge the old Nationalist Party. Three Independents who had been closely involved with the movement stood in the election. In Derry John Hume and Ivan Cooper defeated the sitting Nationalist candidates, including the leader of the party, and Paddy O'Hanlon was returned for South Armagh. A further step in unifying and consolidating the Catholic reformist interests at Stormont and in local government was taken in August 1970, when the Social Democratic and Labour Party was formed. The six MPs and one Senator who were initially involved included the three Independents and former members of the Labour, Republican Labour and Nationalist Parties. The new party described itself as non-sectarian and promised radical policies on economic and social issues. It aimed to 'promote co-operation, friendship and understanding between North and South with a view to the eventual reunification of Ireland through the consent of the majority of people in the North and South.'[12]

The SDLP's acceptance of Faulkner's committee proposals, despite the absence of any substantive power that could be derived from them, clearly illustrated their commitment to working within the existing constitutional arrangements. However, at a time of increasing sectarian violence and Catholic disillusionment with the progress of reform, the SDLP's claim to represent the united voice of the Catholic community was continually being challenged. With the emergence of the Provisional IRA early in 1971 to defend the Catholic ghettoes, traditional republicanism found a new and powerful voice. In addition, the Official IRA was attracting the support of socialists. The increasing involvement of the British Army in attempts to subjugate the IRA necessarily alienated large sections of the Catholic population who were subjected to endless harassment and searches. This development, together with the increasing hostility of large numbers of loyalists, severely dented the minority's faith in the possibility of genuine reform. With the introduction of internment it was obvious that the SDLP would lose all credibility if they were to return to Stormont.

The nature of the Catholic response to internment in 1971 is of particular interest in that it highlights the degree to which the political situation had changed since it was last introduced in the 1950s. Traditionally the Catholic population expressed its opposition to the Unionist Government through the military efforts of the IRA and through the Nationalist Party's boycott of Stormont, neither of which strategies had ever presented much of a threat to the Unionist system. In 1971 the reaction took the form of a strike against the State, and hence against the Unionist

Government. Rent and rate payments to councils and local authorities were withheld, and Catholic MPs, councillors and other nominated officials left office. It was an enormously effective form of protest, striking at the heart of the authority of the Unionist State.

Since 1971 day-to-day life in Northern Ireland has been dominated by battles on the streets, and parliamentary politicians have been in constant danger of being overtaken by events. Against such a background the SDLP appears as a rather weak alliance of interests which is constantly in danger of being forced out of the contest. However, the party represents the victory of the Catholic professional middle class over the old Nationalist Party and the mainly petty bourgeois interests it represented. Discussing the parties which supported the monopoly capital interest, Bayley and Boehringer conclude that: 'its politics consist of an up-dated version of those of the old National Unity grouping: participation in administration and politics for the Catholic middle class, reform of the administrative structure to secure the allegiance of the Catholic working class, co-operation between Northern Ireland and the Republic, deferment of the border issue until reunification became acceptable to a majority in Northern Ireland.'[13] From the beginning the SDLP had the support of the Dublin Government, and were largely financed by Southern businessmen.

It was precisely this reformist stance that exacerbated the crisis of the Orange State. First, in the form of the early civil rights movement, with its demands for limited and specific reforms within the existing constitutional framework, they succeeded in splitting the Unionist monolith. By focusing on issues like the franchise, unemployment, housing and patronage, they were highlighting contradictions that were already emerging within the Unionist system. Inasmuch as their demands were not only for an end to discrimination against Catholics but also for the centralisation of State powers in order to deal with problems general to the province as a depressed area, they attracted the support of some working class and middle class Protestants. Second, the reforms that the SDLP sought through Parliament were the direct outcome of fundamental economic and social changes that had been at work in the province for many years, and had produced an articulate Catholic middle class. The party's policies on central planning and economic development, which included support for the integration of the province into the EEC, provided them with powerful allies in Dublin, Westminster and Brussels.

It was the imposition of direct rule in March 1972 that gave the SDLP the opportunity to reassert its position in the Catholic community, despite the continued detention of hundreds of Catholics under the Special Powers Act, and mounting Protestant extremist opposition. The announcement of direct rule provided sufficient evidence of Westminster's willingness to support reform to spark off 'peace initiatives' in the Catholic community. Under these conditions the SDLP were able to play a central role in the discussions which led to the establishment of the reconstituted Northern Ireland Assembly. They were rewarded with widespread support in the first elections to the Assembly in June 1973, and, at the party's annual conference in December of the same year, the principle of power-sharing was enthusiastically and convincingly accepted by the 500 delegates.

THE NORTHERN IRELAND ASSEMBLY

In March 1973, one year after the suspension of the Northern Ireland Parliament at Stormont, the British Government introduced its White Paper outlining the constitutional proposals for the restoration of devolved government in the province.[14] The reforms involved in establishing a new Assembly were considerable. First, the simple majority vote system using single member constituencies, which together with gerrymandered constituency boundaries had so favoured the Unionist Party, was dropped in favour of the single transferable vote method of proportional representation. Elections were to be held on the basis of the twelve Westminster constituencies instead of the fifty-two Stormont ones. This system was intended to get the accurate reflection of minority-group opinion in the Assembly and to break the stranglehold that Unionism and Nationalism had held over the two communities. Second, the size of the Assembly was increased from fifty-two to seventy-eight, to permit the functioning of an inter-party committee system. Third, it was established that the Executive, to be made up of the new Heads of Departments, 'can no longer be solely based upon any single party, if that party draws its support and its elected representation virtually entirely from only one section of a divided community.'[15] And, finally, on the question of relations with the Republic, it stated that 'following elections to the Northern Ireland Assembly, the Government will invite the Government of the Republic of Ireland and the leaders of the elected representatives of Northern Ireland opinion to participate with them in a conference' to discuss the question of a Council of Ireland.[16]

In June 1973, on the basis of these proposals, elections were held for the seventy-eight seats in the new Assembly. The field was dominated by candidates from the new political parties which had appeared during the previous five years in response to the radical realignment of forces in Ulster. The results were as follows:

Official Unionists	22
Unofficial Unionists	11
West Belfast Loyalist Coalition	2
Social Democratic and Labour Party	19
Alliance	8
Northern Ireland Labour Party	1
Loyalist Coalition:	
Democratic Unionist Party (Paisley)	8
Vanguard Unionist Progressive Party (Craig)	7

The most significant division lay within the Protestant community, with the Loyalist Coalition pledged to stop the Assembly getting off the ground. The increased representation of the Catholic community through the SDLP, however, together with Faulkner's Official Unionists presented a workable majority, able to govern through the committee system of power-sharing. These parties had the support of the Alliance Party, a moderate, non-sectarian group formed by liberal Unionists in 1969. In October, under pressure from the Westminster and Dublin Governments, agreement was reached between these parties over the allocation of executive posts, and an executive designate was formed, under the leadership of Faulkner.

It now seemed as though political alliances reflected more accurately the altered balance of interests in the province. However, the problem of the Unionist Parliamentary Party's relationship to the many sectarian social and political institutions of the old Orange State was far from solved. In July the Official Unionists' willingness to break away from the Orange Order did receive some publicity when an Orange meeting was held for Members of the Assembly. Only twelve out of the total of thirty-four Unionist Members attended, and all but four of these were outside Faulkner's Official group. But, as their title implies, Faulkner's supporters had not succeeded in 'taking-over' the Unionist Parliamentary Party. A further eleven Unionists had been elected to the Assembly who opposed the settlement, and acted as an independent group. The struggle to retain control of the Unionist machine was only just beginning.

THE REPUBLIC AND THE SUNNINGDALE AGREEMENT

The radical changes that have occurred in the relations of the Republic with both Westminster and Northern Ireland are clearly manifested in the Dublin Government's participation in the constitutional discussions that led to agreement on power-sharing and a Council of Ireland. William Whitelaw's Green Paper, *The Future of Northern Ireland. A Paper for Discussion*, published in October 1972, states the British Government's position quite frankly:

> It is, therefore, clearly desirable that any new arrangements for Northern Ireland, should, whilst meeting the wishes of Northern Ireland and Great Britain, be so far as possible acceptable to and accepted by the Republic of Ireland, which from 1 January 1973 will share the rights and obligations of membership of the European Communities.

The question of a Council of Ireland arose directly from the declining economic significance of the border, and the development of common interests between sections of the ruling class in Belfast, Dublin and London. Against the background of common membership of the EEC, questions of political jurisdiction have faded into the past for the big bourgeoisie, and have been replaced by an over-riding mutual concern with creating a stable environment for investment. Politically this is reflected in the emphasis on facilitating governmental co-operation between North and South in matters of economic and social planning.

It should be noted here that to speak of the Republic's altered policies in no way implies a popular national consensus on the new line, but simply the ability of the Government to pursue such policies without significant opposition. In the North the growing pressures for reform of the decentralised clientage system on which the Unionist State had been founded finally came violently into conflict with the parochial forces of loyalism and Orangeism. In the South it was the forces of traditional republicanism and nationalism that threatened Lemass and Lynch, and their 'new deal' internationalism. However, the transition was easier in the South, for, as McCann points out: 'The establishment in the South was better placed. There was no equivalent to the Orange Order resistant to change and controlling central and local government apparatus.'[17]

Amongst the ideologists of the 'new deal' in the Republic, the case for international capitalism is most eloquently argued by Garret FitzGerald in his book, *Towards a New Ireland.*[18] A confirmed marketeer, he is concerned with the elimination of out-dated loyalties, and their replacement with more 'normal' and stable patterns of political affiliation. Thus he argues that:

> Because of Partition, politics both North and South have tended to remain frozen in a pre-ideological state. This is most obvious, of course, in Northern Ireland, where the Protestant and Catholic working-classes continued after 1920 to support extremely conservative parties lacking in any political programme intended to or likely to serve the interests of these workers. But Partition has also had somewhat similar effects in the Republic, where the astute playing of the "anti-partition" card, especially at election times, has contributed to the ability of the latterly very conservative Fianna Fail party to remain in power throughout 85% of the forty years from 1932 to 1972.[19]

FitzGerald is at pains to defend not only his particular class and party philosophy, but also a total political system in which the major political divisions are derived from class affiliation; a model presumably derived from the British two-party system. With regret, he remarks that:

> The small Irish Labour Party never succeeded in making much progress in the face of this situation — it never won more than 15% of the seats in the Dail — and only a leftward shift in the principal opposition party, Fine Gael, in and after 1964, has so far offered any prospect of creating a more normal and constructive party alignment in the Republic.[20]

There is little doubt in FitzGerald's mind about the factors favouring the development of co-operation between the North and the South of Ireland. 'Membership of the European Communities may well prove to be the most important single factor influencing events in a positive direction in the years ahead.'[21] 'Within a vast European Community the two parts of Ireland, sharing common interests in relation to such matters as agriculture and regional policy, must tend to draw together.'[22]

It is this view of the future which determines what FitzGerald has to say concerning ways of settling the upheavals in the North. 'The first stage of any solution must lie in a reform of the institutions of government within Northern Ireland.'[23] He proceeds to outline a possible framework for a new Government which includes several of the elements that were in fact included in the power-sharing settlement, concluding that, 'hopefully over time, the proposed system of joint government could lead to an end to the sectarian polarisation of Northern Ireland politics and to the emergence of some other division, possibly on the basis of divergent economic ideologies.'[24]

It was within the framework of such ideas that the Dublin Government participated in the talks at Sunningdale in December 1973 on the setting up of a Council of Ireland. However, Irishmen were by no means united in their support for the changes that Lemass and his successor, Lynch, sought to introduce. Many groups recognised the weakness of their position in the face of integration into a large free trade area. Thousands of small farmers were watching the 'rationalisation' of agriculture, with emigration the only alternative to unemployment. Ireland's small-scale industrial enterprises which had struggled to establish themselves behind protective tariffs, faced extinction or the 'take-over' under such conditions. In addition to these conflicting class interests, traditional republican sympathies were still widespread in the South. Only forty years had passed since partition and the civil war.

As the situation deteriorated in the North, some Fianna Fail Ministers and other members of the party attempted to revive the memory of the time when that party had been the true 'republican party'. They refused to fall in with what they claimed was a policy of 'appeasement'. And so, in August 1969, when the Catholics of the Bogside were under siege, and sectarian violence was spreading, the Dublin Government was obliged to respond. On the basis of a very narrow majority the then Prime Minister, Mr Lynch, announced that Irish Army units were moving to the border, and would set up army field hospitals. The realisation that the Republic might acutally become seriously involved in the struggles in Northern Ireland brought out into the open many underlying confused attitudes. As Liam de Paor puts it:

> Many people who had subscribed unthinkingly to a policy of reunification based on the proposition that Ireland was one nation were suddenly faced with the realization that it was at least one small island. Even those who were not interested in reunification had brought home to them that an upheaval such as was happening in the north must affect the country as a whole in some ways. Admiration for the early achievements of the civil

rights movement and for its moderate leadership — which was widespread — was matched by distrust and fear of its radical leaders especially when these attacked the policies and attitudes of the southern government almost as vehemently as they did those of the northern.[25]

When the British Army moved in, the tone of the Republic's pronouncements changed. In September Mr Lynch publicly abandoned the old anti-partition line. He no longer pointed to the border as the main issue, and renounced the use of force to solve the Irish problem. His Government's programme of economic expansion, and the Free Trade Agreement with Britain left him with little genuine independence. However, Lynch was not without opposition from within his own party. Three of his Ministers, Blaney, Boland and Haughey, were openly talking of their sympathy with the Northern republicans. In May 1970 Lynch dismissed Haughey and Blaney from the Government, and accepted Boland's resignation together with that of some junior Ministers. Later in the same year these three senior Ministers were involved in preliminary hearings concerning charges of obtaining arms and conspiring to smuggle them into Northern Ireland. In October Haughey and Blaney, having been acquitted, attempted to take over the leadership of Fianna Fail, appealing to the spirit of the old 'republican party'. Their attempt failed, and Mr Lynch's position was reinforced by the vote of confidence which followed.

Since that time the Republic's policy on Northern Ireland has moved consistently into line with British policy, even to the extent of introducing 'Special Powers' to detain suspected members of the IRA. Here again there was considerable opposition within the Republic. In December 1972 the Dail debated the 'Offences against the State (Amendment) Bill', which would permit the police to detain a person simply by alleging membership of the IRA. Support for the Bill was lukewarm, and many of Lynch's own party were far from enthusiastic. There was in fact a real danger of his being defeated. However, while the debate was in progress two bombs exploded in Dublin, killing two and injuring more than a hundred. Concern for civil liberties melted away, and the Bill was passed immediately. The timing of the explosions was fortuitous enough for some suspicion to fall on the activities of British agents in Ireland.[26]

The economic and political changes occurring in the Republic during the 1960s, and its increasingly cosmopolitan outlook had inevitable repercussions for the cultural traditions associated with de Valera's Gaelic nation. In particular it led to a reassessment of the Catholic Church's influence in the spheres of education and public morality. The recent moves in the South to sever the knots between Church and State should not be seen merely as concessions to long-standing Protestant fears on this subject. These moves have their roots in changes occuring within the Republic. However, there is no doubt that there were those who might otherwise have been content to allow these reforms to develop at their own pace, but who, in their desire to see a rapid rapprochment with the North, brought out many questions into public debate; for example, the issues of contraception and censorship. It was in this context that Lynch introduced a referendum at the end of 1972, as a result of which the article in the de Valera constitution which gave the Roman Catholic Church a special position in the State was removed.

The British Government's White Paper, *Northern Ireland: Constitutional Proposals*, gave due recognition to the Republic's efforts. It noted that:

> There have been a number of significant developments since the publication of the Paper for Discussion. First, on 1 January 1973 the United Kingdom and the Republic of Ireland both became member countries of the European Economic Community, a development which is bound to have an ever-increasing impact upon the lives of all who live in these islands. (para 7)

> Second, the then Government of the Republic of Ireland introduced, and the Oireachtas carried into law, new legislation designed to cope with terrorist activity, and the authorities of the Republic have subsequently brought before the courts under these new powers some of those persons involved in the organisation and direction of I.R.A. terrorism throughout Ireland. (para 8)

The stage was now set, and in December 1973 the British and Irish Governments and the newly constituted Northern Ireland Executive met at Sunningdale. The Conference agreed that a two-tier Council of Ireland should be established, with a Council of Ministers and a Consultative Assembly. There would be equal representation for both parts of Ireland, and all decisions would have to be unanimous. The Council's main function would be to facilitate economic and social co-operation. The 'Agreed Communique' issued after the talks announced that: 'The Irish Government fully accepted and solemnly declared that there could be no change in the status of Northern Ireland until a majority of the people of Northern Ireland desired a change in that status.'

THE ASSEMBLY DEFEATED

At the same time as the Council of Ireland Conference was meeting at Sunningdale, the loyalist opposition in the new Assembly regrouped its forces under the umbrella of an organisation to be called the United Ulster Unionist Council. Its primary objective was to prevent the Council of Ireland getting off the ground, and to bring down the Executive. The Sunningdale agreement further weakened Faulkner's grip on the Unionist machine, and in January 1974 he was defeated at a meeting of the Ulster Unionist Council, which rejected the agreement by a majority of eighty. As a result Faulkner was obliged to resign the party leadership, conceding to the Unofficial Unionists full control of the party headquarters and organisation. Despite this development Faulkner continued to lead the Northern Ireland Executive until its collapse in May. In February the British Conservative Government decided to call a snap general election over the miners' strike, a decision which could not have been more ill-timed from the Executive's point of view.

> It played straight into the hands of the Loyalist parties and anti-Sunningdale Unionists, whose previous tactics of disruption in the Assembly had served only to advertise their impotence. These groups agreed to fight the election in harness as the United Ulster Unionist Council, giving approval to one candidate in each constituency, on the simple policy of opposition to the Sunningdale agreement.[27]

The UUUC won eleven of the twelve seats with this remarkable show of solidarity.

THE LOYALIST RESPONSE

The Sunningdale system of reformed political relations both within Northern Ireland and between Northern Ireland and the Republic was, in one sense, the logical outcome of the economic changes described earlier. The decline of the main traditional industries in the North, and the inability of private owner-managed businesses to compete in a market increasingly dominated by the corporations of monopoly capitalism, led to direct financial dependence on Britain, and to the growth of State intervention into the reproduction of the relations of production. In the South, the failure to establish an independent national economy capable of withstanding competition from international capital led to an end to protectionism, and reintegration into the British market with the Free Trade Agreement of 1965. In order to avert stagnation and economic decline, the Stormont and Dublin Governments adopted similar policies of attracting foreign investment through financial inducements. The foundations of partition in the historic development of two different modes of production in Ireland were being steadily undermined, together with the basis of ruling class sectarianism in Ulster. The Orange system was further threatened by the way in which Catholics in the North were tempering their opposition to the Six County State. The growth of the Welfare State reduced the pressure to emigrate, and shielded many Catholics from the worst privations of the system, and this, together with the changing economic conditions, contributed to the rise of a reformist Catholic middle class.

The monopoly interest in Ireland has been greatly weakened, however, by the international economic recession that began in the early 1970s, and the fall off in world trade that has resulted. British capital has been particularly severely hit by this slump. In the South the Government's policy of subsidising capital investment through increased taxation and massive borrowing has resulted in greatly increased debts, while unemployment and the rate of inflation continue to increase. In 1975 unemployment was 9%, while the cost of creating a new job has risen from £5,000 in the 1960s to over three times that sum. As a result, political support for the 'new deal' of the 1960s has declined. In the North the economic outlook is equally gloomy, and the reform programme has met with sharp resistance from sections of the Protestant community. Since 1969 there has been a proliferation of political and military groups within the Protestant community, reflecting a variety of responses to the reform movement, most of which were hostile. In May 1974 the Ulster Workers' Council strike, in support of the demand for the removal of the Council of Ireland from the Assembly's agenda, clearly revealed Orangeism as a relatively autonomous institution. The new-born Assembly could not survive, and a spectre of the pre-O'Neill era of Protestant solidarity was raised.

In separating out the different structural and ideological bases of these opposition groups, it is important to note, however, the degree to which this apparent solidarity had been fundamentally undermined by the changes described previously. For this reason I have eschewed a detailed chronological account of the appearance of these groups in favour of a more selective approach, which focuses on the nature of the class interests threatened by the structural changes in the economy, on the political interests challenged by the reform of the clientilist, locally based system of patronage, and on the ideological responses to the new emphasis on ecumenism and a secular social order. If the forms of political struggle were direct, unmediated reflections of underlying contradictions between 'the material forces of production in society' and the 'existing relations of production', then one would expect to find class based inter-Unionist factional strife predominating. Indeed, there has been widespread inter-Unionist conflict, but only rarely has it dominated the political scene, as for example in the mid-sixties, personified in the opposition of Paisley to O'Neill. However, far more severe has been the escalation of working class sectarian conflict, and the military struggle between the IRA and the British Army.

In outlining the central features of the Orange State that emerged after partition I draw attention to the fact that the structural determination and reproduction of classes in that social formation involved ideological and political processes as well as economic ones. It is the nature of the dialectical relationship between the political and ideological institutions of the Orange State and the underlying economic structure that is central to any analysis of the forms of political struggle. Thus, conflict within the economic region could not be resolved through the 'reform' of that region without the equally significant 'reform' of the political and ideological superstructures. The mobilisation of class interests over economic issues (e.g. by the working class over improved housing and job opportunities and by the bourgeoisie over the need for the rationalisation and centralisation of economic planning) inevitably undermined certain aspects of traditional Unionism and Protestantism. The picture is further complicated by the fact that there has been little secularisation of ideology, and religious modes of thought continue to affect profoundly the economic and political struggles, as well as being affected by them. Widespread religious fundamentalism is not unique to Northern Ireland's Protestant population, but seems to be a feature of various settler or frontier societies, divided along ethnic or racial lines, which perceive themselves as constantly embattled. It is an essential element in understanding the phenomenon of Paisleyism in Northern Irish politics, and certain forms that the political struggle has taken in recent years.

In addition to the particular significance of religion in the social formation, there is the question of the relationship between the existing political institutions (and their roots in a particular set of class relations) and the mobilisation of emergent class interests over economic issues. This involves some consideration of the fundamental economic strengths of the various classes and fractions of classes, and the extent to which the existing political system is capable of functioning as an autonomous social force, challenging the economic domination of monopoly capital. In Northern Ireland the rise of monopoly capital has not prevented the continued economic decline of the province and its relegation to increasingly peripheral status within the broader British and European economies. O'Neill's economic reformism may have provided a means of arresting certain aspects of the decline through the active encouragement of foreign investment, but the benefits were small in the first place, and unevenly distributed in the second. Some of the political opposition to O'Neill derives directly from the uneven impact of his new policies.

> In the border areas the relatively high solidarity of the anti-
> O'Neill Unionists of all social classes probably depends not only
> upon the fact that they felt themselves particularly threatened by
> Catholic demands but also on the fact that O'Neillism provided
> very few compensating benefits to those areas. Unemployment
> had always been higher the further one moved away from the
> East coast and from Belfast. If one looks at the number of "New
> Jobs promoted" in different areas up to and including 1967, just
> under 17,000 of a total of 24,000 were promoted in Co. Antrim,
> Belfast, North Down and North Armagh.[1]

Thus, the reformism of certain sections of the Protestant middle class may well have reflected the interests of the most advanced and economically significant section of capital, but it could not mobilise the political support of other sections which gained little from O'Neillism, and had most to fear from any concessions which O'Neill might make to the civil rights movement. The indigenous bourgeoisie were particularly vulnerable to any increase in working class militancy. 'With a much higher level of productivity, the new capital operating in the North was less concerned with keeping wages down through sectarian divisions in the northern working class than its local counterpart.'[2]

The political weakness of the reformist interest was exacerbated by the internal structure of the Unionist Party, in which the local constituency associations have full powers over the selection of their candidates, without any reference to a central controlling body. This potential for grass-roots involvement creates a key role for any well-organised body within the

Unionist movement.

The lack of tangible material benefits from reform also had direct implications for the autonomous working class consciousness that began to appear in the early 1960s, manifested in the growth of trade union militancy. Unemployment was increasing in such a way that even skilled Protestant workers were being laid off, and by 1963 the issue could no longer be defined simply as a Catholic problem. In the 1930s, under similar conditions, Unionist leaders had combated this development by redistributing jobs in favour of Protestants. 'Unionist politicians had been known to fight elections in working class Protestant areas while advocating the end of welfare payments'.[3] It did seem, initially, as though O'Neill's policies might foster the development of non-sectarian political and economic demands amongst the Protestant working class, by severing the traditional alliance between local capital and the Protestant labour aristocracy. However, in the south and west regions of the province there was little real improvement in economic conditions as a result of his policies, and nothing conducive of a more tolerant attitude toward Catholic demands. In Belfast, what improvement there was failed to provide a basis for any realistic alternative to the system of excluding Catholics from the major industrial strongholds. These facts are central to the consideration of the significance of such organisations as the Loyalist Association of Workers, and the ability of the Protestant labour aristocracy to dominate the broader working class.

VANGUARD

In February 1972 William Craig, a major figure in the Unionist Party, called a press conference to announce details of his new Vanguard movement. His central aim was to mobilise as many elements as possible of the old Unionist alliance round the demand for a return to the traditional Stormont system of government. Failing this, Craig stood for a Unilateral Declaration of Independence; for breaking the link with Britain. It is with this policy that Craig emerges as the representative of the small, locally-based capitalists, in conflict with those groups whose interests now lay in the wider markets of Britain and the EEC, and with the corporate agents of international capital. Craig and his associates openly articulated the implications of UDI; it would be necessary to reduce wages, and cut social security, though by implication it would be the Catholic population who suffered most from such policies.[4]

The leadership of Vanguard was strongly imbued with the attitudes and values of Unionism as they were expressed at the height of Ulster's fight against Home Rule before the First World War. In his attempt to recreate the old Unionist alliance, Craig played on the Unionist heritage. He organised mass rallies, at which, flanked by a motorcycle escort, he inspected serried ranks of 'Ulster Volunteers', 'shaking hands now and then and nodding greetings to men with war medals on their breasts and bowlers on their heads.'[5] At the first rally in Lisburn, in February, Craig read out a long and detailed Ulster Covenant reminiscent of the 1912 document which pledged the Northern Unionists to fight Home Rule for Ireland. In 1911 Carson had addressed a huge rally on the outskirts of Belfast, at which he said: 'We must be prepared . . . the morning home rule passes, ourselves to become responsible for the government of the Protestant province of Ulster.'[6] Echoing these sentiments in April 1972, the Ulster Vanguard Central Committee announced that the movement had plans to establish an effective Parliament and Government in Northern Ireland.

Since 1967 Craig had been the most consistent opponent of reform within the Unionist Party. In December 1968 O'Neill sacked him from the post of Minister of Home Affairs following his criticism of the Prime Minister's 'Crossroads' speech. In 1971 he was easily defeated by Faulkner in the election for the leadership of the Unionist Party, following Chichester-Clark's resignation, and he was then excluded from the Cabinet. Commenting on the earlier sacking, O'Neill remarks that: 'Once or twice I had made him drop a proposed paragraph from a speech, which seemed to me almost to propose UDI.'[7] In his 'Crossroads' speech O'Neill had forcefully put the case for protecting the British link, and added the following:

> There are, I know, today some so-called loyalists who talk of independence from Britain . . . Rhodesia, in defying Britain from thousands of miles away, at least had an Air Force and an Army of her own. Where are the Ulster armoured divisions or the Ulster jet planes? They do not exist and we could not afford to buy them.[8]

It was differences over such fundamental questions as the possibility of UDI that separated Craig and his supporters from the rest of the right-wing within the Unionist Party. Many MPs opposed reform, but, like the farmers who depended on British agricultural subsidies, they were well aware of the necessity of Britain's support. The opposition of this group to the Sunningdale settlement was later organised within the Unionist Party, under the leadership of Harry West. It was with these 'Unofficial Unpledged Unionists' that Enoch Powell was most closely associated. In fact, the middle class elements that Craig sought to represent no longer existed as an independent social force. Craig might have the complete support of the sold-out representatives of Ulster's once independent linen industry, and some retired army officers, but there are only a few producers left who are independent of the British link.

For similar reasons, Craig found that support for his policies among the Protestant working class was conditional and unreliable. The experiences of the early sixties had heightened their awareness of the need for the protection of the Welfare State and the encouragement of outside investment. Gusty Spence, leader of the Ulster Volunteer Force, expressed the distrust of the working class for the old Unionist Party in a television interview in June 1973.

> One has only to look at the Shankhill Road, the heart of the empire that lies torn and bleeding. We have known squalor. I was born and reared in it. No one knows better than we do the meaning of slums, the meaning of deprivation, the meaning of suffering for what one believes in, whatever the ideology. In so far as people speak of fifty years of misrule, I wouldn't disagree with that. What I would say is this, that we have suffered every bit as much as the people of the Falls Road, or any other underprivileged quarter — in many cases, more so.[9]

In a Sunday Times Story, Dave Fogel told how the Ulster Defence Association mistrusted both Faulkner and Craig.[10] Both were middle class politicians from the old Unionist Party, and were no friends of the working class.

The contradictory nature of Protestant working class opposition to reform will be dealt with more fully later. For the moment it is important to investigate the reasons why Vanguard was able to mobilize such large numbers of supporters in the early months of 1972. One factor is the form that the movement took initially, and the other concerns the timing of its appearance. At the opening press conference, reporters were told that Vanguard was not a political party, but an 'association of associations', 'an umbrella for traditional loyalist groups.'[11] Membership of Vanguard, at this stage, was not incompatible with membership of the Unionist Party, or any other political organisation. On the contrary, the aim was to recreate the unity of loyalist organisation. Unconditional support for the political extremism underlying Craig's appeal was limited to those elements of the Orange system who sought the maintenance of Protestant power at *any* price. Craig was aware of the need for the support of a much broader stratum of the population, and the policies he expounded were tailored, at first, to this necessity.

Craig's speeches focused on bitter criticism of the Government's handling of the security situation, built around regret at the changes introduced in 1969; i.e. the disarming of the RUC and the disbanding of the B Specials. Here at last was a vehicle through which the Protestant people might express their anger and frustration over their sufferings in the last two years. At the positive level his policies were rather more vague. At the first major Vanguard rally, held in Lisburn in February, Craig summed up his position in this way: 'We are determined, ladies and gentlemen, to preserve our British traditions and way of life. And God help those who get in our way.'[12]

Before tracing the development of Vanguard into a narrower political party, it is important to understand the 'mass' nature of the following it created in the early months of 1972. The key lies in the events of the preceding nine months, during which time large sections of the Protestant

119

community had been directly exposed to experiences which created an overwhelming atmosphere of anger and betrayal. The policy of internment, introduced in August 1971 had manifestly failed to improve the security situation, and indeed appeared to have provoked even more determined opposition to the State amongst the Catholic community. In the following months life in the province's towns became increasingly intolerable under pressure of the Provisionals' bombing campaign. The situation was exacerbated by the existence of 'no-go' areas in the Catholic enclaves; barricaded areas in which the British Army tacitly refrained from operating.

The SDLP had withdrawn from Stormont, and in response to internment were now actively encouraging a widespread rent and rate strike against the State. For three years the Protestant community had watched successive Governments push through the reform programme to redress the initial grievances of the civil rights movement, only to discover that the situation continued to deteriorate.

> They felt betrayed by the attitude of successive British governments, both Conservative and Labour, none of whom had made a real effort to arrest the process. The governments in Westminster seemed too often, to the ordinary Protestant in Belfast, to be more concerned with maintaining good relations with the government of the Irish Republic in Dublin. And yet it was this very government, led by John Mary Lynch, that was turning a blind eye to the activities of the IRA and allowing its territory to become a safe haven for wanted terrorists from the North.
>
> Ulster's Protestants, it seemed, had no friends anywhere. The world's press was virtually unanimous in its hostility to their cause.[13]

Then, in January 1972, a Protestant who was due to give evidence at the trial of three local IRA men charged with hijacking a bus was assassinated by the IRA. The killing horrified the province, arousing a genuine and widespread fear in Protestant areas that no one was safe from the IRA. It was against this background that Vanguard appeared, with Craig's hard line reflecting the gut-feelings of many loyalists. Developments in the following six months only served to validate Craig's claims about the betrayal of Ulster. His specific demands for the full return of the old Ulster C Special Constabulary fell on receptive ears, for the Provisional campaign and its effects on the province's urban centres had already sown the seeds of a Protestant paramilitary defence force. The 'C' men were originally an additional force of small shopkeepers and local men who supplemented the A and B Specials of the twenties.

Four days prior to the announcement of direct rule, Craig made a speech foreshadowing the coming crisis, in which he declared that:

> The great majority want no political juggling. The course of action is pretty clear — liquidate the IRA. That is, put down the IRA. Any truce or agreement with the IRA will only last as long as is convenient for them . . . The days of the union

may be drawing to a close but our British heritage and way of life will be saved. We may be moving into a situation close to war.[14]

Direct rule was imposed on 24th March, and on 26th June the IRA and the British Government began a truce. These two events finally unleashed the much talked-of Protestant backlash, in the form of an assassination campaign. Craig's support for such a campaign can hardly be doubted from the evidence of his public statements. In July, in a speech in Scotland, he claimed that Vanguard was establishing a loyalist army for action, if the need arose.

An army was indeed coming into existence, but Vanguard had not established it, and its loyalty to Craig was never to be particularly reliable. The relationship between the paramilitary Ulster Defence Association, the Loyalist Assocation of Workers and Vanguard is a complex one, but in February Craig had had the open support of LAW on the Vanguard platform. LAW represented that section of the Protestant working class who had most to lose with the break-up of Protestant power in Ulster. LAW was based mainly, though not entirely, in Belfast's Harland and Wolff shipyard, which employs over 10,000 workers, almost all of them Protestant. In addition, the level of wages for skilled labour there is amongst the highest in Belfast. Within this labour aristocracy, support for the economic reformism of O'Neill was likely to be severely limited by the immediate calculus of profit and loss. However, Craig's demands for a return to the old regime, and failing this for UDI, had less support in the broader working class which was becoming increasingly distrustful of all middle class politicians. Furthermore, although UDI might protect local capital and the Protestant ascendancy, it would do so at the cost of greatly reduced working-class living standards.

In the year following the imposition of direct rule, during which time plans for the reconstituted Northern Ireland Assembly were being worked out, Craig maintained his uncompromising position. Addressing a rally in April he stated that it was the duty of loyalists to destroy the Whitelaw administration. In July this was backed up by a call to all Vanguard supporters to take part in a rent and rates strike until their demands were met. Two days later the UDA announced that it was splitting from Vanguard, and did not support the plan for a rent and rates strike. A week later Vanguard decided to postpone the strike. In September, however, the UDA, Vanguard and LAW announced that they had settled their differences and would unite under the United Loyalist Front. Only two days had passed before the UDA again found it necessary to issue a statement contradicting a Vanguard report about its objectives, and describing as madness the suggestion that the UDA had plans for attacking Catholic areas, or would assist in stopping industry.

In the same month Craig announced that he would be boycotting the forthcoming Darlington conference on the future of the province. As these talks progressed, Craig's total opposition to power sharing and any kind of British intervention in the province's affairs became more vehement. In a speech to the Monday Club in October he said: 'Let us put bluff aside. I am prepared to kill and those behind me have my full support. We will not surrender.'[15] He claimed to be able to mobilise 80,000 men. This speech was only one of many which reflected the growing tension between the extremism of Vanguard and the other conservative strands of Unionist opinion.

In January 1973 Craig published a full page advertisement in the *Newsletter* in which he presented a series of statistics designed to show that UDI was a real alternative to the Union. It was becoming increasingly obvious that membership of Vanguard was hardly compatible with membership of the Unionist Party. However, it was not until the British Government's White Paper on the future of Northern Ireland was published in March 1973 that the split was formalised. At the end of the month Craig announced the formation of a new political party, to be called the Vanguard Unionist Progressive Party, which would contest the coming Assembly elections. In April Craig resigned from the Ulster Unionist Council, and called on others to join him. Membership of both organisations was now incompatible. Significantly, on 4th May, both the Rev. Martin Smyth, Grand Master of the Orange Lodge of Ireland, and Captain Austin Ardill, both Vice-chairmen of Vanguard, announced their resignation from Vanguard and their continued membership of the Unionist Party.

In their election manifesto, VUPP proposed that control over the police be returned to the Assembly, and called for a federal system of government in Britain, with up to a dozen regional Parliaments. It also proposed to end recognition of the Irish Congress of Trade Unions. At the election the VUPP won seven seats out of the total of seventy-eight, and entered into a coalition with Paisley's Democratic Unionist Party (DUP), which won eight, and with the Unofficial Unionists who opposed the constitution.

In the following months while the composition of the new Executive was being worked out, Craig remained the most outspoken opponent of power-sharing, emphasising VUPP's intention of making the Assembly unworkable, and reiterating the claim that if the Constitution Act was the price of peace in Ulster, then 'war would be preferable'. Paisley, on the other hand, had committed himself to the view that full integration into the United Kingdom was the best alternative to a powerless Assembly. Despite these fundamental differences, yet another alliance between the opponents of the settlement appeared in December, just as the Sunningdale agreement was being negotiated. The United Ulster Unionist Council (UUUC) was established in order to provide common leadership on an anti-power-sharing platform. Craig announced that it would be the means of finally restoring unity to the Unionist cause.

By the spring of 1974 the split between those committed to the new Assembly and those dedicated to its destruction dominated the political life of the province. The Unionist Party's hegemony was destroyed, but for the moment the unity of opposition to the settlement was enshrined in the UUUC, and ratified by its success in the British general election held in February. However, the foundations of the loyalist alliance had been greatly weakened. Vanguard played a major role in the realignment of forces in Ulster politics by mobilising and articulating many aspects of Protestant opposition to reforms and the Sunningdale settlement, but at the same time it was constantly confronted with the contradictory bases of this opposition. Vanguard's extremism was in danger of provoking further splits within the loyalist community for at root it was based on interests that were directly opposed to those of the Protestant proletariat, as well as those of important fractions of the bourgeoisie.

As the political organisation reflecting the interests of the most reactionary sections of the province's business community, Vanguard was able to mobilise support from those Protestant groups to whom the benefits of the Union with Britain were not sufficient to outweigh the loss of privileges, both economic and political, stemming from the reform programme. In particular Craig had the support of the petty bourgeoisie.

> The structural changes in the economy towards greater emphasis on modern capital-intensive industries have benefited some groups of skilled workers and the professional classes, but unskilled workers and others are paying the cost in the form of deteriorating employment opportunities. The lower middle class of small self-employed in sales and services have also been among the losers. Many small shopkeepers were ruined when the British chain stores moved in in the mid-sixties. Many streets in Belfast present the desolate picture of small shops which are never going to open again.[16]

In addition, this petty bourgeois element included precisely those groups which suffered so immediately from the Provisional bombing campaign. Their support for Craig's extremism directly reflects their experience of being squeezed on all sides. Vanguard also attracted those elements of the old Unionist alliance whose political and social influence was being radically undermined by different aspects of the reform movement, like the Orange Order which traditionally played a central role in maintaining the cohesion of the Protestant community. However, it is interesting to note that it was Paisley and the DUP who took up the issue of the defence of 'Protestantism', rather than Craig. In fact Craig welcomed the ecumenical moves of the early sixties.[17]

Vanguard's hostility to 'reformist' Unionism and the Sunningdale settlement is matched by the equally vociferous opposition of Paisley's Democratic Unionist Party, which won eight seats in the new Assembly. The alliance between the DUP and VUPP was based on a common agreement to give a written undertaking to reject totally the constitution proposed for Northern Ireland in the White Paper, and to oppose any administration or executive that might emerge from the Assembly. In

December 1973 while the tri-partite talks were in progress at Sunningdale, these parties were joined by the anti-Faulkner Unionists.

However, the history of relations between Vanguard and the DUP reflects many deep-rooted antagonisms, and suggests that there is little in common between these parties beyond their opposition to the settlement envisaged by the White Paper. My object here is to examine the support for, and the policies of the DUP since its formation in 1971, and to suggest that its development is intimately rooted in the specifically working class response to O'Neill's policies in the sixties, in contrast to Craig's base among the small capitalists. The relationship of the DUP with the Protestant petty bourgeoisie and working class is not direct or simple, and this is reflected in the wavering allegiance of such populist organisations as the Ulster Defence Association. However, an analysis of the phenomenon of Paisleyism as it emerged in the mid-sixties, and its development into the DUP, provides an essential insight into the birth of some kind of autonomous Protestant working class political action, and the manner in which religion continues to mediate political experiences. Furthermore, it is an essential element in understanding the fundamental rupture which O'Neill's policies inflicted on the old Unionist alliance.

Two years before the civil rights movement mounted its first major demonstration in the reform campaign, and five years before the Provisional IRA made its appearance, the Province experienced the worst outbreak of street violence since the 1920s. Already, in 1966, Protestant grass-roots opposition to O'Neill's reformism, and the general climate of rapprochement with the Republic over economic and theological issues, was making itself felt in a variety of ways. The turmoil among loyalists was focused around three men, Ian Paisley, Noel Doherty, and Gusty Spence, and the organisations which grew up behind them: the Ulster Constitution Defence Committee, the Ulster Protestant Volunteers, and the Ulster Volunteer Force. Their activities in 1966 ranged from demonstrations against the 'Romeward trend' in the Presbyterian Church, and what they described as the 'rot in Ulster Unionism which began when Captain O'Neill got in touch with Mr Lemass', to the petrol bombing of Catholic-owned premises, and sectarian assassination attempts.

Before turning in more detail to the issues around which this opposition was mobilised and the form it took, it is important to return to the broader question of how the Protestant working class had been integrated, politically and ideologically, into the Unionist alliance. Against this background it is then possible to begin to analyse the impact of O'Neill's policies, and to explain why they met with such violent opposition at this early stage.

The original strength of the Unionist party lay in the alliance that the Conservative industrialists formed with the essentially proletarian-based Orange Order. From its inception in the late 18th century, the Orange movement had been co-opted by the land-owning ruling class in its struggle against the United Irishmen, and in 1798 the leadership of the lodges had been taken over by the gentry. With the active membership of the ruling class in the Order, the lodges gave the rural and industrial proletariat an outward and visible assurance of its part in the ruling ascendancy. 'If he shared nothing else with the gentry in the big houses, the common rhetoric of the lodges gave him an illusion of equality. Their victory at the Boyne was his victory, their responsibility to uphold Protestant law and Protestant order was his responsibility.'[18]

During the first half of the 19th century, under the shelter of the Act of Union, the gentry's connections with the Order weakened considerably, though the latter remained a powerful sectarian organisation amongst the rural population and the growing industrial proletariat in Belfast. Despite the periodic rioting and violence that the Order provoked, its existence was tolerated since it provided a way of containing the dangers that the industrial revolution created for the ruling class. As Ulster developed into an increasingly urban society in the second half of the 19th century, the Orangemen remained loyal to the Protestant ascendancy. This loyalty was not simply the product of ideological manipulation, as Frank Wright points out: 'The existence of Orange Lodges bearing the titles of different occupations such as 'Shipwrights', 'Bricklayers', 'Mechanics', 'Bakers', 'Artisans' is indicative of the fact that Orangeism is closely linked to the preservation of the Protestant character of certain skilled occupations.'[19]

In the 1880s, threatened with Gladstone's first Home Rule Bill, Ulster's industrialists once again turned to the Orangemen. The national and the religious questions were firmly entwined in the politics of Orangeism, through which the Protestant working class articulated and defended their interests. In Britain the working class was developing an independent labour ideology and flexing its political muscles against Whigs and Tories alike, while Ulster's proletariat was joining the Ulster bourgeoisie behind the barricades. Unionism, Protestantism and Orangeism united to combat Home Rule, and after the settlement of 1920, a political system emerged which institutionalised the relationships upon which this alliance was founded.

When, in later years, some Unionists attempted to play down the sectarian image of the party, they found themselves greatly hampered by its institutional links with Orangeism, for by its constitution the Order is a sectarian organisation. Membership involves the promise to 'love, uphold and defend the Protestant religion, and sincerely desire and endeavour to propagate its doctrines and precepts', and to 'strenuously oppose the fatal errors and doctrines of the Church of Rome, and scrupulously avoid countenancing (by his presence or otherwise) any act or ceremony of Popish worship.'[20] A prominent Unionist MP was in fact expelled from the Order in 1968 for attending a Roman Catholic ceremony as part of his public duty.

The achievement of a 'Protestant Parliament' at Stormont did not result in any modification of the nature of working class allegiance to the Unionist Party. On the contrary, the strength of the Unionist alliance was reinforced and reproduced through the sectarian political and ideological apparatuses of the Unionist State. A positive role was assured the working class loyalist militants in 1920, when the Ulster Volunteer Force was reorganised into the Ulster Special Constabulary. In the early months of its existence, the threat of the newly independent Irish Free State, and widespread mistrust of Westminster's intentions, created a sense of siege in Northern Ireland, and the Specials immediately assumed a crucial paramilitary role. 'The Specials were permitted to carry their arms even when off duty and in plain clothes, a privilege which lasted until their transformation in to the Ulster Defence Regiment in 1969. For fifty years they played the role of Unionism's private army.'[21] The Protestant proletariat cannot be characterised simply as the passive tool of Ulster's ruling class, for the real strength of the Unionist alliance lay in the mass participation and sense of purpose found in such organisations as the Orange Order and the Specials. Indeed it was precisely the symbiotic nature of the alliance that was to thwart the later attempts of leaders like O'Neill to effect some kind of reforms from within the Unionist Party.

It is against this background of institutionalised political and economic discrimination that we must examine the phenomenon of the pervasive influence of fundamentalist religious beliefs. Wright notes that:

> Working-class areas of Belfast are particularly heavily exposed to such forms of Protestantism in many aspects of their daily lives. A quick look at the number of churches, mission halls and religious meeting houses on the Shankhill today reveals at least the large presence of such influences, even if it tells us nothing about how successful they are.[22]

In his autobiography, *No Surrender*, Robert Harbinson tells of his life as a child in the Protestant working class Sandy Row. He describes at some length what Sandy Row boys thought about Catholics:

> It was our firm belief that every sin had to be payed for in hard cash, and that was why so many Catholics were publicans — unlike so many others, their tills were always full of cash . . . For one particular crime we would never forgive the Mickeys, their hatred of the Bible. All Catholics were under orders, we were told, to burn any scripture they found, especially New Testaments.[23]

Schools did little to remedy the situation. Harbinson describes his experience in this way:

> Crowding out any other aspect of History, our schools dinned into us over and over again the Protestant story. On leaving school . . . I had no notion of the world's past other than a few prehistoric tales and dreary details concerning our Protestant faith and the unrelieved darkness of Rome . . . And yet in spite of such entrenched opinion our ignorance of

the Catholic world was profound. I, for instance, believed that Mickeys existed only in parts of Belfast, and nowhere else except the Free State and Rome itself.[24]

The kind of ideas to which many Protestants were exposed received widespread publicity during Paisley's campaign against ecumenism in the 1960s.[25] However, it is not the doctrinal substance of Protestant Evangelicalism that concerns us here, but rather the function of such an ideology in the reproduction of social relations. As Wright concludes in his study, *Protestant Ideology and Politics in Ulster:*

> This type of ideological perspective sharpens the conflict in Ulster. There is today and there always has been a large section of the population who are prepared to take up these types of issues. For these people the conflict *is* essentially a religious conflict. But in fact it seems unlikely that issues of this kind could ever develop the significance they do develop if it were not for the fact that for many people they are an ideological expression of a conflict with a deeper, socio-economic and political meaning.[26]

The absence of any secular labour ideology and independent working class political organisations derives from the hegemonic position established by Ulster's industrial bourgeoisie at the end of the 19th century. The internal and external factors which contributed to their hegemony were described earlier, and the Protestant labour aristocracy's willingness to take up class positions that were in fact bourgeois testifies to its strength. However, this lack of class consciousness and autonomous working class political organisation should not be taken to imply the absence of class struggle, of antagonistic class relations within Unionism. The Orange Order was indeed co-opted into the Unionist Party, but there have been numerous occasions on which the ideology of Orangeism has revealed its relative autonomy as a vehicle for expressing working class antagonism toward the ruling class. Thus, in the general election of 1868, held at a time when the linen industry was hit by recession, causing widespread unemployment, Conservative candidates were challenged over their ability to defend the interests of the working class. The articulation of socio-economic grievances was constantly mediated by the dominant religious ideology through which the mass of Protestants interpreted and integrated their experiences, so that, for example, the criticism of Conservatism was usually expressed in terms of a general distrust of the candidates commitment to true Protestantism.

The odd mixture of radicalism and religious fundamentalism which characterised Paisleyism in the 1960s was not a new phenomenon. At the beginning of this century the militant Independent Orangemen broke with the Conservatives because of the latter's concession to 'Popery' on the question of whether convent laundries should be exempted from the Inspection of Laundries Act, and went on to take a leading part in organising the Belfast Dock Strike.[27] In the thirties there was the Ulster

Protestant League, and in the fifties Paisley played a leading role in an organisation called Ulster Protestant Action, formed to keep Protestants and loyalists in employment in times of depression, in preference to their Catholic fellow-workers. The redress of all working class grievances became inextricably linked with the defence of Protestantism. In this lay the roots of the intense hostility provoked by the ecumenical movement of the early 1960s, and the bitterness of feeling engendered by O'Neill's tentative moves toward some kind of improved relationship with the Catholic community in the North and the Government of the South.

THE REVEREND IAN PAISLEY

The common identification 'Protestant', however, conferred only the illusion of unity between the Shankhill Road worker and the landowning aristocrat. Behind that illusory unity was the constant antagonism of class interests. So reactionary and anachronistic a system could hold together only as long as Ulster remained isolated from the main currents of British politics. By the mid-1960s the province was caught up in both the economic and ideational currents of broader British and Irish politics.

Paisley's mobilisation of popular support on the streets in defence of traditional Protestantism and the constitution, and the reappearance of paramilitary groups like the UVF, were only the traditional, and once officially sanctioned, response of loyalists to any threat to the established social order. The difference was that under the changed conditions of the sixties, Official Unionism was anxious to disassociate itself altogether from that part of its own past that persisted in lingering on as 'Paisleyism'. 'Unionist Party leaders fell over themselves to get their protestations on record. To Roy Bradford, Paisley was "this latter-day Luther of the lumpen-proletariat" whose preaching was "the very rabies of religion".'[28] O'Neill denounced the movement, comparing it with the rise of fascism in Germany. A sense of bewilderment and betrayal swept over loyalists.

It is interesting to note the issues over which the rift in the Unionist alliance first occurred, and the early date at which the split began to manifest itself. The election of O'Neill occurred shortly after Pope John XXIII had convened the historic second Vatican Council and caused an upheaval within the Roman Catholic Church and a reorientation of its rigid institutional framework. Ecumenism was in the air. When Pope John died in 1963, the Belfast City Hall lowered the Union Jack in mourning, before an incredulous Protestant audience. The ecumenical controversy had, inevitably, a special relevance for Northern Ireland. The great mass of Protestants neither knew nor cared that the leadership of their Churches had long since abandoned Calvinism and Bible fundamentalism. The significance of the ecumenical movement lay in its political implications, for behind this preoccupation with questions of theology and the constitution lay an essential substantive issue. In Ulster, ecumenism carried a threat of Catholic integration, a threat to Protestant privilege in jobs, housing, and access to political power. Thus, anyone who preached the doctrine of fundamentalism was making a stand for traditional Unionism. Herein lay the popular appeal of Paisley's attack on the leaders of the major Churches, who, arm in arm with the political elite, were preaching ecumenism, were selling out to Rome.

Although Paisley's central theme was his outright denunciation of the theological liberalism of the official Presbyterian Church, he and his supporters were involved in demonstrations and rioting over a variety of issues in the early sixties. Their activities were soon focused around the slogan 'O'Neill must go!' Long before the civil rights movement appeared on the streets, the problem of mounting any kind of reform programme from within the Unionist Party had been amply demonstrated. O'Neill was asking for a complete reversal of all traditional loyalties, those loyalties which had been drummed in over years of Unionist rule. And he could not even provide the concrete benefits which might have sugared the pill. In the early 1960s the province was hit by a depression, and his talk of economic planning did little to compensate for the loss of privilege that his plans for the centralisation of power entailed.

The movement conjured up by Paisley in the sixties derived support from a wide variety of Protestant groups. In the countryside he mobilised the smaller farmers and tenant workers. In Belfast he had a wide religious following amongst the respectable petty bourgeoisie, and he was rumoured to have contacts with the extreme paramilitary working class organisation, the Ulster Protestant Volunteers, and the Ulster Volunteer Force. This coalition of interests inevitably began to weaken as the conflict developed, fragmenting into a variety of splinter groups. However, in 1966, when Paisley was released from prison after serving three months for refusing to sign a pledge of good behaviour, it was estimated that he had a potential 200,000 supporters.[29] He had effectively succeeded in transferring the conflict onto the streets, and by 1969 his supporters achieved one of their major objectives with the resignation of O'Neill.

In the 1930s Orangeism had intervened decisively to divert class antagonism into religious conflict. In the 1960s the Protestant working class again responded by organising to defend Protestant privilege in Northern Ireland. This time it seemed as though they would carry out their threat to form a new Unionist Party 'which would make the State more genuinely Protestant'.

THE DEMOCRATIC UNIONIST PARTY

In the Stormont elections held in February 1969, Paisley fielded six candidates under the title of Protestant Unionists. Five of them took second place, with Paisley himself coming very close to unseating the Prime Minister, Captain O'Neill. In April 1970 Paisley won the seat at a by-election, with his colleague the Rev. Beattie taking South Antrim. Two months later Paisley also won a seat at Westminster. The political situation was deteriorating, with the Unionist Party, under the leadership of Chichester-Clark, grudgingly proceeding with the reform programme under heavy pressure from Westminster. There was growing distrust amongst the Catholic population and increasing opposition from disillusioned loyalists. Paisley maintained his attacks on the Unionist Party, vehemently opposing those moves which most offended Protestant working class opinion, such as the disbanding of the B Specials.

However, Protestant Unionism was not the simple anti-Catholic phenomenon that many commentators asserted it to be. Harbinson describes it thus:

> It is certainly anti-republican, and no doubt many of its adherents equate Catholicism and republicanism. But it is fundamentally a working class movement whose policies in the social, economic and libertarian fields differ very little from such Catholic movements as the Social and Democratic Labour Party. It has attacked Unionist Governments on their economic policies, castigated Unionist controlled local authorities over their performance in housing and public health, and opposed internment.[30]

Paisley's opposition to internment brings to light the complex nature of the relationship between his parliamentary party and his grass roots support. The Protestant Unionist Party, and its successor the Democratic Unionist Party, consistently defended the rights of the Protestant working class, and sought to lead that section of the community. However, in many respects the relationship between the two was insecure. During the upheavals of this time the working class began to throw up its own leaders, at least at the local level, through a variety of organisations, mostly of a paramilitary nature. Furthermore, the workers' allegiance was now being courted by Craig from within the Unionist Party. Paisley's opposition to internment was rooted in his defence of working class interests, in the knowledge that it could be used equally well against loyalists as against republicans. Yet he chose to announce his opposition, in the spring of 1971, just at a time when the vast majority of opinion in the province was moving toward support for its introduction. It was at this moment that the Provisionals launched their bombing offensive.

In August 1971, Faulkner introduced internment in an attempt to retain the support of the rank and file of the Unionist Party. He succeeded in provoking an explosion of Catholic violence, and in sowing the seeds of the territorially-based Protestant vigilante groups which later joined together in the Ulster Defence Association. Suddenly Faulkner's leadership was as insecure as ever O'Neill's had been, and the battle for the allegiance of the loyalist masses began in earnest. Paradoxically it began with an alliance between Faulkner's main opponents, Craig, Paisley and Boal; the 'Unionist Alliance'. It was, however, merely a tactical alliance, which only temporarily disguised fundamental disagreements. Craig hoped to reunite the traditional elements of Unionism and Orangeism in his own bid for power. 'Paisley and Boal, on the other hand, saw the Alliance as the nucleus of a new party which would attract the disaffected Protestant working class. Boal, in particular, saw the new party taking the opposition seats in Stormont vacated by the SDLP boycott. If and when the SDLP returned, the new party might join with them, on social if not on constitutional issues, as a non-sectarian working class opposition.'[31]

Desmond Boal, an erudite barrister, was elected to Stormont in 1960 as Unionist MP for the Shankill, an overwhelmingly working class Protestant area of Belfast. In any other political system his politics would be labelled social democratic. In 1961 he had the privilege to be the first Unionist MP to have the whip withdrawn for voting with the Northern Ireland Labour Party on an economic censure motion. He was also consistently opposed to the policies of O'Neill and Chichester-Clark. A week after the formation of the Unionist Alliance, Boal announced his resignation from the Unionist Party, together with John McQuade, MP for the Woodvale constituency of Belfast, who was a former docker. The following day these two formally joined forces with Paisley in his renamed Democratic Unionist Party. Boal described the party as being 'right-wing in the sense of being strong on the constitution and restoring security, but to the left on social policies.'[32] Real success for the DUP depended on its ability to provoke defections from the Unionists, and in this, despite widespread support, they failed. Traditional ties with official Unionism were very strong. Furthermore, their claim to represent the loyalist masses was being undermined by events on the streets. The failure of internment, and the chaos that followed, was driving Protestants into local Defence Associations.

In December 1971 the DUP took their places as the Official Opposition at Stormont, and from this position took the development of non-sectarian politics to previously undreamed of lengths. In the same month Paisley met with the SDLP secretly, and it is reported that while agreeing to differ on the constitutional question, they found themselves in agreement on their opposition to internment and to 'community government', and the need for urgent measures to combat unemployment. A few days later Boal launched an unprecedented attack on Unionism's link with the Orange Order. Not surprisingly the DUP's broad mass of supporters were confused by these developments, and their faith was greatly shaken by the spectacle of Paisley being welcomed as a hero by such traditional enemies as the Dublin Government and the Provisional IRA's high command. Paisley and Boal had gone too far, and once again it was apparent that although they might be 'for' the working class, they were not 'of' it. In November, in the UDA Bulletin, it was noted that 'at one time we would have followed

Paisley anywhere'. Now, however, while offering 'thanks for his original efforts in forging all Loyalists together', the loyalist masses were withdrawing their support.[33]

In March 1972, shortly before the imposition of direct rule, Paisley attacked Craig's talk of UDI, claiming that 'it was certainly not acceptable to the majority of loyalist people.'[34] He went on to say that if Stormont were to be tampered with it might be better to integrate Northern Ireland into the United Kingdom. His opposition to Vanguard's policies on UDI, and his stated preference for full integration was a central obstacle in attempts to recreate a united opposition to the Sunningdale settlement. Despite the fact that his policy in this respect contradicted the feelings of the loyalist working class at this time, Paisley managed to maintain better relations with the emerging UDA than his rival, Craig, who in many ways succeeded in catching their mood more accurately. The conflicts that emerged within the UDA over support for Vanguard or the DUP are dealt with more fully below, but it is interesting to note that the UDA has been consistently critical of the middle class nature of Vanguard leadership, and has often expressed regret at its differences with Paisley.

In opposition to the Sunningdale agreement, the DUP, Vanguard and the Unofficial Unionists regrouped in the United Ulster Unionist Council, with the backing of the UDA. The inherently unstable nature of their allegiance to one another is a reflection of the extent to which all political relationships had been challenged by the clash between traditional Unionism and the pressures for reform. The battle for the political support of the Protestant working class continued, and was of no less significance than the sectarian war on the streets.

POLITICS IN THE STREETS

In discussing the political struggles provoked by the growing contradictions within the structure of the Unionist State, I chose to focus on the attempt to establish a new Northern Ireland Assembly and a Council of Ireland. However, it was not the party political manoeuvrings that kept the province in the newspaper headlines. Since 1971 parliamentary politics have been overshadowed by the politics of the streets, by sectarian rioting, by the war between the IRA and the British Army, and by the steady growth of community-based paramilitary organisations.

The political conflict between the supporters of reform and its opponents was transformed into sectarian confrontations on the street by the impossibility of resolving the growing contradictions within the Unionist alliance without shattering the Unionist State. Reform under a Unionist Government depended on two mutually exclusive conditions: first, the maintenance of credibility in the eyes of the Catholic minority, and second, the preservation of the Government's power base amongst the loyalist masses. With the direct intervention of Westminster in August 1969 and the arrival of the British Army, followed by the reform of the province's security forces, it seemed as though the latter was to be sacrificed to the former.

Westminster, however, having preferred to ignore totally the Irish question since the settlement of 1920, understood little of the forces at work, and showed no inclination to follow up their military intervention with any determined political initiatives. In 1969 Britain saw the problem essentially in terms of 'community relations', ameliorable through a gradualist programme of legislation to outlaw discrimination. The implementation of this policy of the 'long slow haul' was left in the hands of Chichester-Clark, with the British Army ostensibly retained in a simple peace-keeping role. In essence, O'Neill, Chichester-Clark and Faulkner were engaged in a series of attempts to pacify the minority with the promise of reform whilst assuring the loyalists that the substance would be withheld. The net result was the massive alienation of broad sections of both communities, and the proliferation of paramilitary organisations.

THE PARAMILITARY ORGANISATIONS

The Ulster Defence Association was not a unified organisation with a centralised leadership and clearly defined objectives, but rather an association of territorially based groups, constantly divided amongst themselves, and adopting contradictory class stands. Nonetheless, the possibility of socialist intervention in the resolution of the Northern Ireland crisis depends crucially on the ultimate allegiance of those people who were active in, and supported the UDA. In discussing the phenomenon of Paisleyism, I described the political and ideological history of the Protestant working class, the essential background to understanding its response to the changes of the O'Neill era. The emergence of the UDA, however, is directly related to the subsequent transformation of the political battle over reform into a military struggle on the streets. In considering the development of the UDA it is necessary to take account of the Catholic community's response to the failure of reform, the growth of no-go areas, increasing hostility toward the British Army, and the launching of the Provisional IRA's military offensive.

THE IRISH REPUBLICAN ARMY

After the collapse of the 1950s border campaign, the old IRA was forced to re-examine its traditional strategy. Those elements that wished to turn to more political work were hampered by the fact that Sinn Fein was pledged to a policy of abstentionism. Also, they were opposed by the more traditionally minded old guard in the movement, whose objectives were purely military.

> It thus proved impossible to build up a united body of opinion within either Sinn Fein or the IRA's Army Council in favour of terminating the principle of abstention from parliamentary attendance. What was achieved, however, was the reintroduction of radical socialist republicanism into the movement, and its subsequent association with practical courses of action, in both the north and south of Ireland.[1]

The influence of socialist ideas encouraged the IRA to take some account of the interests and aspirations of the Protestant working class. The organisation developed a gradualist strategy which involved working towards reform *within* the Six Counties. The creation of a united working class movement in the North was seen as a prerequisite of any campaign toward a united, socialist Ireland. As a result, their activities in the North in the 1960s were limited to supporting the civil rights campaign as it developed.

In the process of this ideological transformation they virtually surrendered their traditional role as military defenders of the Catholic urban enclaves. When rioting Protestants invaded the Catholic Falls Road in August 1969, there were virtually no arms in the Catholic community. As a result of this experience, and in fear of a more sustained pogrom against the Catholic minority, a number of older, more traditionally minded men in the movement took steps to recapture the leadership of the IRA, and to turn it into a physical force organisation again. During the latter part of 1969 the republican movement was torn apart over this issue, and all over Belfast sharp factional fighting broke out within the organisation.

The same fight was going on at the national level. The leadership of the movement was about to abandon one of the major planks of republicanism, abstention from parliamentary elections. In December and January the issue was put to the vote at meetings of the Army Council and Ard Fheis, as a result of which the republican movement was split into two sections. Official Sinn Fein continued to represent the new 'political' line, while the more traditionally minded Provisional Sinn Fein were intent on rebuilding their armed strength.

By the beginning of 1970 the Provisional IRA was established as a small armed force in Belfast. They had obtained weapons and were concentrating on training and setting up organisational procedures, but they were as yet uncertain of their tactics. Throughout the early part of 1970 the Provisional IRA represented a minority tendency inside the Catholic working class. However, they were an indication of growing Catholic apprehension that the British Army would be turned against them as soon as the necessity to prop up Chichester-Clark and the Unionist Government took precedence over 'peace-keeping'.

Just as the SDLP's credibility was progressively undermined by the obvious lack of genuine reform, so the Official IRA's position was weakened by the apparent failure of their political strategies. In July 1970 the British Army attempted an arms raid in the Falls Road area, provoking a violent confrontation with the inhabitants. This event marked the beginning of a new phase in the 'troubles', with the shattering of the Catholic community's faith in the British Army and Westminster's intentions. Five civilians were killed during the operation, and fifteen soldiers and sixty civilians injured. This and subsequent arms raids incensed the Catholics, since it was common knowledge that the Protestant enclaves had always bristled with legally held guns, and even now, after the disbandment of the B Specials, were well protected through alternative organisations like gun clubs.

With the responsibility for the reform programme left in the hands of the Unionist Government it was inevitable that the British Army's role should become increasingly partisan, and that with its all-pervasive presence along the community boundaries, it should become the focal point of Catholic hostility. After the Falls Road curfew, recruitment to the Provisional IRA increased dramatically, and in the absence of any new political initiatives, a genuine military republican force developed. An important feature of this development was the way in which the centre of political activity was transferred on to a residential, territorial basis. Given the segregated structure of working class residential patterns in Belfast and other major towns, and a long tradition of symbolic confrontations over territory (such as the Orange marches), there was inevitably growing tension along the boundaries. In 1969 the Catholics had responded to the danger from Protestant rioters by barricading themselves into the Bogside, from where they proclaimed 'Free Derry'.

As the situation worsened there were mass migrations of Protestants and Catholics, leading to even more clearly segregated communal boundaries. In both communities, distrust of the British Army, and a growing need for physical defence led to the proliferation of residentially based defence organisations. By the Spring of 1971 the defence of the Catholic communities had passed into the hands of the Provisionals, who were now in a position to mount a more positive attack on Stormont. Within the Protestant community the development was slower, and there was no centralised organisation. The introduction of internment, however, provoked a startling increase in activity in both communities. The SDLP had withdrawn from Stormont, and were now deprived of any mandate to return, leaving the Provisional IRA the dominant tendency within the Catholic community. The massive rejection by the minority of the whole Unionist system was reflected in the ensuing rent and rates strike, and the springing up of numerous 'no-go' areas, from within which the Provisionals launched their bombing campaign. Amongst the Protestant working class there was growing disillusionment with Faulkner, and a real fear of a Catholic uprising. '. . . in July 1971 there was probably no more than a score of active UVF men, most of them long-time associates of Gusty Spence. The explosion of Catholic violence that followed internment in August was to change that. As homes burned and refugees fled, Protestant vigilante groups sprang up everywhere.'[2] The Ulster Defence Association had been born.

THE ULSTER DEFENCE ASSOCIATION

A prototype of the form the organisation took had in fact emerged earlier, in 1969, under the title 'Shankill Defence Association'. This group, based in a solidly working class slum area of Belfast, had formed an armed vigilante force at the time when the Catholics in the neighbouring Ardoyne area were involved in serious riots with the police. They were subsequently involved in the intimidation of Catholics and in the formation of gun clubs. However, it was not until August 1971 that any widespread systematic organisation took place. Three days after the introduction of internment a leaflet appeared on the streets of Belfast, which read:
Being convinced that the enemies of the Faith and Freedom are

determined to destroy the State of Northern Ireland and thereby
enslave the people of God, we call on all members of our loyalist
institutions, and other responsible citizens to organise themselves
immediately into platoons of twenty under the command of
someone capable of acting as sergeant. Every effort must be made
to arm these platoons, with whatever weapons are available. The
first duty of each platoon will be to formulate a plan for the
defence of its own street or road in cooperation with platoons in
adjoining areas. A structure of command is already in existence
and various platoons will eventually be linked in a coordinated
effort.[3]

By the end of August there were vigilante groups or 'defence associations'
in Shankill, Woodvale, Ormeau, Carrick, Donegall Pass and many other
areas. Early in September, a founder member of the Woodvale Defence
Association took the initiative of bringing them all together under a central
council: the Ulster Defence Association. Their distrust of traditional
loyalist leadership was clearly manifested in the stipulation that no MPs
and no religious mentors were to be admitted.

Since its formation the UDA has been involved in a wide variety of
different activities, such as organised military action against the British
Army, running drinking clubs, running protection and extortion rackets,
organising neighbourhood advice centres, torture and assassination
campaigns, blockades of the Province, and the construction of no-go areas.
It is important to recognise the several conflicting strands in their policies,
and the existence of major sources of tension within the Association. Only
in this way can the UDA's present and future relationship to the central
question of reform of the Orange system be evaluated. Their hostility
toward republicanism may not be in doubt, but their relationship with the
different fragments of the old Unionist alliance is clearly in the balance.

The Ulster Defence Association, as its name implies, has its roots in the
need for defence: political defence of the *status quo*, and physical defence
of territory. It was not formed in order to launch an attack on the Catholic
population. In spite of provocation, and the constant talk of a Protestant
'backlash', sanctioned by extremists like Craig, its military activities have,
for the most part, been very restrained. Nor was it formed to prosecute a
defined political programme. However, the fact that it was established on
the basis of local residential patterns is reflected in the ideological framework within which its political development has occurred. The historical
division of Belfast into numerous, clearly demarcated enclaves, and the
decentralised political system based on vertical patronage relationships,
had combined to give the petty bourgeoisie an important role in local
politics. Within the enclaves the shops and small businesses provide the
focal points of the area. The likelihood of petty bourgeois leadership was
further increased by the fact that, as a class, it was their power and
privileges that had most seriously been undermined by the changes of the
sixties. The advent of British and international chain stores, the

redevelopment of urban areas, the centralisation of power from a local council to central level, and the shift of power within the Unionist Party had all been trends that had militated against their interests.

The dominance of the petty bourgeois element was reflected in the composition of the first UDA Council, which was headed by the owner of a small glazier's business, and included drapers and newspaper shop owners. It is the interests of this class that are reflected in the UDA's demands for a massive campaign against the IRA and the restoration of the old Stormont, and in the organisation's initial support for Vanguard. The petty bourgeoisie received positive support from the more reactionary elements of the Protestant working class, and in particular from the Loyalist Association of Workers (LAW), the organisation of the Protestant labour aristocracy. From this perspective the UDA are the staunch defenders of the Orange system and the sectarian basis of its politics.

However, these tendencies are not unopposed within the organisation. There have been many serious disagreements within the UDA since its formation. Some of these merely reflect the factional strife that inevitably developed because of the autonomy of individual associations and the lack of centralised leadership, and the different conditions obtaining in the various enclaves. Some of the disagreements, on the other hand, are more deep-rooted, and stem from the organisation's dependence on broad working class support, and the underlying conflicts of interest between this class and the petty bourgeois element. The description of some of the UDA's activities that follows is not intended to be exhaustive, but rather to illustrate the existence of these conflicting strands in their political behaviour and ideological development.

Through the autumn of 1971 and spring of 1972 the security situation continued to deteriorate. Internment provided a new impetus to the Provisionals' bombing campaign, and led to a dramatic widening in the scope of their targets, bringing home to almost the whole population the experience of violence. Life in Belfast's city centre, and in other towns, ground to a halt with shops and pubs closing early, and a severe fall-off in trade. The extent of Catholic alienation and increasingly active opposition to Stormont was visible to all in the rent and rates strike, the no-go areas and huge illegal demonstrations against internment. Under such conditions, support for the UDA grew inexorably.

In February, after the launching of Vanguard, Craig made his bid for the support of the UDA, and after some initial disagreements, succeeded in forming an alliance. He organised a series of monster rallies, at which the UDA were in evidence, dressed in the now familiar combat jackets. The spectre of a united loyalist backlash was raised. In fact the UDA never accepted the role of military wing to Vanguard, despite Craig's claims and encouragement. There was indeed to be a backlash, provoked by the imposition of Direct Rule and the British Government's subsequent truce with the IRA. But it did not take the form envisaged by Craig, nor was it in any way subject to Vanguard's control.

The backlash took the form of an assassination campaign. A detailed study of this campaign can be found in M. Dillon and D. Lehane's book, *Political Murder in Northern Ireland*. In this they conclude that: 'The story of the sectarian assassinations in Ulster is the story of the Protestant backlash. There can be no questioning the simple truth that the greater part of the near-200 such assassinations were committed by Protestants organised in groups, often for this specific purpose.'[4] Willingness to distinguish between the IRA and the wider Catholic community had been totally undermined by the events of the previous year, and the loyalist community saw no alternative means of expressing their opposition to developments in the province, having despaired of progress by constitutional means. 'The sectarian assassinations were a counter-attack by a group of Ulster Protestants who agreed with Austin Currie and the IRA that the Catholics were winning and the Unionist system was about to be destroyed.'[5] The success of the Provisional bombing campaign in hastening the collapse of Stormont resulted inevitably in the emergence of this sectarian response, and the involvement of the UDA in the assassination campaign.

Whilst it succeeded in bringing terror to the streets of the province, the campaign did little to alter the political situation. As a result of direct rule the Catholic community were greatly encouraged, and gave the SDLP a new mandate to negotiate. Furthermore the Official IRA decided to cease all military activities. Through the summer and autumn of 1972 William Whitelaw pressed ahead with a series of negotiations with the parliamentary parties on the future of the Province. Meanwhile, on the streets the UDA was coming increasingly into direct conflict with the British Army. In May and June the organisation had adopted a policy of setting up their own no-go areas as part of a campaign to protest against the continued existence of Catholic ones. Confrontations with the British Army had two significant effects on the thinking of the Protestant working class. First, it gave them first-hand experience of what the Catholic community had undergone for two years, and led to complaints about the Army's behaviour that directly echoed those of the Catholic working class. Second, an increasing number of Protestants were picked up under the Special Powers Act, which led to some rethinking about the merits of internment.

These developments combined to produce a demand amongst some elements of the UDA for a more coherent political programme. Evidence of growing dissension within the organisation appeared in its ambivalent relationship with Vanguard. In August the UDA denounced Vanguard as a prop for the Official Unionist Party, a reflection of the intensifying conflict between the middle class, conservative leadership of Vanguard, and the working class leaders in the UDA. Craig and his close allies, still working within the traditional Orange-Unionist framework of Lodge and Party, were intensely suspicious of independent working class action. It looked as though a real split might occur, when, in the same month, it was announced that LAW, 'after consultations with the UDA (with which, in any case, it was so closely linked as to be, in effect, the Association's political wing), was considering the formation of a new working-class "loyalist" party aiming at "government of the people, by the people and for the people, and one man one vote." '[6] Craig, however, managed to rescue the situation by promising the Party that it would have Vanguard's full support if it became clear that the Unionist Party could not be captured from within. The UDA and LAW withdrew their suggestion shortly after.

In September the rifts opened up again, when the then Chairman of the UDA Council announced in a newspaper interview that his personal choice as 'loyalist' leader was Ian Paisley. James Anderson criticised successive Unionist Governments for neglecting the ordinary people of Northern Ireland.[7] He was sharply attacked by other UDA members over this statement, for the rift was not merely between Vanguard and the UDA but reflected class conflict within the UDA. In October a circular was distributed to the press.

> It claimed that 'socialist-oriented and class-conscious elements of the UDA' were forming 'active service units of the Ulster Citizen Army' for the protection of Protestant working class areas. 'Growing dissatisfaction, frustration and anger within UDA ranks' was 'the result of the increasing influence of Vanguard leadership and ex-Unionist politicians' upon the UDA command. These parasites, who never in the past were the friend of the Ulster worker, have not changed. Their sole aim is still pursuit of power at any price.[8]

This thread of independent, increasingly class-conscious thinking developed within a section of the UDA through the autumn of 1972. It went so far as to contemplate the possibility of an accomodation with the Catholic working class, and with this in mind, secret meetings were arranged with the Official IRA.

The reaction of the petty bourgeois and hard-line elements within the UDA was dramatic. In December, Ernie Elliott, the lieutenant-colonel of Woodvale UDA, who was known to support this radical line of thinking, was assassinated by the right wing of his own organisation.[9] Six weeks later Elliott's first-in-command, Dave Fogel, defected from the UDA and fled to England. His story, which he sold to the *Sunday Times*,[10] tells of the extent to which the development of non-sectarian, working class ideology had gone within the UDA, and of the attempt of certain members to translate this into new political relations with the Catholic community. In this context Fogel mentions the efforts of Tommy Herron, the UDA Vice-chairman from East Belfast. In January 1973 Herron announced publicly that the UDA had ordered the assassins on both sides to stop the killings, and hinted that the UDA would deal with any Protestants who ignored the order.[11] In the following month there was not a single assassination of a Roman Catholic. The subsequent collapse of this initiative, and the manner in which those elements who wished to preserve the Orange system regained control of the organisation are dealt with in detail by Dillon and Lehane. Herron was in fact assassinated in September 1973 by a faction of the UDA.

The rifts in the UDA that had emerged in 1972-3 had been contained, but they were not eliminated. The Association's leadership was continually divided over a variety of issues, and there were a number of splinter groups. At one extreme a group calling themselves the Ulster Freedom Fighters came to prominence in June 1973, claiming responsibility for the continued assassination of Catholics. At the other extreme the Ulster Volunteer Force attempted to 'go political' between 1972 and 1974, in opposition to right wing populist tendencies, and established further links with the Official IRA. The moderate element responsible for this development was, however, overthrown by loyalist militants in November 1974. The question of the Protestant working class's ultimate allegiance, either to the petty bourgeois leadership of the UDA or to Vanguard, Paisley or some political organisation of its own, is still unresolved.

THE ULSTER WORKERS COUNCIL

When direct rule was announced in March 1972, Craig called for a two-day general stoppage in protest. The strike was organised by the Loyalist Association of Workers. LAW had been influential in getting the emergent defence associations to integrate into the UDA, and there were close links between the two bodies. Both these organisations, the industrial and the paramilitary, were suspicious of the established loyalist political leaders, yet unclear about their own political objectives. In the first half of 1973 LAW broke up because of disagreements about strategy and tactics. By the end of the year, however, it had been reformed as the Ulster Workers Council, and was concentrating on the idea of using industrial tactics to topple the new Executive. From a tactical point of view, the UWC's major asset was the support of workers in key industries such as Short Bros., Harland and Wolff, and most importantly, the power stations. The strikers' ability to close down the power stations was their trump card.

In January 1974 the UWC had completed its strike plans, and informed the leaders of the United Ulster Unionist Council of them. The UWC now got together with the paramilitary organisations to set up a 21-man executive, and co-opted Paisley, Craig and the leader of the anti-power-sharing Unionists, Harry West. These three, however, were very wary of the political risks involved and procrastinated about the timing of the strike. As a result, on the 14th of May, the UWC took the initiative and presented them with a *fait accompli*. As the Northern Ireland Executive voted to support the Sunningdale agreement, the UWC announced the start of their strike. The central demand of the strikers, about which there had been considerable disagreement, was for fresh elections to the Assembly.

The progress of the two-week strike, which brought the province to a complete standstill, is described in great detail by Robert Fisk in his book, *The Point of No Return*.[12] The key factors behind its success were first, the UWC's control of the power stations; second, the existence of widespread support in the loyalist community and the equally widespread use of intimidation; and third, the failure of the British Army to take any stand against the strikers. On the 28th of May Faulkner and his Unionist Ministers resigned, bringing down the Executive. Westminster prorogued the Assembly and restored direct rule. The loyalists returned to work.

The strike had a significant impact on British policy in Northern Ireland, and encouraged speculation about gradual disengagement. Within one month of the collapse of the Assembly, Westminster produced a new White Paper which announced the setting up of a new constitutional Convention, to be given the responsibility of finding some new political compromise. The 78 members of the Convention were to be elected on the old Assembly principles, from all the parties in Northern Ireland, but this time there were no terms of reference which insisted on power-sharing, and the London and Dublin Governments were specifically excluded from the discussions. This was very much what the UWC and Paisley had called for at the end of the strike. Early in 1975, three months prior to the Convention election, Merlyn Rees, the Labour Government's Secretary of State in Northern Ireland, negotiated a truce with the Provisional IRA, apparently on the basis of an agreement about the phasing out of internment. However, it was widely believed that the discussions between Rees's officials and the Provisionals had included the topic of British withdrawal.

The loyalists' claim that their action had been supported by the vast majority of the Protestant community appeared to be vindicated by the electoral success of the UUUC. In the British general election held in October 1974, they won 58% of the total vote, taking ten of the twelve Northern Ireland seats. In the elections for the Convention, in May 1975, the UUUC won 46 seats.[13] These developments were regarded with grave concern by those socialists who had identified British imperialism as the main enemy in Northern Ireland. In his book, *Northern Ireland: the Orange State*, Michael Farrell was obliged to admit that: 'Orangeism, once the mere tool of the Unionist bourgeoisie, had become the dominant force in Northern Politics.'[14] He, together with most other nationalist observers, concluded: 'The Loyalists are intent on restoring the Orange system and returning to the pre-1968 set-up. They even want greater powers than the old Stormont had. They have won a majority of the electorate for this line in three successive elections, and with a solid majority in the constitutional Convention they are demanding power and control of security.'[15] Such a loyalist regime, Farrell claims, would be 'violent, brutal and semi-fascist in character.'[16]

Loyalist solidarity in opposing power-sharing and any form of constitutional links with the Republic did indeed raise the spectre of Protestant unity as it existed under Carson and Craig. But it was more a spectre than a reality, for the objective conditions favouring a Protestant all-class alliance had been fundamentally transformed in the preceding decade. Once the strike was over the Protestant community was once again divided by class antagonisms. Fisk reports that: 'The 21 members of the UWC's co-ordinating committee held a largely unpublicized meeting to decide their future early in June. But the politicians and paramilitary leaders quickly retreated to their old positions of mutual distrust. The men whose faces became best known during the stoppage also began to quarrel among themselves.' [17] A minority within the UWC wished to make some kind of conciliatory gesture to the Catholic population over the phasing out of internment, and there were suggestions about starting a peace movement. The UDA, unable to agree on a political programme, split apart when the East Belfast officers accused those in West Belfast of racketeering. Early in 1975 the UVF, who were also riven with internal dissension, became involved in a murderous gangland war with the UDA.

The British Government and the nationalists credited loyalism with the status of a coherent political movement, and were dismayed by the UUUC's success in the Convention elections. However, Farrell's assertion that: 'Under Loyalist control, party and state would become virtually one as they did under the old regime, and the para-military groups would be absorbed into the forces of the state',[18] totally ignores the class antagonisms that emerged with the collapse of Unionism. As Rumpf and Hepburn have noted:

> There has thus been a certain amount of speculation on the nature of the party political system that is evolving in the light of proportional representation and the changed circumstances since 1972. While the UUUC has indicated its potential as a Protestant monolith in three successive elections, it is a three-party coalition which has not yet attained even the minimum level of domination which the Unionist Party was able to maintain in the old Stormont parliament. A one per cent swing in the eight most marginal returns at the Convention election would have reduced the number of UUUC seats to thirty-nine, exactly half the total.[19]

The appearance of unity within the UUUC was further undermined in September 1975, when Craig made an extraordinary *volte-face*, and called for a three-year, all-party coalition of reconstruction which would subsequently give way to conventional party government. Craig had the support of the UDA leadership for this proposal, but was opposed by the other parties in the UUUC, and by the majority of his own party. As a result a much reduced Vanguard withdrew from the UUUC. By March 1976, the Convention had failed to present an agreed report to Westminster on how the Province might govern itself, and it was dissolved.

Direct rule was restored on an indefinite basis.

The UWC strike was an essentially defensive political move, led by the Protestant working class, and subsequent events proved that Protestant unity at this moment could *only* be maintained on such negative issues as opposition to a Council of Ireland. Indeed, once the struggle had taken on this industrial form, the tensions between the working class and the bourgeoisie were likely to increase. The overall cost of the fifteen-day strike was estimated at £100 million and did nothing to improve the longer-run economic prospects. One week after the strike ended, a Swiss engineering firm withdrew from a joint venture with Harland and Wolff which would have provided 1,500 jobs. While Craig may have had visions of a corporatist, 'neo-fascist' State in Ulster, the militancy of the Protestant working class made it impossible for him to maintain political domination. His conversion to power-sharing, which Bell dismisses as 'tactical',[20] is more likely to reflect the fact that local capital is no longer an independent social force, and is ultimately dependent on monopoly capital. Despite the conflicts between these capitals, the central contradiction remains that between the bourgeoisie as a whole and the working class.

In May 1977, when the UUUC began another indefinite strike for stricter security measures and a return to majority rule, they were opposed by Vanguard, West's Official Unionist Party, and the Orange Order. The UUUC split apart, with the Official Unionists reaffirming their support for the link with Britain, and accusing Paisley's DUP and the rump of Unofficial Unionists of seeking UDI. The strike was not a success, for this time the power-workers refused to come out, and despite widespread intimidation and the backing of the UDA, it failed to gain mass support. The net result was a further weakening of the UDA, and increased dissension within the Protestant community.

8

CONCLUSION

During the 1960s profound changes occurred in the structure of Anglo-Irish relations. In Northern Ireland the declining profitability of local capital led to increased dependence on British subsidies and foreign investment. In the Republic the failure to establish an independent centre of capital accumulation provoked a radical reappraisal of economic strategies, resulting in the abandonment of protectionism. Both the Stormont and Dublin regimes began to adopt similar policies of attracting foreign investment with financial incentives. At the political level these developments were accompanied by a marked reduction in nationalist hostilities, symbolised in the retirement of Brookeborough and de Valera. The new era of co-operation between O'Neill, Lemass and Westminster necessitated a complete reversal of class alliances within Ireland and a radical change in ideological perspectives. In the South this meant the abandonment of the small farmers, small businessmen and the petty bourgeoisie, and an attack on orthodox republicanism and its traditional protagonists, the Irish Republican Army. In the North it meant challenging the foundations of the Unionist state which had been established to defend the interests of Ulster capital and the privileges of the Protestant labour aristocracy. The logic of partition which derived from the historical development of two different modes of production in Ireland was being steadily undermined.

The Sunningdale settlement arrived at in 1973, which included a reformed political Assembly in the North, and a Council of Ireland to co-ordinate the common interests of the main bourgeois parties, represented the culmination of these trends. The settlement was the product of a major political initiative by the British government, although as Bayley and Boehringer point out,

> 'It is not to be supposed that the whole arrangement was designed on some drawing board and then gradually implemented over the course of a number of years. The British ruling class interest in Ireland throughout the crisis was and is the interest of monopoly capital. That interest is simply defined — stability, and the protection of investment. Beyond that basic consideration the attitude of the British government has been completely pragmatic.'[1]

The Sunningdale settlement failed partly because of the re-emergence of militant republicanism in the North, but more importantly because of determined opposition from sections of the Ulster bourgeoisie and the Protestant working class. Integration into the international economy does not guarantee prosperity for countries like Ireland. On the contrary, the backwardness of a region in the capitalist system is cumulative and generally irreversible, and such areas find themselves totally vulnerable to economic fluctuations in the major capitalist metropolises. The monopoly interest in Ireland was greatly weakened by the international economic recession that began in the mid 1970s. The large-scale industry which is typical of advanced capitalism is usually only weakly represented in peripheral regions, and international capital imposes only a 'formal domination', without fundamentally transforming the material conditions of production. This is an important factor in explaining the absence of a unified working class in either the North or the South of Ireland, able to intervene as an autonomous force in the present struggles. The working class and the petty bourgeoisie find themselves at the bottom of the ladder within this broader capitalist social formation in terms of employment opportunities, consumption and social development. They are exploited twice over: by international capital and by being tied to old and peripheral modes of production.[2]

In Northern Ireland the pressure for reform led to the total destabilisation of existing political and ideological relations, and the fragmentation of the Protestant alliance. The hegemony of the capitalist class was broken by the development of internal contradictions, allowing the Protestant working class to intervene in the political struggle. However, this intervention has been of a confused and contradictory nature; first because of the dominance of Orange ideology within the traditional Protestant labour aristocracy, and second because of the potential for petty bourgeois leadership of the broader working class.

In the light of this analysis it is now possible to examine critically the two major socialist strategies which have been developed in Northern Ireland: strategies which have been clearly articulated by Farrell on the one hand, and Boserup on the other.[3] The position adopted by Farrell, which is close to that of the Provisional IRA, the Troops Out Movement in Britain and most other revolutionary groupings, is determined by the traditionally nationalist perspective described in the Introduction. With the collapse of the Assembly and Britain's failure to confront loyalist opposition to the settlement, Farrell concludes that 'no compromise is possible in the North any longer. To get power and hold on to it, the Loyalists must defeat and destroy minority resistance. To avoid enslavement the minority must destroy Loyalism. No one can be neutral in this struggle.'[4] 'The choice in Ireland has become devastatingly simple: between, on the one hand, a semi-fascist Orange statelet in the North matched by a pro-imperialist police state in the South, and, on the other hand, an antiimperialist and socialist revolution.'

The major weakness of this position derives from the assumed identity between nationalist and socialist objectives, and the extremely superficial analysis of Protestant politics. The fight for minority rights in the North and for socialism in Ireland is not synonymous with the demand for reunification or the fight against British imperialism. The Protestants of Ulster are an independent force in Ireland, claiming the right to self-determination, and the Irish working class has nothing to gain from 'driving them into the sea'. The objective basis of Orangeism, as the sectarian ideology of the Protestant labour aristocracy, has been eroded by the decline of Ulster's traditional industries and the rise of monopoly capital. The Protestant working class has only just begun to free itself from the Unionist alliance, and as yet has failed to throw up an independent political leadership. Its essentially defensive stance and vacillating class positions cannot be said to constitute the basis of a fascist alliance. Furthermore, the present conflict cannot be considered as a nationalist, anti-imperialist struggle for the liberation of Ireland. In a brief article on 'Some basic problems of the contemporary situation',[5] Gibbon has raised several criticisms of those who identify the imperialist/anti-imperialist conflict as the primary contradiction in Ireland today. Gibbon develops his critique by referring to Lenin's position on the national question, emphasising Lenin's distinction between national wars and anti-imperialist wars. The anti-imperialist nature of any struggle cannot simply be deduced by identifying the parties involved, but must depend on the balance of forces in those particular international circumstances. 'Where these determine that the *conditions of existence* of monopoly capitalism's reproduction are directly or indirectly touched upon, then one can speak of anti-imperialist struggles.' In this book I have attempted to show that, as Gibbon puts it, 'the object of British intervention in Northern Ireland has been to stabilize a conflict which in no foreseeable way has the significance which has been attributed to it.'[6] In addition, as I pointed out in the Introduction, the nationalist objectives of the Republican movement have been consistently rejected by the nation it seeks to represent, and the movement has failed to establish a mass base even in the North.

In his article, 'Contradictions and struggles in Northern Ireland', Boserup is also critical of the influence of nationalist ideology on socialist analysis. He concludes: 'If it is to engage effectively in the struggle against the Orange system the left must necessarily dissociate itself from 32-County nationalism and accept the existence of the Northern State.'[7] In support of this view, however, Boserup resorts to what has become known as the 'Two Nations' theory, which claims that the Protestants and Catholics in Ireland constitute two distinct nations, each with the right to statehood. The central flaw in this approach is that it relies on a totally ahistorical conception of nationalism, and fails to recognise successive transformations in Irish modes of production. Thus, Boserup claims:

'Northern Irish nationalism is no new phenomenon, but it has not been clearly visible hitherto because it took the form of Unionism as long as the Union with Britain was the best safeguard for Northern Ireland's independence from the South . . . It was a reaction to Catholic nationalism and a self-assertive settler-ideology dressed up as Unionism.'[8]

Such a view is theoretically inadequate, for in Lenin's words, 'the categorical requirement of Marxist theory in investigating any social question is that it be examined within *definite* historical limits.'[9] There is no simple continuity between the United Irishmen, Carson's Unionists and the Ulster nationalists of the 1970s; nor can the intimate economic and political ties between Britain and Ulster be dismissed in this way.

In his discussion of Lenin's views on the right of nations to self-determination, Gibbon also raises doubts about the Ulster nationalists' claims, pointing out that: 'It is difficult to see how partisans of either national bloc could demonstrate that its victory could improve this democracy [as established in 1923], or simplify class antagonisms . . . On the contrary, it appears more likely that the complete victory of either bloc could only be enforced through *restrictions* upon democracy.'[10] Furthermore, it has been argued here that a central element in the present conflict has been precisely the emergence of contradictions *within* the Unionist bloc.

Boserup's insistence on the 'national rights' of the Protestants in Northern Ireland is in any case partially contradicted by his main strategic argument, that socialists in Ireland should enter into a tactical alliance with 'British imperialism' and the Protestant liberals for the purpose of crushing Orangeism. 'It needs to be recognised that the destruction of the Orange system and its replacement by the 'welfare state' of managerial capitalism is historically necessary and historically progressive. It is progressive from a socialist point of view, and it is so despite the certainty that the new order will be of a neo-colonialist type.'[11] The definition of 'progressive' adopted by Boserup is in this case, however, a formalistic one rather than an analytic one. Thus he is arguing that, because monopoly capital in Ulster is in conflict with certain aspects of the Orange system, it is *ipso facto* progressive. But, as Gibbon notes, 'to look at things in terms of who is in the ring fighting is purely formalistic . . . Lenin rejected this approach, defining the nature of conflicts according to the significance invested in them by the balance of forces in given conjunctures.'[12] Indeed, Boserup's claim that the victory of 'managerial capitalism' over Orangeism 'is progressive in much the same way as were the French Revolution and Europe's conquest of the world' is not only theoretically inadequate but also practically misleading. For, as Parker and Driver's economic study, 'Capitalism in Ireland', seeks to demonstrate, monopoly capital is incapable of 'crushing' Orangeism. The crisis in Northern Ireland has coincided with a crisis for British capital and world capitalism generally, and the 'troubles' have further reduced the likelihood of vigorous capitalist expansion, capable of sweeping away a 'stagnant social order'. While the rise of monopoly capital may have challenged the objective economic basis of sectarian division within the working class and broken the Ulster bour-geoisie's political hegemony, it has failed to create majority support for democratic reforms.

Boserup is of course correct to emphasise the importance of ideological struggle in winning over sections of the Protestant working class to socialism. However, the major objective of this activity must surely be to unite the working class in Northern Ireland to defend their interests against both local and monopoly capital. The Sunningdale settlement may have had much to recommend it to the British and Irish ruling classes, but it had little to offer the workers, either Catholic or Protestant. In their last strike bulletin the UWC stated: 'It is our aim to have fresh elections, so that all elected representatives can sit down round a table and, without interference from Dublin and London, find a way whereby this province can be governed for the benefit of all.' The Convention subsequently collapsed, but its general acceptance of this principle was an important step towards the establishment of democratic institutions in Northern Ireland, and it succeeded in attracting tentative support from sections of the IRA and the Catholic community. Such a demand should not be confused with threats of UDI, or claims for a new 'nation-state'. Rather, the establishment of a genuinely democratic assembly is a prerequisite of any settlement in which the working class may have a political voice.

The progressive elements in the present conflict must, as Gibbon has said, be identified according to more substantive criteria, such as position on the general class struggle, and disposition toward democratic accommo-dation. On these grounds Gibbon considers the Official Republican move-ment, the Communist Party of Ireland and the traditional wing of the Northern Ireland Labour Party to be progressive, and the Provisional Republican movement, loyalist paramilitary groups and official Unionism to be reactionary. However, by focusing on existing political organisations, Gibbon ignores the existence of severe conflicts within loyalist organis-ations and the Unionist movement generally, as well as within both wings of the Republican movement. A major feature of the conflict over the years since Stormont was suspended has been the constant fragmenting of existing organisations and the existence of widespread internal feuding. The real battle for working class unity in Northern Ireland has only just begun, for the dominance of nationalist ideology within the Catholic working class is almost as strong as that of Orange ideology within the Protestant working class. In both communities the hesitant development of non-sectarian socialist perspectives has met with determined and violent opposition.

The political and ideological tasks are enormous, for as yet the pro-gressive forces have failed to find significant forms of political activity around which they can unite. However, it is essential to challenge the analyses put forward by both Farrell and Boserup. The former's failure to develop an adequate theoretical framework prevents any serious consideration of the nature of Protestant politics and leads him to a position of *de facto* support for the Provisional IRA as the basis of a national liberation movement. Boserup's economistic interpretation of the conflict as a contradiction between the 'Orange system' and 'managerial capitalism' results in an essentially fatalistic strategy for socialists, and *de facto* support for Ulster nationalism. Neither of these views examines seriously the possibility of working class unity in Northern Ireland, denying its relevance in the present struggle largely on the basis of the lack of historical precedent. It is, however, essential that both 'national' demands be assessed from the angle of their relevance to working class struggles. It is precisely this angle which, as yet, has hardly been explored in the development of socialist strategy in Northern Ireland. And a rigorous class analysis of the present conflict is an essential component in the discovery and implementation of that strategy.

REFERENCES

INTRODUCTION

1. See Sunday Times Insight Team, *Ulster*, (Harmondsworth, 1972), pp.66, 76, 126.
2. See for example Robert Moore, 'Race relations in the six counties: colonialism, industrialisation, and stratification in Ireland', *RACE*, XIV (1972), pp.39-41.
3. This is the conclusion reached by Geoffrey Bell in his survey of approaches to Protestant behaviour in *The Protestants of Ulster*, (London, 1976), p.14.
4. *Hibernia*, January 30 1976.
5. For a more detailed discussion of this question see Nicos Poulantzas, *Political Power and Social Class*, (London, 1975), pp.11-33.
6. G. Therborn, *Science, Class and Society*, (London, 1976), p.408.
7. Sunday Times Insight Team, *Ulster*, p.143.
8. P. Berresford Ellis (ed.), *James Connolly: Selected Writings*, (Harmondsworth, 1973), p.283.
9. Quoted in E. Rumpf and A.C. Hepburn, *Nationalism and Socialism in Twentieth Century Ireland*, (Liverpool, 1977), p.12.
10. C. Desmond Greaves, *The Irish Crisis*, (London, 1972), p.34.
11. Anders Boserup, 'Contradictions and struggles in Northern Ireland', *Socialist Register*, (1972), p.181.
12. Greaves, *The Irish Crisis*, p.214.
13. V.I. Lenin, *Critical Remarks on the National Question: The Right of Nations to Self-Determination*, (Moscow, 1971), p.45.
14. *Ibid.*
15. *Ibid.*, p.44.
16. *Ibid.*, p.54.
17. *Ibid.*, p.55.
18. Boserup, 'Contradictions and struggles', p.184. Boserup even goes so far as to suggest that monopoly capital is playing a progressive role in Northern Ireland! This view is strongly challenged by Stephen Parker and Ciaran Driver in 'Capitalism in Ireland', *Bulletin of the Conference of Socialist Economists*, 4, (1975), p.6.
19. Parker and Driver, 'Capitalism in Ireland', p.9.

20.   Quoted in Rumpf and Hepburn, *Nationalism and Socialism*, p.12.

21.   *Ibid.*, p.162.

22.   Serrge Van der Straeten and Philippe Daufouy, *The Counter-Revolution in Ireland*, (Detroit, 1974), p.41. This pamphlet first appeared as 'La contre-revolution Irlandaise', *Les Temps Modernes*, No.311. (1972). For a critique of this position see Parker and Driver, 'Capitalism in Ireland', pp.5-6.

23.   Paul Bew, 'The problem of Irish Unionism', *Economy and Society*, 6, (1977), p.103.

24.   Rumpf and Hepburn, *Nationalism and Socialism*, p.159.

25.   *Ibid.*, pp.159-163.

26.   'People's Democracy: a discussion on strategy', *New Left Review*, 55 (1969), p.5.

27.   See P. Arthur, *The People's Democracy 1968-73*, (Belfast, 1974).

28.   'People's Democracy: a discussion on strategy', *op. cit.* p.6.

29.   Eamann McCann, *War and an Irish Town*, (Harmondsworth, 1974), p.83.

30.   *Ibid.*

31.   Karl Marx, 'The Eighteenth Brumaire of Louis Bonaparte', in David Fernbach (ed.), *Surveys from Exile*, (Harmondsworth, 1973), p.146.

32.   McCann, *War and an Irish Town*, p.83.

33.   Louis Althusser, *For Marx*, (London, 1969), p.111.

CHAPTER ONE

1.   Patrick O'Farrell, *Ireland's English Question*, (New York, 1971), p.15.

2.   *Ibid.*, p.11.

3.   A.T.Q. Stewart, *The Ulster Crisis*, (London, 1967), p.29.

4.   V.I. Lenin, *Critical Remarks on the National Question*, (Moscow, 1971), p.40.

5.   W.E.H. Lecky, *The History of Ireland in the Eighteenth Century*, (Chicago, abr. ed., 1972), p.36.

6.   *Ibid.*, p.54.

7.   E.R.R. Green, 'The Beginnings of Industrial Revolution', in T.W. Moody and J.C. Beckett (ed.), *Ulster Since 1800*, first series, (London, 1955), p.28.

8.   Lecky, *History of Ireland*, p.161.

9.   *Ibid.*, p.167.

10.   J.C. Beckett, *The Making of Modern Ireland 1603-1923*, (London, 1969), p.207.

11.   *Ibid.*, p.259.

12.   Gibbon, *Ulster Unionism*, p.26.

13.   Lecky, *History of Ireland*, p.332.

14. Gibbon, *Ulster Unionism*, p.32.
15. *Ibid.*
16. *Ibid.*, p.33.
17. Althusser, *For Marx*, p.113.
18. Gibbon, *Ulster Unionism*, p.41.
19. Quoted in Liam de Paor, *Divided Ulster*, (Harmondsworth, 1972), p.26.
20. Beckett, *Modern Ireland*, p.264.
21. *Ibid.*, p.306.
22. J.M. Goldstrom, 'The Industrialisation of the North-East', in L.M. Cullen (ed.), *The Formation of the Irish Economy*, (Cork, 1969), p.101.
23. Beckett, *Modern Ireland*, p.290.
24. *Ibid.*
25. This was the view taken by C. Gill in his influential work, *The Rise of the Linen Industry*, (Oxford, 1925). See also Brian Kennedy, 'Tenant-Right Before 1870', in Moody and Becket (eds.), *Ulster Since 1800*, first series, and Bell, *The Protestants of Ulster*.
26. Gill, *The Linen Industry*, p.48.
27. Barbara Solow, *The Land Question and the Irish Economy, 1870-1903*, (Cambridge, Mass., 1971).
28. Gibbon, *Ulster Unionism*, p.13.
29. W.H. Crawford, 'The Rise of the Linen Industry', in Cullen (ed.), *The Irish Economy*.
30. Gibbon, *Ulster Unionism*, p.14.
31. *Ibid.*, p.16.
32. Goldstrom, 'Industrialisation of the North-East', in Cullen (ed.), *The Irish Economy*, p.107.
33. Gibbon, *Ulster Unionism*, p.16.
34. Bell, *Protestants of Ulster*, pp.17-23.
35. See for example Joseph Lee, *The Modernisation of Irish Society 1848-1918*, (Dublin, 1973), p.14.
36. Gibbon, *Ulster Unionism*, p.18.
37. *Ibid.*, p.19.
38. E.R.R. Green, 'Industrial Decline in the Nineteenth Century', in Cullen (ed.), *The Irish Economy*, p.94.
39. F.S.L. Lyons, *Ireland Since the Famine*, (London, 1973), p.42.
40. K. Marx and F. Engels, *Ireland and the Irish Question*, (Moscow and London, 1971), p.147.
41. J. Lee, 'Capital in the Irish Economy', in Cullen (ed.), *The Irish Economy*, p.56.
42. Marx and Engels, *Ireland*, p.138.
43. *Ibid.*, p.144.
44. The words of Fintan Lalor, quoted in Lyons, *Ireland Since the Famine*, p.108.
45. Lyons, *Ireland Since the Famine*, p.26.

46. Gibbon, *Ulster Unionism*, p.11.
47. Marx and Engels, *Ireland*, p.72.
48. Lyons, *Ireland Since the Famine*, p.179.
49. de Paor, *Divided Ulster*, p.56.
50. O'Farrell, *Ireland's English Question*, p.224.
51. Green, 'Industrial Decline', p.97.
52. Beckett, *Modern Ireland*, p.417.
53. Rumpf and Hepburn, *Nationalism and Socialism*, p.8.
54. Lenin, *The National Question*, p.49.
55. See Rumpf and Hepburn's chapter on 'The social structure of Irish nationalism and republicanism, 1922-3', in *Nationalism and Socialism*.
56. McCann, *War and an Irish Town*, p.166.
57. Gibbon, *Ulster Unionism*, p.12.
58. See Gilbert A. Cahill, 'Some nineteeth-century roots of the Ulster problem, 1829-1848', *Irish University Review*, 1, (1970).
59. de Paor, *Divided Ulster*, p.44.
60. See Andrew Boyd, *Holy War In Belfast*, (Tralee, 1969).
61. See Gibbon, *Ulster Unionism*, Ch.4.
62. Patrick Buckland, 'The unity of Ulster Unionism 1886-1939', *History*, 60 (1975), p.211.
63. See J.W. Boyle, 'The Belfast Protestant Association and the Independent Orange Order, 1901-10', *Irish Historical Studies*, XIII (1962-3).
64. Beckett, *Mo dern Ireland*, p.399.
65. Gibbon, *Ulster Unionism*, p.137.
66. Buckland, 'The unity of Ulster Unionism 1886-1939', p.214.
67. T.A. Jackson, *Ireland Her Own*, (London, 1971), p.372.
68. *Ibid.*, p.374.
69. Beckett, *Modern Ireland*, p.426.
70. D.G. Boyce, 'British conservative opinion, the Ulster question, and the partition of Ireland, 1919-21', *Irish Historical Studies*, 67 (1970-1), p.107.
71. Greaves, *Irish Crisis*, p.14.
72. Van der Straeten and Daufouy, *The Counter-Revolution in Ireland*, p.23.
73. Boserup, 'Contradictions and Struggles', *Socialist Register*, (1972), p.184.

CHAPTER TWO

1. Stewart, *The Ulster Crisis*, p.81.
2. Nicholas Mansergh, *The Government of Northern Ireland*, (London, 1936), p.244.
3. Sunday Times Insight Team, *Ulster*, p.80.
4. Althusser, *For Marx*, p.112.

5.   The information in this section was derived primarily from K.S. Isles and N.C. Cuthbert, *An Economic Survey of Northern Ireland*, (HMSO Belfast, 1957).

6.   *Ibid.*, p.57.

7.   *Ibid.*, p.107.

8.   *Ibid.*, p.112.

9.   *Ibid.*, p.119.

10.   *Ibid.*, p.120.

11.   K.S. Isles, 'Northern Ireland: an Economic Survey 1920-54' in Moody and Beckett (eds.), *Ulster Since 1800*, p.116.

12.   *Ibid.*, p.117.

13.   McCann, *War and an Irish Town*, p.155.

14.   *Ibid.*, p.156.

15.   David Kennedy, 'Catholics in Northern Ireland, 1926-1939', in F. MacManus (ed.), *The Years of the Great Test*, (Cork, 1967), p.138.

16.   Bell, *Protestants of Ulster*, p.21.

17.   Edmund Aunger, 'Religion and occupational class in Northern Ireland', *Economic and Social Review*, 7 (1975), p.15.

18.   John F. Harbinson, *The Ulster Unionist Party*, (Belfast, 1973), p.36.

19.   *Ibid.*, p.55.

20.   *Ibid.*, p.38.

21.   D.P. Barritt and C.F. Carter, *The Northern Ireland Problem: A Study in Group Relations*, (London, 1962), p.42.

22.   Quoted in J.L. McCracken, 'The Political Scene in Northern Ireland, 1926-1937', in MacManus (ed.), *The Years of the Great Test*, p.156.

23.   Quoted in Farrell, *Northern Ireland*, p.111.

24.   Mansergh, *The Government of Northern Ireland*, p.179.

25.   *Ibid.*, p.245.

26.   *Ibid.*, p.241.

27.   J.W. Good, *Irish Unionism*, (Dublin and London, 1920), p.228.

28.   Quoted in de Paor, *Divided Ulster*, p.105.

29.   *Hibernia*, 21 January, 1972.

30.   Buckland, 'The Unity of Ulster Unionism', p.218.

31.   *Disturbances in Northern Ireland: Report of the Commission Appointed by the Governor of Northern Ireland*, (Cameron Report), Cmd. 532, (HMSO Belfast, 1969), para. 229.

32.   Frank Gallagher, *The Indivisible Island*, (London, 1957).

33.   Martin Wallace, *Northern Ireland: Fifty Years of Self-Government*, (Newton Abbot, 1971), p.145.

34.   Northern Ireland Parliamentary Debates (Hansard), House of Commons, 20 May 1958, Col. 61.

35.   *Cameron Report*, paras. 128-130.

36.   *Ibid.*, para. 138.

37.   *Ibid.*

38.   Quoted in Harbinson, *The Unionist Party*, p.56.

39.   Quoted in de Paor, *Divided Ulster*, p.105.
40.   *Irish Times*, 4 May 1951.
41.   *Sunday Independent*, 21 May 1961.
42.   Harbinson, *The Unionist Party*, p.95.
43.   *Ibid.*, p.93.
44.   M.W. Dewar, *Why Orangeism?* (Belfast, 1959), p.23.
45.   Bell, *Protestants of Ulster*, p.93.
46.   Buckland, 'The unity of Ulster unionism', p.216.

CHAPTER THREE

1.   Parker and Driver, 'Capitalism in Ireland', p.8.
2.   Farrell, *Northern Ireland*, p.92.
3.   M. Blades and D. Scott, *What Price Northern Ireland?* Young Fabian Pamphlet, No. 22, (London, 1970).
4.   *Ibid.*, p.6.
5.   *Ibid.*, p.4.
6.   Isles and Cuthbert, *An Economic Survey of Northern Ireland*, p.155.
7.   *Ibid.*, p.158.
8.   Wallace, *Northern Ireland*, p.123.
9.   Blades and Scott, *What Price Northern Ireland?*, p.12.
10.   Parker and Driver, 'Capitalism in Ireland', p.10.
11.   Blades and Scott, *What Price Northern Ireland?*, p.12.
12.   McCann, *War and an Irish Town*, p.215.
13.   Blades and Scott, *What Price Northern Ireland?*, p.13.
14.   Parker and Driver, 'Capitalism in Ireland', p.13.
15.   *Ibid.*
16.   Bell, *Protestants of Ulster*, p.31.
17.   Blades and Scott, *What Price Northern Ireland?*, p.13.
18.   *Report of the Committee on Financial Relations between the State and Local Authorities*, (HMSO Belfast), Cmd. 131.
19.   Blades and Scott, *What Price Northern Ireland?*, p.16.
20.   de Paor, *Divided Ulster*, p.105.
21.   Quoted in Farrell, *Northern Ireland*, p.138.
22.   Bew, 'The problem of Irish Unionism', p.104.
23.   Harbinson, *The Unionist Party*, p.220.
24.   Buckland, 'The unity of Ulster Unionism', p.222.
25.   McCann, *War and an Irish Town*, p.178.
26.   Harbinson, *The Unionist Party*, p.220.
27.   *Sunday Times*, 11 February 1938.
28.   Thomas Wilson (ed.), *Ulster Under Home Rule*, (London, 1965), p.65.
29.   Barritt and Carter, *The Northern Ireland Problem*, pp.107-8.
30.   de Paor, *Divided Ulster*, p.130.

31.   Parker and Driver, 'Capitalism in Ireland', p.11.

CHAPTER FOUR

1.   Isles and Cuthbert, *An Economic Survey of Northern Ireland.*
2.   *Report of the Joint Working Party on the Economy of Northern Ireland,* Cmd. 1835, (HMSO London, 1962)
3.   Quoted in Wallace, *Northern Ireland,* p.70.
4.   Terence O'Neill, *The Autobiography of Terence O'Neill,* (London, 1972), p.47.
5.   *Ibid.,* p.40.
6.   *Economic Development in Northern Ireland,* Cmd 479, (HMSO Belfast, 1965).
7.   *Belfast Regional Survey and Plan: Recommendations and Conclusions,* Cmd 451, (HMSO Belfast, 1965).
8.   McCann, *War and an Irish Town,* p.217.
9.   Alan Robinson, 'Londonderry, Northern Ireland: a border study', *Scottish Geographical Magazine,* 86, (3 December 1970), p.211.
10.   Farrell, *Northern Ireland,* p.241.
11.   McCann, *War and an Irish Town,* p.208.
12.   James Meenan, 'From Free Trade to Self-Sufficiency', in MacManus (ed.), *The Years of the Great Test,* p.70.
13.   de Paor, *Divided Ulster,* p.110.
14.   Meenan, 'From Free Trade', p.75.
15.   D.R. O'Connor Lysaght, *The Republic of Ireland,* (Cork, 1970), p.104.
16.   Buckland, 'The unity of Ulster Unionism', p.222.
17.   Jackson, *Ireland Her Own,* p.468.
18.   Rumpf and Hepburn, *Nationalism and Socialism,* p.118.
19.   Jackson, *Ireland Her Own,* p.470.
20.   *Ibid.*
21.   Lysaght, *The Republic,* p.170.
22.   Lyons, *Ireland Since the Famine,* p.629.
23.   Jackson, *Ireland Her Own,* p.474.
24.   Parker and Driver, 'Capitalism in Ireland', p.8.
25.   *Ibid.,* p.2.
26.   Joseph Johnston, *Why Ireland Needs the Common Market,* (Cork, 1962).
27.   Lysaght, *The Republic,* pp.171-2.
28.   Quoted in de Paor, *Divided Ulster,* p.138.
29.   O'Neill, *Autobiography,* p.73.
30.   *Ibid.,* p.75.
31.   McCann, *War and an Irish Town,* p.210.
32.   Quoted in de Paor, *Divided Ulster,* p.118.

33.   J. Bowyer Bell, *The Secret Army: A History of the IRA, 1916-70*, (London, 1970), p.421.
34.   de Paor, *Divided Ulster*, pp.140-1.
35.   *Cameron Report*, para. 44.
36.   Quoted in de Paor, *Divided Ulster*, p.175.
37.   Sunday Times Insight Team, *Ulster*, p.66.
38.   *Cameron Report*, para. 177.

CHAPTER FIVE

1.   Boserup, 'Contradictions and struggles', p.173.
2.   For a general discussion of the relationship between monopoly and non-monopoly capital and the State see Nicos Poulantzas, *Classes in Contemporary Capitalism*, (London, 1975), especially Part 2, 'The bourgeoisies: their contradictions and their relations to the State'.
3.   A full text of the 'Crossroads' speech, broadcast on 9 December 1968, appears in O'Neill, *Autobiography*, pp.145-149.
4.   O'Neill, *Autobiography*, pp.122-3.
5.   *Guardian*, 8 January 1974.
6.   *Report of the Advisory Committee on Police in Northern Ireland*, Cmd 535, (HMSO Belfast, 1969).
7.   *Violence and Civil Disturbances in Northern Ireland in 1969: Report of Tribunal of Enquiry*, Cmd 566, 2 vols, (HMSO Belfast, 1972).
8.   Quoted in Henry Kelly, *How Stormont Fell*, (Dublin, 1972), p.13.
9.   Harbinson, *The Unionist Party*, p.159.
10.   Kelly, *How Stormont Fell*, p.25.
11.   See Farrell, *Northern Ireland*, pp.281-290, and Sunday Times Insight Team, *Ulster*, ch. 16.
12.   Wallace, *Northern Ireland*, p.84.
13.   J. Bayley and K. Boehringer, *The Struggle in Northern Ireland 1968-73*, (London, 1976), p.8.
14.   *Northern Ireland Constitutional Proposals*, Cmd. 5259, (HMSO) London, 1973).
15.   *Ibid.*, para. 52.
16.   *Ibid.*, para. 112.
17.   McCann, *War and an Irish Town*, p.217.
18.   Garret FitzGerald, *Towards a New Ireland*, (London, 1972).
19.   *Ibid.*, p.60.
20.   *Ibid.*, p.61.
21.   *Ibid.*, p.103.
22.   *Ibid.*, p.105.
23.   *Ibid.*, p.124.
24.   *Ibid.*, p.141.
25.   de Paor, *Divided Ulster*, p.210.

26. McCann, *War and an Irish Town*, p.252. See also *Observer*, 19 August 1973, p.2.
27. Rumpf and Hepburn, *Nationalism and Socialism*, p.212.

CHAPTER SIX

1. Frank Wright, 'Protestant ideology and politics in Ulster', *European Journal of Sociology*, XIV (1973), 273.
2. Parker and Driver, 'Capitalism in Ireland', p.9.
3. Wright, 'Protestant ideology', p.238.
4. See Kennedy Lindsay, *Dominion of Ulster?*, (Ulster Vanguard Publication, 1972).
5. Kelly, *How Stormont Fell*, p.123.
6. Quoted in de Paor, *Divided Ulster*, p.66.
7. O'Neill, *Autobiography*, p.107.
8. *Ibid.*, p.147.
9. Quoted in Martin Dillon and Denis Lehane, *Political Murder in Northern Ireland*, (Harmondsworth, 1973), pp.170-1.
10. *Sunday Times*, 28 January, 1973.
11. Kelly, *How Stormont Fell*, p.122.
12. *Ibid.*, p.124.
13. Dillon and Lehane, *Political Murder*, p.50.
14. *Ibid.*, p.62.
15. Quoted in R. Deutsch and V. Magowan, *Northern Ireland 1968-73: A Chronology of Events*, vol. 2 (Belfast, 1974), p.230.
16. Boserup, 'Contradictions and struggles,' p.177.
17. Wright, 'Protestant ideology', p.270.
18. David Boulton, *The UVF 1966-73: An Anatomy of Loyalist Rebellion*, (Dublin, 1973), pp.13-14.
19. Wright, 'Protestant ideology', p.241.
20. Harbinson, *The Unionist Party*, pp.89-91.
21. Boulton, *The UVF*, p.21.
22. Wright, 'Protestant ideology', p.244.
23. Robert Harbinson, *No Surrender: An Ulster Childhood*, (London, 1960), p.68.
24. *Ibid.*, p.70.
25. For a more detailed illustration of popular Protestant culture in this period see Bell, *Protestants of Ulster*, Ch. 4.
26. Wright, 'Protestant ideology', p.229.
27. See Boyle, 'The Belfast Protestant Association'.
28. Boulton, *The UVF*, p.44.
29. *Ibid.*, p.60.
30. Harbinson, *The Unionist Party*, p.224.
31. Boulton, *The UVF*, p.142.

32. *Ibid.*
33. *Ibid.*, p.149.
34. Deutsch and Magowan, *Northern Ireland 1968-73*, Vol.2, p.163.

CHAPTER SEVEN
1. Rumpf and Hepburn, *Nationalism and Socialism*, p.158.
2. Boulton, *The UVF*, p.144.
3. Dillon and Lehane, *Political Murder*, p.51.
4. *Ibid.*, p.24.
5. *Ibid.*, p.26.
6. Boulton, *The UVF*, p.176.
7. Deutsch and Magowan, *Northern Ireland 1968-73*, Vol.2, p.218.
8. Boulton, *The UVF*, p.178.
9. *Ibid.*, p.182.
10. *Sunday Times*, 28 January 1973.
11. Dillon and Lehane, *Political Murder*, p.165.
12. Robert Fisk, *The Point of No Return*, (London, 1975).
13. The full results were as follows: United Ulster Unionist Council, 46 (Vanguard 14, DUP 12, Official Unionists 19, Independent 1); Independent Loyalist, 1; Unionist Party of Northern Ireland (Faulkner), 5; SDLP, 17; Alliance, 8; NILP, 1.
14. Farrell, *Northern Ireland*, p.331.
15. *Ibid.*
16. *Ibid.*, p.332.
17. Fisk, *Point of No Return*, p.231.
18. Farrell, *Northern Ireland*, p.332.
19. Rumpf and Hepburn, *Nationalism and Socialism*, p.215.
20. Bell, *Protestants of Ulster*, p.140.

CHAPTER EIGHT
1. Bayley and Boehringer, *The Struggle in Ireland*, p.10.
2. See Emmanuel Terray, 'L'idee de nation et les transformations du capitalisme', *Les Temps Modernes*, (August-September, 1973).
3. For a recent statement of Farrell's views see his 'Northern Ireland — an anti-imperialist struggle', in *Socialist Register*, (1977).
4. Farrell, *Northern Ireland*, p.333 and p.335.
5. Peter Gibbon, 'Some basic problems of the contemporary situation', *Socialist Register*, (1977).
6. *Ibid.*, p.85.
7. Boserup, 'Contradictions and struggles', p.188.
8. *Ibid.*, p.180.
9. Lenin, *The National Question*, p.44.
10. Gibbon, 'Some basic problems of the contemporary situation', p.83.
11. Boserup, 'Contradictions and struggles', p.186.
12. Gibbon, 'Some basic problems of the contemporary situation', p.85.

BIBLIOGRAPHY

OFFICIAL PUBLICATIONS

Belfast Regional Survey and Plan: Recommendations and Conclusions (Matthew Report), Cmd. 451 (Belfast, 1965).

Disturbances in Northern Ireland: Report of the Commission Appointed by the Governor of Northern Ireland (Cameron Report), Cmd. 532 (Belfast, 1969).

Economic Development, (Dublin, 1958).

Economic Development in Northern Ireland (Wilson Report), Cmd. 479 (Belfast, 1969).

Future of Northern Ireland: A Paper for Discussion, (London, 1972).

Northern Ireland Constitutional Proposals, Cmnd. 5259 (London, 1973).

Northern Ireland Development Programme, 1970-75, (Belfast, 1970).

Northern Ireland Development Programme, 1970-75: Government Statement, Cmd. 547 (Belfast, 1970).

Report of the Advisory Committee on Police in Northern Ireland, (Hunt Report), Cmd. 535 (Belfast, 1969).

Report of the Enquiry into Allegations against the Security Forces of Physical Brutality in Northern Ireland, arising out of Events on the 9th August, 1971, Cmd. 4823 (London, 1971).

Report of the Joint Working Party on the Economy of Northern Ireland (Hall Report), Cmnd. 1835 (London, 1962).

Report of the Tribunal appointed to Enquire into the Events on Sunday 30th January, 1972, which led to Loss of Life in connection with the Procession in Londonderry on that day (Widgery Report), (London, 1972).

Reshaping of Local Government: Further Proposals, Cmd. 530 (Belfast, 1969).

Second Programme for Economic Expansion, Parts 1 and II, Pr. 7239 and Pr. 7670 (Dublin, 1963-64).

Violence and Civil Disturbances in Northern Ireland in 1969: Report of Tribunal of Enquiry (Scarman Report), Cmd. 566 (2 vols., Belfast, 1972).

BOOKS AND ARTICLES

Althusser, Louis, *For Marx*, (London, 1969).

Arthur, Paul, *The People's Democracy, 1968-73*, (Belfast, 1974).

Aunger, Edmund A., 'Religion and occupational class in Northern Ireland', *Economic and Social Review*, Vol. 7, No. 1 (1975).

Barritt, D.P. and Carter, C.F., *The Northern Ireland Problem*, (London, 1962).

Beckett, J.C., *The Making of Modern Ireland, 1603-1923*, London, 1969).

Beckett, J.C. and Glasscock, R.E. (eds.), *Belfast: Origin and Growth of an Industrial City*, (London, 1967).

Bell, Geoffrey, *The Protestants of Ulster*, (London, 1976).

Bell, J. Bowyer, *The Secret Army: A History of the IRA 1916-70*, (London, 1972).

Bew, Paul, 'The problems of Irish Unionism', *Economy and Society*, 6, No. 1 (1977).

Boserup, Anders, 'Contradictions and struggles in Northern Ireland', *Socialist Register*, (1972).

Boulton, David, *The UVF, 1966-73*, (Dublin, 1973).

Boyce, D.G., 'British conservative opinion, the Ulster question and the partition of Ireland', *Irish Historical Studies*, LXVII (1970-71).

Boyd, Andrew, *Holy War in Belfast*, (Tralee, 1969).

Boyle, John, 'The Belfast Protestant Association and the Independent Orange Order', *Irish Historical Studies*, XIII (1962).

British and Irish Communist Organisation, *The Birth of Ulster Unionism*, (Belfast, 1973).

British and Irish Communist Organisation, *The Economics of Partition*, (Belfast, 1972).

Buckland, Patrick, *Irish Unionism 2: Ulster Unionism and the Origins of Northern Ireland*, (Dublin and London, 1973).

Buckland, Patrick, 'The unity of Ulster Unionism', *History*, 60 (1975).

Cahill, Gilbert A., 'Some nineteenth-century roots of the Ulster problem, 1829-1848', *Irish University Review*, 1 (1970).

Coogan, Tim Pat, *The IRA*, (London, 1970).

Cullen, L.M., *An Economic History of Ireland since 1660*, (London, 1972).

Cullen, L.M. (ed.), *The Formation of the Irish Economy*, (Cork, 1969).

de Paor, Liam, *Divided Ulster*, (Harmondsworth, 1972).

Deutsch, R. and Magowan, V., *Northern Ireland, 1968-73: A Chronology of Events*, (2 vols., Belfast, 1974).

Devlin, Bernadette, *The Price of My Soul*, (London, 1969).

Dewar, M.W., Brown, J., and Long, S.E., *Orangeism: A New Historical Appreciation*, (Belfast, 1967).

Dillon, M. and Lehane, D., *Political Murder in Northern Ireland*, (Harmondsworth, 1973).

Ellis, P. Berresford (ed.), *James Connolly, Selected Writings*, (Harmondsworth, 1973).

Farrell, Michael, *Northern Ireland: The Orange State*, (London, 1976).

Fisk, Robert, *The Point of No Return*, (London, 1975).

FitzGerald, Garret, *Planning in Ireland*, (Dublin and London, 1968).

FitzGerald, Garret, *Towards a New Ireland*, (London, 1972).

Gallagher, Frank, *The Indivisible Island*, (London, 1957).

Gibbon, Peter, 'The dialectic of religion and class in Ulster', *New Left Review*, 56 (1969).

Gibbon, Peter, *The Origins of Ulster Unionism*, (Manchester, 1976).

Gill, Conrad, *The Rise of the Irish Linen Industry*, (Oxford, 1925).

Good, J.W., *Irish Unionism*, (Dublin, 1920).

Greaves, C. Desmond, *The Irish Crisis*, (London, 1972).

Harbinson, John F., *The Ulster Unionist Party, 1882-1973*, (Belfast, 1973).

Harbinson, Robert, *No Surrender: An Ulster Childhood*, (London, 1960).

Hezlet, Sir Arthur, *The 'B' Specials*, (London, 1973).

Isles, K.S. and Cuthbert, N., *An Economic Survey of Northern Ireland*, (Belfast, 1957).

Jackson, T.A., *Ireland Her Own*, (London, 1971).

Kee, Robert, *The Green Flag*, (London, 1972).

Kelly, Henry, *How Stormont Fell*, (Dublin, 1972).

Lawrence, R.J., *The Government of Northern Ireland: Public Finance and Public Services, 1921-1964*, (Oxford, 1965).

Lecky, W.E.H., *A History of Ireland in the Eighteenth Century*, (Chicago, abr., 1972).

Lee, Joseph, *The Modernisation of Irish Society, 1848-1918*, (Dublin, 1973).

Lenin, V.I., *Critical Remarks on the National Question, The Right of Nations to Self-Determination*, (Moscow, 1971).

Lyons, F.S.L., *Ireland Since the Famine*, (London, 1973).

Lysaght, D.R. O'Connor, *The Republic of Ireland*, (Cork, 1970).

McCann, Eamonn, *War and an Irish Town*, (Harmondsworth, 1974).

MacManus, Francis (ed.), *The Years of the Great Test, 1926-39*, (Cork, 1967).

Mansergh, Nicholas, *The Government of Northern Ireland*, (London, 1936).

Mansergh, Nicholas, *The Irish Question*, (London, 1965).

Marx, Karl and Engels, Frederick, *Ireland and the Irish Question*, (Moscow and London, 1971).

Meenan, J., *The Irish Economy since 1922*, (Liverpool, 1970).

Moody, T.W. and Beckett, J.C. (eds.), *Ulster Since 1800*, 2 series:
 (1) A political and economic survey, (London, 1955);
 (2) A social survey, (London, 1957).

Moore, Robert, 'Race relations in the six counties: colonialism, industrialisation, and stratification in Ireland', *Race*, XIV I (1972).

163

Nairn, Tom, *The Break-Up of Britain*, (London, 1977).

O'Brien, Conor Cruise, *States of Ireland*, (London, 1974).

O'Farrell, Patrick, *England and Ireland Since 1800*, (London, 1975).

O'Farrell, Patrick, *Ireland's English Question*, (New York, 1971).

O'Neill, Terence, *The Autobiography of Terence O'Neill*, (London, 1972).

Parker, S. and Driver, C., 'Capitalism in Ireland', *Bulletin of the Conference of Socialist Economists*, IV, 2(1975).

Patterson, H., 'Refining the debate on Unionism', *Political Studies*, XXIV (1976).

'People's Democracy: a discussion on strategy', *New Left Review*, 55 (1969).

Poulantzas, Nicos,*Classes in Contemporary Capitalism*, (London, 1975)

Poulantzas, Nicos, *Political Power and Social Classes*, (London, 1973).

Rose, Richard, *Governing Without Consensus*, (London, 1971).

Rumpf, E. and Hepburn, A.C., *Nationalism and Socialism in Twentieth Century Ireland*, (Liverpool, 1977).

Senior, Hereward, *Orangeism in Ireland and Britain, 1795-1836*, (London, 1966).

Sibbet, R.M., *Orangeism in Ireland and throughout the Empire*, (London, 1939).

Solow, Barbara, *The Land Question and the Irish Economy, 1870-1903*, (Cambridge, Mass., 1971).

Stewart, A.T.Q., *The Ulster Crisis*, (London, 1967).

Strauss, Eric, *Irish Nationalism and British Democracy*, (London, 1951).

Sunday Times Insight Team, *Ulster*, (Harmondsworth, 1972).

Terray, Emmanuel, 'L'idee de nation et les transformations du capitalisme', *Les Temps Modernes*, (August-September, 1973).

Utley, T.E., *Lessons of Ulster*, (London, 1975).

Van der Straeten, Serge and Daufouy, Philippe, 'La contre-revolution Irlandaise', *Les Temps Modernes*, 311 (June 1972).

Wallace, Martin, *Northern Ireland: 50 Years of Self-Government*, (Newton Abbot, 1971).

Whyte, J.H., *Church and State in Modern Ireland, 1923-70*, (Dublin and London, 1971).

Wilson, Thomas (ed.), *Ulster Under Home Rule*, (London, 1955).

Wright, Frank, 'Protestant ideology and politics in Ulster', *European Journal of Sociology*, XIV (1973).

INDEX

ZED PRESS is a new socialist publisher of books on the Third
World. Our first series are: Imperialism and Revolution, Women
in the Third World, Africa, the Middle East and Asia.

Our books are both introductory texts and more advanced
analyses of the complex forms of oppression which Third World
revolutionary forces are struggling to overcome. Most of our
authors use Marxism as their basis for coming to grips with
political history, with the way the world is structured and with
what the future holds. Our writers are people, many of whom
are in active opposition to the forces of imperialist oppression
in its local and international manifestations. We intend our
authors to be equally from the Third World and from the West.

ZED PRESS is committed to taking radical literature out of the
studies of the academics and into the hands of a much wider
circle of intellectuals who feel the need to understand our contradiction and crisis-ridden world. We will encourage manuscripts
which do this.

We aim to distribute ZED's books as widely as possible, especially
in the Third World. We want to get our books directly to those
involved in anti-imperialist struggles. We have a network of
representatives, and are building up a direct mail order service
to make our books accessible anywhere in the world. We are
therefore willing to help other radical publishers in providing a
more comprehensive distribution of their titles in the Third
World, in addition to originating our own titles.

ZED PRESS is financially independent and not tied to any
political faction. Our aim is to encourage broad debate in a
Marxist and socialist framework, to promote radical knowledge
and to build up a climate of opinion favourable to liberation
everywhere.

OTHER BOOKS AVAILABLE FROM ZED PRESS

(Please note: UK prices quoted in sterling; prices for rest of the world in US dollars.)

Annerstedt (Jan) & Gustavsson (Rolf) Towards a New International Division of Labour? Pb £1.95/$3.75 (Not available in Sandinavia)

Caldwell (Malcolm) The Wealth of Some Nations Hb £5.00/$10.00

Davis (Uri) Israel: Utopia Incorporated Hb £5.00/$10.00

Eisen Bergman (Arlene) Women in Vietnam Pb £2.75/$5.40 (Not available in North America)

Elliott (David) Thailand: Origins of Military Rule Hb £5.95/$12.95

Hirson (Baruch) Soweto: Roots of a Revolution? Hb (In preparation)

Kiernan (Victor) America — The Imperial Record Hb £6.95/$12.95

Mandel (Ernest) From Class Society to Communism Hb $10.50; Pb $3.95 (Available Third World only)

Nabudere (Wadada) The Political Economy of Imperialism Hb £7.75/$15.50 (Pb distributed by Tanzania Publishing House in Africa)

Peoples Press With Freedom in their Eyes (Angola) Pb £2.50/$5.00 (Not available in North America)

Peoples Press Our Roots Are Still Alive Pb £2.95 (Not available in North America)

Rodinson (Maxime) Marxism and the Muslim World Hb £8.75/$18.50

Samir Amin The Arab Nation: Nationalism and Class Struggles Hb £6.50/$12.75

Seidman (Ann and Neva) U.S. Multinationals in Southern Africa Pb £4.95 (Not available in Africa and North America)